MW01641675

Godfidence: Real Faith i
©2020 by Randy Garcia
Interior and Cover Design
Copy Editors: Brenda D. Garcia and Shauna Perez
Rising Higher Publishing
San Antonio, TX 78249
www.Godfidencebook.com

All rights reserved.
ISBN: 978-164999599-5

All Scripture quotations, unless otherwise indicated, are taken from the Holy Bible, New International Version®, NIV®. Copyright ©1973, 1978, 1984, 2011 by Biblica, Inc.™ Used by permission of Zondervan. All rights reserved worldwide. www.zondervan.com The “NIV” and “New International Version” are trademarks registered in the United States Patent and Trademark Office by Biblica, Inc.™

Scripture quotations marked BSB are from The Holy Bible, Berean Study Bible, BSB. Copyright ©2016, 2018 by Bible Hub. Used by Permission. All Rights Reserved Worldwide.

Scripture quotations marked ESV are from the ESV® Bible (The Holy Bible, English Standard Version®). Copyright © 2001 by Crossway, a publishing ministry of Good News Publishers. Used by permission. All rights reserved.
Scripture quotations marked TLB are from The Living Bible copyright © 1971 by Tyndale House Foundation. Used by permission of Tyndale House Publishers Inc., Carol Stream, Illinois 60188. All rights reserved.

Scripture quotations marked MSG are taken from THE MESSAGE, copyright © 1993, 2002, 2018 by Eugene H. Peterson. Used by permission of NavPress. All rights reserved. Represented by Tyndale House Publishers, Inc.
Scripture quotations marked NKJV are taken from the New King James Version®. Copyright © 1982 by Thomas Nelson. Used by permission. All rights reserved.

Scripture quotations marked NLT are taken from the Holy Bible, New Living Translation, copyright ©1996, 2004, 2007, 2013, 2015 by Tyndale House Foundation. Used by permission of Tyndale House Publishers, Inc., Carol Stream, Illinois 60188. All rights reserved.

Scripture quotations marked RSV are from the Revised Standard Version of the Bible, copyright © 1946, 1952, and 1971 the Division of Christian Education of the National Council of the Churches of Christ in the United States of America. Used by permission. All rights reserved.

TABLE OF CONTENTS

INTRODUCTION

I remember it well. The year was 1995. At Jackson Middle School, where my church was meeting for worship, I was getting ready to stand in front of a congregation of people and teach the Word of God. I was nervous. I was shaking. And three minutes before I took the microphone, I pulled off to the side of the stage and threw up. I went through the sermon as best I could, and I was fine after that. Until the following Sunday, when the same thing happened again. And then the following Sunday, repeat. This was becoming a pattern.

At first, I thought it was a simple case of nerves. There were people saying I didn't have what it took to fulfill my calling as a pastor. They were doing their best to strip me of my confidence, and for a while, they did; but they couldn't strip me of my Godfidence. I asked the Lord if there was a spiritual lesson I needed to learn.

Here is the lesson I learned: God was intentionally taking my confidence away from me because I needed to let go of relying on my own abilities and begin trusting in what God can do. He wanted me to increase my Godfidence.

GODFIDENCE LESSON

I am so glad I lost my confidence,
because I gained something much more powerful:
Godfidence.

Godfidence? Yes, I made up a word. You won't find this word in *Webster's Dictionary*. In fact, every time I type this word on my laptop, the Word program places a red squiggly line under it to tell me that I have misspelled this word. No, I haven't misspelled Godfidence. It just hasn't made its way into the dictionary. Yet.

We know what the word confidence is. Confidence is defined as "full trust; belief in the powers, trustworthiness, or reliability of a person or thing."[1] Some people have confidence in their job. Their bank account. Their abilities. The stock market. Some even have confidence in the horoscope. I call this wrongfidence. But what word do we use to describe placing your confidence in God? Godfidence.

> **GODFIDENCE (N):**
> the assurance one receives when they place their faith 100% in God Almighty; the knowledge that God is in control of every situation; the anointed confidence that takes an individual to their spiritual potential.

In this Scripture from Philippians, the Apostle Paul describes the battle between confidence in the flesh and confidence in God.

> *For it is we who are the circumcision, we who serve God by his Spirit, who boast in Christ Jesus, and who put no confidence in the flesh. (Philippians 3:3)*

Yes, it is easy for any of us to find reason to have confidence in ourselves. When a person has a certain talent or ability, it is easy for them to be confident about it. When you have a nice position at work and a successful career going, it usually brings you confidence. The degree you obtained, the money you've earned, the victories you've won, and the people you know often lead you to gain more confidence in life. But God has something more for you. Those who rely on confidence limit their potential. But those who live with Godfidence "raise the lid" on their potential.

> **GODFIDENCE LESSON**
> Confidence in your own abilities may or may not bring you good results. Confidence in what God can do (Godfidence) will change your life.

In this Philippians 3 passage, Paul addresses the

problem of believers beginning to lose confidence in the Lord and therefore raising their confidence in themselves. Dangerous territory. Even today, there are those who go overboard and think too much of themselves. Their level of self-confidence is through the roof. Instead of having confidence in God, their confidence is in themselves. No matter how much confidence you have in your flesh, there comes a time when your flesh will fail you.

There is nothing wrong with having confidence. You need it. But the big question is this: Where is your confidence? If your confidence is in the Lord, everything changes.

What matters is not how much confidence you have but rather where you put it.

In 2016, the Barna Group reported that 73% of Americans identify themselves as Christian. [2] I thought, "Wow, that is a significant number of believers in America." But as I continued to read this report, it revealed that only 31% are committed Christians, consistent in their church attendance, Bible reading, prayer life, serving, etc. It was then that I quickly realize that these statistics were quite sad. If my math is correct, this means that 42% of Americans fall into the category of uncommitted Christians. Many know how to talk the talk. But not everyone walks the walk. America, we have a problem.

I believe that this "non-committed" mentality is an issue from many angles. First of all, it hinders the unchurched people from coming to faith in the Lord. The Christian community is giving the non-believers a bad testimony. Secondly, as the number of uncommitted Christians continues to rise, the morality of our nation declines. Spiritual and moral compromise is contagious. And third of all, non-committed Christians are taking advantage of the grace of God.

> "Lead the person in the mirror first. The very first step of leadership is leading yourself. Be a lifelong learner. Seek opportunities for personal growth."
> – Matt Garcia

In speaking with a group of young adults about this issue, most agree that they are turned off by a lack of authenticity. There is way too much fake Christianity. What does it take to be real? How can we get to the place of being a Christ follower who is a Spirit-filled, sin-defacing, Jesus-loving, soul-winning, ministry-reaching, disciple-making, overcoming child of God? Well, it doesn't happen overnight. It begins by building a strong spiritual foundation. That is what this book is about. We will focus on fourteen aspects of spiritual formation that lead to real Christianity. No more going through the motions. Are you ready for this journey? It begins with Godfidence. Do you have it?

CH. 1: BIBLICAL GODFIDENCE

Growing up, I was a very shy, introverted boy who never liked being around people much. When Sunday church service was over, it was a tradition for my parents to take us out to eat. More times than not, I would take the option of staying at our house next to the church building to read or watch football on TV, asking my parents to bring me back a to-go plate of food. I just didn't have any confidence to be around people.

I remember a particular day well when I was about twenty years old. My dad and mom, who served more than sixty-six years in pastoral ministries, asked me to join them in my dad's office. When I got there, I noticed we were joined by a few other church leaders. The message everyone conveyed to me in the room that day was that God had a special calling over me, and they wanted to anoint me with oil and pray over me. They did.

Could God use a shy, introverted young man for the purpose of His kingdom? That day, I learned that God could indeed do that. From that day on, I have lived with Godfidence!

> ## GODFIDENCE LESSON
> God has great plans for you. He is just waiting for you to have the Godfidence to step into those plans.

The Bible is filled with great stories of men and women whose lives were changed once they began to live with Godfidence. Here are a few examples…

In 1 Samuel 17, we read about a teenage boy named David taking some food to his older brothers who were being threatened by a big giant named Goliath. When everyone else was afraid of this giant, there was something that rose up in the heart of David that made him want to confront Goliath. It was Godfidence.

He told the giant, "You come against me with sword and

spear and javelin, but I come against you in the name of the LORD Almighty" (v. 45). His confidence was in the God within him. And the result? David defeated Goliath.

In the book of Ruth, we read about Naomi, a godly woman whose husband and two sons passed away, and the decision she made to move back to her home town of Bethlehem, primarily because of her faith in God. Each of her two daughters-in-law had a decision to make. They could either stay where they grew up (Moab) or consider going with Naomi where the people worship the Lord God Almighty. One daughter-in-law chose to stick with the familiar, Moab. The other daughter-in-law, Ruth, chose to go with Naomi to Bethlehem, as she said, "Where you go I will go, and where you stay I will stay. Your people will be my people and your God my God" (Ruth 1:16).

What gave Ruth the ability to step out and go with her mother-in-law to a land that was unfamiliar and agree to worship a God Whom she didn't grow up serving? Godfidence. What was the result? God gave Ruth a new beginning with a godly husband (Boaz) and a fulfilled promise. Everything changed because Ruth had the Godfidence to make the godly choice.

GODFIDENCE LESSON

Everything changes when you have the Godfidence to make godly choices.

In Luke 10:25–37, Jesus tells the story of a man who was beaten and robbed and left on the side of the road to die. Two religious men (a priest and a Levite) walked by this man and did nothing. Their relationship with God was not authentic. But then, a Samaritan who walked by stopped, bandaged him up, took him to an inn, and paid his bill. What did the Samaritan man have that the others did not have? Godfidence to take the initiative to help others. Remember this: you don't need to be religious to have Godfidence.

In the book of Esther, we find that an evil advisor, Haman,

convinced the king of Persia to execute all the Jews in the empire. Hatred. Racism. Just evil. The king also was in the market for a new queen, and a young lady named Esther had the Godfidence not only to pursue a role as queen but also to do something about saving her people from annihilation.

This would not be an easy task. People who approached the king without proper protocol potentially faced death. Few people would take that chance. Her cousin, Mordecai, gave her some great words of life when he said, “Who knows but that you have come to your royal position for such a time as this?” (Esther 4:14). So, after the people of God prayed and fasted, Esther gained the Godfidence to approach the king and influence his change of heart. What was the result? Success!! And the people of God were saved.

GODFIDENCE LESSON

As long as you maintain your Godfidence, miracles happen.

In Matthew 14:22–33, we read that the disciples were in a boat when strong winds came against them. They saw what at first looked like a ghost but then realized it was Jesus Himself walking on the water toward them. While most of the guys were terrified (no Godfidence), one did have Godfidence: Peter. He stepped out of the boat and began walking on the water toward Jesus. That is Godfidence. Then, when he took his eyes off Jesus, losing his Godfidence, he began to sink. What lesson can we learn from Peter? As long as you maintain your Godfidence, miracles happen.

In the book of Jonah, we read about a man who God called to go preach in the city of Nineveh, but he resisted. He didn’t have any Godfidence. He ran away. But God didn’t give up on Jonah, just like He doesn’t give up on you. Through a series of events, God got Jonah’s attention, and he finally said “yes” to God.

What was the result? Jonah was used by God to preach to a people who greatly needed to hear the gospel message. What made him have a change of heart? Godfidence. When Jonah embraced it, it made a world of difference.

In 1 Kings 18:16–39, we read about a man of God named Elijah who was challenged by 450 prophets of the false god, Baal. The odds were definitely against him. 450 to 1. Each side was to build an altar with a sacrifice to their god. Then, each was to call on their god to answer from heaven and consume their sacrifice with fire. What did Elijah have within him that brought him to the place of agreeing to this great challenge? Godfidence. And what was the result? Baal didn't respond, but our Lord God Almighty answered with fire from heaven and consumed the altar. And because of that, everyone turned to God.

GODFIDENCE LESSON

When the odds are against you,
all you need is some Godfidence.

In Daniel 3, we are told of the story of King Nebuchadnezzar and his plan to force everyone in his kingdom to bow down to the golden image he created. Those who disobeyed the king's decree would face dire circumstances – they would be thrown into a fiery furnace. Everyone obeyed the king's decree, except for three young godly men: Hananiah, Azariah, and Mishael (I prefer using their Hebrew names instead of their Babylonian names). What did they possess that gave them the ability to stand when everyone else bowed to an evil king? Godfidence. Confidence and faith in God. What was the result? They were thrown into that fiery furnace, but they didn't die. They weren't even singed. Then, miraculously, a fourth man appeared in the furnace. It was like God sent His Son to be with these three Godfident young men. It changed a kingdom.

...and Godfidence can change you as well.

TAKING CONFIDENCE TO ANOTHER LEVEL

A number of Scriptures teach us that Godfidence makes a difference in our spiritual life. Here are twenty-five of them. As you read the following verses, think of the word *Godfidence* as you read the word *confidence* and make a note of what Godfidence can do for you.

- **Faith is defined by Godfidence.** "Now faith is **confidence** in what we hope for and assurance about what we do not see" (Hebrews 11:1).
- **Godfidence places your faith and hope in God.** "Through him you have **confidence** in God, who raised him from the dead and gave him glory, so that your faith and hope are in God" (1 Peter 1:21 RSV).
- **Godfidence is quite different from self-confidence.** "Forget about **self-confidence**; it's useless. Cultivate God-confidence" (1 Corinthians 10:12 MSG).
- **Godfidence makes you competent to do God's will.** "Such **confidence** we have through Christ before God. Not that we are competent in ourselves to claim anything for ourselves, but our competence comes from God" (2 Corinthians 3:4–5).
- **Godfidence gives you faith to approach God.** "In him and through faith in him we may approach God with freedom and **confidence**" (Ephesians 3:12).
- **Godfidence rescues you from danger.** "And he did rescue us from mortal danger, and he will rescue us again. We have placed our **confidence** in him, and he will continue to rescue us" (2 Corinthians 1:10 NLT).
- **Godfidence can be contagious.** "And because of my imprisonment, most of the believers here have gained **confidence** and boldly speak God's message without fear" (Philippians 1:14 NLT).
- **Godfidence takes you to the place of God's grace and mercy.** "Let us then approach God's throne of grace with **confidence**, so that we may receive mercy and find grace to help us in our time of need" (Hebrews 4:16).
- **Godfidence opens the door to the promise of**

eternal life. "Because of his grace he made us right in his sight and gave us **confidence** that we will inherit eternal life" (Titus 3:7 NLT).

• **Godfidence assures you that God is up to something good.** "'God intends something gloriously grand here and is making the decisions that will bring it about. I say this with absolute **confidence**'" (John 8:50–51 MSG).

• **Godfidence gives you supernatural hope in the Lord.** "For you have been my hope, Sovereign LORD, my **confidence** since my youth" (Psalm 71:5).

• **Godfidence empowers you to preach the gospel.** "'And now they're at it again! Take care of their threats and give your servants fearless **confidence** in preaching your Message, as you stretch out your hand to us in healings and miracles and wonders done in the name of your holy servant Jesus'" (Acts 4:29–30 MSG).

• **Godfidence rises when you are filled with the Spirit.** "While they were praying, the place where they were meeting trembled and shook. They were all filled with the Holy Spirit and continued to speak God's Word with fearless **confidence**" (Acts 4:31 MSG).

• **Godfidence gives you a blessed hope of Christ's return. "**We can tell you with complete **confidence** – we have the Master's word on it.... The Master himself will give the command. Archangel thunder! God's trumpet blast! He'll come down from heaven and the dead in Christ will rise – they'll go first. Then the rest of us who are still alive at the time will be caught up with them into the clouds to meet the Master. Oh, we'll be walking on air! And then there will be one huge family reunion with the Master." (1 Thessalonians 4:15–18 MSG)

• **Godfidence will bring you great reward.** "Therefore do not cast away your **confidence**, which has great reward. For you have need of endurance, so that after you have done the will of God, you may receive the promise" (Hebrews 10:35–36 NKJV).

- **Godfidence takes you to the Most Holy Place.** How does **confidence** make a difference in drawing near to God? "Therefore, brothers and sisters, since we have confidence to enter the Most Holy Place by the blood of Jesus, by a new and living way opened for us…" (Hebrews 10:19–20).
- **Godfidence captures God's listening ear.** "And this is the **confidence** that we have toward him, that if we ask anything according to his will he hears us" (1 John 5:14 ESV).
- **Godfidence reminds you of the promises of God.** "LORD, never forget the promises you've made to me, for they are my hope and **confidence**" (Psalm 119:49 TPT).
- **Godfidence is a result of God's presence.** "Because you are close to me and always available, my **confidence** will never be shaken, for I experience your wrap-around presence every moment" (Psalm 16:8 TPT).
- **Godfidence opens the way to boldness.** "Since this new way gives us such **confidence**, we can be very bold" (2 Corinthians 3:12 NLT).
- **Godfidence gives you the ability to overcome fear and intimidation.** "Fear and intimidation is a trap that holds you back. But when you place your **confidence** in the LORD, you will be seated in the high place (Proverbs 29:25 TPT).
- **Godfidence makes your spiritual steps sure.** "For the LORD will be your **confidence**, | And will keep your foot from being caught" (Proverbs 3:26 NKJV).
- **Godfidence creates a safe place for your children.** "The Fear-of-GOD builds up **confidence**, | and makes a world safe for your children" (Proverbs 14:26 MSG).
- **Godfidence and trust in the Lord result in blessings.** "But blessed is the one who trusts in the LORD, whose **confidence** is in him" (Jeremiah 17:7).
- **Godfidence can make you fearless.** "So we say with **confidence**, 'The Lord is my helper; I will not be afraid'" (Hebrews 13:6).

GODFIDENCE LESSON

Godfidence takes you out of the rut of the average Christian life.

To encourage you to put all you have into the commitment of your faith, the Apostle Paul uses this phrase in Philippians 2:12: "continue to work out your salvation with fear and trembling." He is not saying that you obtain your salvation by works. Perhaps you can get the picture of what he is saying in this analogy. You have been blessed by God with a physical body. You didn't pay for it; it was a gift from God. But it is up to you to take care of your body, e.g., exercise, eating right, etc. To be physically healthy, you need to work out, build your muscles. Likewise, we have a responsibility to "work out" our spiritual life. If you want to be spiritually healthy, it is going to take some work. Paul says, "work out your salvation." This is much of what this book is all is all about. Working our spiritual muscles.

GODFIDENCE LESSON

It doesn't matter when you start your race, it only matters if you finish.

THE "I KNOW" ATTITUDE

I am not ashamed, for I know whom I have believed, and I am convinced that he is able to guard until that day what has been entrusted to me. (2 Timothy 1:12 ESV)

The individual who chooses to live with Godfidence does not doubt their faith in God nor their purpose in life. They have an "I know" attitude. Here is what this looks like:

Because I know that Jesus is the Way, the Truth and the Life, I don't have to look anywhere else.
Because I know that God has forgiven me, I have Godfidence to forgive others and even forgive myself.
Because I know that my eternity is in heaven, I believe that the problems I face today are worth it all.
Because I know that God's truth has set me free, I have

Godfidence to live in freedom.
Because I know that God is control of my health, I don't have to worry.
Because I know that God is in control of my finances, I have Godfidence that God will provide for my every need.
Because I know that God desires to bless me, I have Godfidence to obey His Word.
Because I know that God desires to bless those around me, I have Godfidence to speak words of life over them.
Because I know that God holds my tomorrow, I have Godfidence to live for Him today.
Because I know that I can do all things through Christ, I have Godfidence that He will give me victory.
Because I know that God's protection is over me and my family, I have no reason to fear.
Because I know Who God really is, I have Godfidence to make worship a lifestyle.
Because I know that I am Spirit filled, I have Godfidence that I am Spirit led.
Because I know that God has a plan for my life, I have Godfidence to follow Him and His will.

This is *Godfidence*. It's the way I live.

WORDS OF LIFE

I can do all things through Christ Who strengthens me. I am an overcomer. I am victorious. I will not be defeated. I am forgiven. I am blessed and highly favored. I am saved. I may not know what tomorrow holds, but I know Who holds tomorrow. I am a child of God!

GODFIDENCE CHECKUP

1) What are two obstacles that have kept you from reaching your spiritual potential, and how can you overcome them?

2) Have you ever found yourself lacking confidence? In your career? In a relationship? In your abilities? In life? What can you do to overcome your lack of confidence?

3) The Biblical stories mentioned in this chapter speak of how Godfidence took ordinary men and women of God and used them in supernatural ways. How can Godfidence separate you from the average, uncommitted Christian in our world today?

PRAYER FOCUS

Lord God Almighty, I come to You in the name of Jesus. Today, I ask for Godfidence. It is my desire to have an unwavering, supernatural faith in You, in Your will, and in Your purpose for my life. I recognize that there are obstacles that are keeping me from reaching my potential. I ask for You to remove anything that is keeping me from being the Christ-follower I am called to be. I believe in Your promises, and I am ready to take my spiritual life to another level. Amen. So be it.

CH. 2: REAL FAITH

Now faith is confidence in what we hope for and assurance about what we do not see.
Hebrews 11:1

In March of 2020, I was diagnosed with a large cyst on my spleen. The surgeon recommended that I have a splenectomy done to remove the cyst and also remove my damaged spleen. What made my option for surgery a bit more complicated was that our world was dealing with the coronavirus, and there were people in that particular hospital who were being treated for COVID-19.

Was it safe for me to have surgery? Would I be exposing myself to the ugly virus? The other option would be to wait and have the surgery after COVID-19 ran its course. If I postponed the surgery, I would run the risk of the cyst rupturing, which would not be good at all.

After Brenda and I prayed about this decision, I had the Godfidence to proceed with the surgery, trusting that God would take care of me. The surgery went well, and like always, God came through for me. All it took was some Godfidence on my part.

Godfidence and faith go hand in hand. What I love about both our Godfidence and faith is that they grow and mature as I personally grow and mature. When I was eleven years old, praying on the front row pew of the church my parents pastored, I needed faith to ask Jesus Christ to be my Lord and Savior. But my faith didn't stay at that level. My faith has grown.

My Godfidence has grown as well. I have noticed that the primary way my Godfidence grows is when I am faced with a challenging situation. When God called me to be a pastor, my Godfidence grew as I made the decision to leave my job and step into ministry. My Godfidence grew when the Lord spoke to me to launch a new church.

In my everyday life, my Godfidence grew when my first wife made the choice to walk out on our three children and me to pursue a different path in life. I didn't expect to raise three children on my own, but I gained the Godfidence to do so. With every financial challenge, my Godfidence grew. Every time someone let me down or treated me wrong, I took it as an opportunity to grow my Godfidence. Yes, Godfidence has changed my entire outlook on life. I no longer see issues as problems – I see them as opportunities to gain more Godfidence.

GODFIDENCE LESSON

Godfidence sees the invisible,
believes in the impossible,
and experiences the incredible.

WHAT DO YOU BELIEVE?

For God so loved the world that He gave His only begotten Son, that whosoever believes in Him shall never perish, but have everlasting life.
John 3:16 (KJV)

This is the most quoted verse in all of the Bible. The message is simple. "Whosoever believes in Him..." Are you a "whosoever"? Do you believe? It is one thing to say, "I believe there is a God." It's another thing to say, "I believe in God."

But what does it mean to "believe"? In the Greek, the word "believe" here is the word pistueon, which means "to have faith in; to entrust." The idea here is this: believing in God and gaining eternal life begins when you entrust your life to Him. Have you done this? Entrusting your life to the Lord is the best decision you can ever make.

Today, many people in America claim to believe in God, but they haven't entrusted their life to the Lord. To many of them, identifying themselves as a Christian is simply the thing to do because their parents identified as Christians. These individuals have a claim to Christianity but have not fully entrusted their lives to the Lord. They lack Godfidence.

If you were to ask 100 people the question, "Do you believe you are going to heaven?" I would say that at least 85% would say, "Yes." Then, if you were to ask a follow-up, "Why?" most would say, "Because I am a good person."

This is a misconception. The Bible never says that we get to heaven because we are good people. Many cults preach this message of "salvation by works," but it is not the truth. The Bible embodies a message of a personal relationship with Jesus Christ and entrusting your life to Him.

> **GODFIDENCE LESSON**
> When your faith is tested, it is your Godfidence that will help you pass the test.

WHEN GODFIDENCE TAKES OVER - NO MORE FEAR

Life is filled with challenges. One after another. And the enemy will do his best to bring you down by taking advantage of your issues. For example, instead of living by faith, he wants you to live in fear. There are many types of fears; here are a few specific examples:

Claustrophobia – the fear of confined spaces

Acrophobia – the fear of heights

Hydrophobia – the fear of water

Androphobia – the fear of men

Arachibutyrophobia – the fear of peanut butter sticking to the roof of your mouth

Chaetophobia – the fear of hairy people

Ergasiophobia – the fear of work (I call this laziness)

Novercaphobia – the fear of your stepmother

Ecclesiophobia – the fear of church

Phobophobia – the fear of being afraid

Fear is the opposite of faith. And the answer to

> Faith is the indefinable certainty of God behind every thing.
> – Oswald Chambers

overcoming fear is Godfidence!

In addition to fear, there are many other obstacles the enemy places in your way to keep you from increasing your Godfidence. The following Scriptures teach us what happens when Godfidence takes over.

• When you want to give up, Godfidence says, "I can do all things through Christ who strengthens me" (Philippians 4:13 NKJV).

• When it seems that you cannot see the light of day, Godfidence says, "God is my Light and my Salvation – whom shall I fear?" (Psalm 27:1).

• When there seems to be no more hope, Godfidence says, "I have…plans to give you hope and a future" (Jeremiah 29:11).

• When you are dealing with financial issues, Godfidence says, "My God will meet all your needs according to the riches of his glory in Christ Jesus" (Philippians 4:19).

> Faith is the not the absence of doubt,
> it's the means to overcome it.
> – Steven Furtick

• When you are dealing with a health issue, Godfidence says, "'I am the LORD who heals you'" (Exodus 15:26).

• When you are dealing with fears, Godfidence says, "I sought the LORD, and He heard me, | And delivered me from all my fears" (Psalm 34:4).

• When you need direction in life, Godfidence says, "Trust in the LORD with all your heart, | And lean not on your own understanding; | In all your ways, acknowledge Him, | And He shall direct your paths" (Proverbs 3:5–6).

• When you are dealing with anxiety, Godfidence says, "Do not be anxious about anything, but in every situation, with prayer and petition, with thanksgiving, present your requests to God" (Philippians 4:6).

•When you feel alone, Godfidence says, "'I will never leave you nor forsake you'" (Hebrews 13:5 ESV).

• When you are dismayed, Godfidence says, "'Do not

fear, for I am with you. | Do not be dismayed, for I am your God'" (Isaiah 41:10).

GODFIDENCE LESSON

Worry, fear, and doubt are simply a lack of Godfidence.

WHEN GODFIDENCE TAKES OVER - NO MORE WORRY

In 2011, my kids and I went up to Estes Park, Colorado for a family reunion. One afternoon, we decided to go horseback riding at Rocky Mountain National Park. We got on our horses and began our ride. As we ascended higher up the mountains, portions of the trail were about five feet from the edge of the mountain. As I looked to the right, all I could see was about a 30-foot drop. I got worried. I was thinking the worst was going to happen. One wrong step by my horse and I was a goner. I was fine riding a horse, but when the horse was a few feet away from a drastic drop, that's where worry set in. My kids were laughing at me because they saw how scared I was. I started to pray. I was repenting of every sin I could think of. "God, if You get me out of this, I will..."

Ever been there? Has worry ever played with your mind?

WORRY (v):

to torment oneself with or suffer from disturbing thoughts; to torment with cares and anxieties.

One man was always worrying. He worried about his children, his job, his wife, and his health. One day a friend of this man noted that he was extremely calm and peaceful. "Why are you so calm?" he asked. "You always worry about everything. What happened?"

The former worrier replied, "I just hired a man to do the worrying for me."

"Well, how much are you paying him?" his friend inquired.

"A thousand dollars a week," the man replied.

"A thousand a week? You can't afford a thousand dollars

a week."

The worrier responded, "That's his problem!"

GODFIDENCE LESSON

Worry makes me think that the worst is going to happen. Faith gives me the Godfidence to know that God has the final word.

Worry depletes your faith. In the story of David and Goliath, everyone was scared of the giant. They were worried about what might happen. David had a choice to make. Did he choose to worry or to have great faith?

Daniel was placed in a den of lions. Did he get worried, or did he choose to have great faith? Hananiah, Mishael, and Azariah were three Hebrew young men who received a death threat if they would not bow down to the idol. Did they choose to worry, or did they have great faith?

Stress is a sister to worry. Is that what you are dealing with? When I am "stressed," I simply turn the letters of that word around and find my solution: "desserts". Just kidding – or am I?

GODFIDENT PEACE

Cecilia tells a story about the peace of God that carried her through a pregnancy:

> When I was twelve weeks pregnant with my first child, my doctor did the standard blood test to check for abnormalities with my baby. About the same time, I had my first sonogram. Just as the technician was about to click to get the measurement, my baby turned around with the back facing towards me. The technician tried to hide her annoyance by pointing out the baby's spine since my baby was now in the fetal position, facing away from us, instead of the profile side view she needed to get the measurement.
>
> She took the sonogram probe and poked at my

belly to try and get my baby to turn back so she could complete the test. My baby was a bit stubborn, though after a bit of probing, my baby finally turned so she could get the measurement she needed.

Two weeks later, my doctor called about 8:30 p.m. Knowing my doctor doesn't normally call this late, my husband and I were alarmed. I answered and heard my doctor say, "Hello Mrs. Gipson, this is Dr. Sabella. I am calling to tell you your baby tested positive for spina bifida, and we need you to see a specialist. My office will be contacting you over the next few days to set up your appointment with a specialist." I said, "Okay," and then had to tell my husband what the doctor had said.

At that moment, I was scared and went into another room. I did exactly what I was supposed to do. I went to my Father and started to pray. I said "God, please don't let my baby have spina bifida…"

Before I said another thing, God spoke to me and said, "But I've already shown you your baby's back," and I knew that my baby was fine. I was filled with the peace that only God can give. Praise God – only He would or could orchestrate an event two weeks prior to give me exactly what I needed at that moment, His peace.

Two weeks later at sixteen weeks pregnant, I saw the specialist. I kept the appointment because I would never pass up a chance to see my baby, and I wasn't sure if my husband would accept or believe my answer that the God of the universe spoke to me and showed me our baby would be fine.

The day of the appointment, I walked into the specialist's office with complete confidence and faith, knowing my baby was fine. The specialist confirmed what I already knew. We had a false positive, and my baby did not have spina bifida.

As a bonus, this happened three weeks before my own doctor would have done a sonogram to see the gender – so we found out we were having a healthy baby boy just before the community garage sale in my neighborhood. I got to purchase things for my son, saving quite a bit of money that weekend. God is so good!

Cecilia said that she walked into the specialist's office with confidence and faith. That, my friend, is what I call Godfidence!

GODFIDENCE LESSON

When your problem gets bigger, thank God, because your Godfidence is about to grow.

HOW BIG IS YOUR GOD?

Some people have just enough faith to get them into heaven with a D-minus. For years, they've struggled with the circumstances in life because they've never been able to muster up enough faith to trust God in their everyday life.

How about you? Are you a big Godder or a small Godder? By that I mean do you trust God with every situation and circumstance you deal with, or do you worry about certain things in life? Those who worry about life have a small God, but those who trust God with everything worship a big God, knowing that He will take care of everything. So, I ask, "How big is your God?"

"When a train goes through a tunnel and it gets dark, you don't throw away the ticket and jump off. You sit still and trust the engineer."
– Corrie ten Boom

In Numbers 13, we are given the story of God telling Moses to send out twelve spies into the promised land to check it out and determine a strategy to overtake it. With one man representing each of the twelve tribes of Israel, it was evident that only two had Godfidence and ten did not. As you read, take note of the different responses of the spies.

> Then Caleb silenced the people before Moses and said, "We should go up and take possession of the land, for we can certainly do it."

> But the men who had gone up with him said, "We can't attack those people; they are stronger than we are." And they spread among the Israelites a bad report about the land they had explored. They said, "The land we explored devours those living in it. All the people we saw there are of great size. We saw the Nephilim there (the descendants of Anak come from the Nephilim). We seemed like grasshoppers in our own eyes, and we looked the same to them." (vv. 30–33)

The majority of the spies (ten of the twelve) had what I call the Grasshopper Mentality. They didn't believe they could overcome their enemy and take possession of the promises of God. A defeated mindset. No faith. No Godfidence.

Question: How many of these ten spies can you name off the top of your head?

Correct answer: Shammua, Shaphat, Igal, Palti, Gaddiel, Gaddi, Ammiel, Sethur, Nahbi, and Geuel.

I couldn't name any of these ten. I had to look it up; in fact, I always thought that Shammua was a killer whale. But I was able to name the two who had Godfidence: Joshua and Caleb.

Think about this: Do people name their children after the two who had Godfidence or the ten with no Godfidence? Two established a legacy. Ten did not. What was the difference? Godfidence. How big is your God?

> **GODFIDENCE LESSON**
>
> Godfidence is believing in God, even when the obstacles seem too big to deal with, and even when your prayers seem to be going unnoticed.

GODFIDENT FAITH

When my mother (Bertha Lopez Garcia) was a teenager, she and her family dealt with many circumstances that challenged their faith in God. Her dad, Pastor Augustin Lopez, was pastoring in Greeley, Colorado, and the opposition was great. Here is a portion of my mom's testimony:

> My family and church were victims of injuries, taunting, bullying, attacks, mistreatment, and threats. Once, someone hung a rat at the entrance to the church building with a note that read, "Mr. Augustin Lopez, you have twenty-four hours to vacate this place or you will be hung." On another occasion, ten men surrounded us, ready to hurt us, but God protected us. The angel of God surrounds those who fear him (Psalm 34:7).
>
> In 1940, my father was invited to preach at tent revival services in Walsenburg, Colorado. It was there that those who opposed their gospel message burned down the tent and everything in it, but my father's faith was strong.
>
> There was another occasion in the middle of the night when someone banged very hard on the door, yelling, "Brother Lopez, your house is on fire!"
>
> This man lived on the street behind the church and the pastor's house. His wife had been very restless and could not sleep. She got up and was looking out the window and could see flames at our house.
>
> When my father went to see what had happened, he saw that the porch was drenched in gasoline. But, miraculously, the only thing that got burned were newspapers and cardboard boxes that were on the side of the house. The power of God stopped the fire. "When you walk through the fire, you will not be burned; the flames will not set you ablaze" (Isaiah 43:2).

GODFIDENCE LESSON

Godfidence rises when your faith is greater than your circumstances.
Godfidence falls when your circumstances are greater than your faith.

THE JESUS FACTOR

For more than twenty years, I've had the privilege of serving on the board for Adult & Teen Challenge (ATC) of Texas. I have seen firsthand how men and women who once were addicted to drugs or alcohol are transformed into a new creation by the power of God. The average government-managed drug and alcohol center has a success rate of about 20%, meaning that five years after completion, about 20% are still clean. But at Adult & Teen Challenge, the success rate is 78%.[4] Wow! What is the difference? It is the Jesus factor. We don't make any apologies that the Word of God is taught and the Holy Spirit is sought at ATC because it makes a world of difference.

Real faith results in real change. In this book, Godfidence, we have been discussing the fact that a great portion of people who identify with Christianity are not really living it out. Here is another reason for this trend. Many of these individuals have never experienced true change. Metamorphosis. Much like we tend to take on certain characteristics of our earthly parents, when we become children of God, we are transformed into the likeness of our heavenly Father, that is, if our faith in God is genuine.

> **GODFIDENCE LESSON**
>
> True repentance is not reflected in how much you cry; it is seen in how much you change.

An individual who willingly keeps on sinning after proclaiming his faith in Christ has not been transformed. They may have said the right words with their mouth, but they have not yet allowed God to transform them into His likeness.

In his book *Irresistible*, Andy Stanley tells the following story:

> In 2007, while spending time in China, we took a tour of an American leather goods factory. I was introduced to

a Chinese girl in her mid-20s who had worked her way from the factory floor to management. She asked me, "Are you a pastor?"

I said, "Yes, I am." What she said next caused the hair on the back of my neck to stand up.

She said, "Two years ago, I was given a CD of your sermon, 'How Good Is Good Enough?' I listened to it over and over and I asked Jesus to live inside me. Before, my life was empty. Now, my life is full. I wanted to go to church, but there are no churches in my city. I began attending a Bible study in an apartment close to where I live. Sometimes, I ride the bus to church, but it is a two-hour ride and the ticket is expensive."

Then she asked, "Why doesn't everyone in America go to church?"

I don't know how to respond to that question. How do you explain thousands of empty churches to a young lady who would ride two hours to get to church? Her participation in the Christian church puts her life at risk. Owning a Bible puts her life at risk.[5]

Perhaps we need more Americans to have that kind of Godfident faith.

GODFIDENCE LESSON

Godfidence is not just adding some Christianity into your life. It is forming your entire life around Him.

GOD-CENTERED PURSUIT

Sometimes, the distractions and idols in life get in the way of our commitment to the Lord. Marcus emailed his story to me, and I want to share it with you.

My martial arts journey began at age five when my dad would pop in Bruce Lee movies. I was instantly hooked to the high-flying action of Enter the Dragon, Fist of Fury (The Chinese Connection), and Game of

Death. I knew instantly that I was going to be a life-long martial artist. What I didn't know was how the martial arts unchecked would become my idol and cause separation from God. My pursuit to become the next Bruce Lee led me down a path of spiritual destruction. Let me explain.

As a kid, I was very athletic, which translated to success. Complex concepts like footwork, head movement, and distancing came naturally to me. Competition was a natural progression because it provided a platform to test my abilities, prove I was the best, and maintain the center-of-attention status. I competed in as many in-house tournaments as possible and completely dominated. I began to realize that when I hit someone, it hurt. Boy did I ever enjoy that sense of power. Truth be told, I was arrogant and cocky. I needed to be humbled, and it needed to happen quickly.

When we moved to Fort Meade, Maryland, I was introduced to the grappling arts. I remember when the coach asked me to roll with one of his students. I was so wrong! I got whooped bad. I was double legged and pinned in under thirty seconds. It was a huge blow to my ego. I finally realized I wasn't the killer I thought I was.

After practice was over, coach pulled me to the side and said, "Boy you have no quit in you, ha." I looked at him and nodded. Then, he said something that would get my total devotion, "Boy, I can make you a champion if you work hard and listen."

What? My ego was restored. I was ready to do whatever it took to learn this new artform, called judo, and be a champion. It felt like I upgraded from the game of checkers to chess. Unfortunately, throughout this whole process, I never gave this amount of devotion to my Creator, who truly deserved it.

Then, catastrophe struck in the form of not one but two severe knee injuries within six months. This was the point in my life where the taste of greatness was an arm's reach away.

I remember the injury as if it were yesterday. We were practicing a throw called a fireman's carry on new mats. Unfortunately, the mats were not secured correctly, and when I attempted the throw, the mat slipped from under me making my uke [the person I was carrying] fall on top of me, causing a huge tear in my meniscus.

I was bummed, but quickly focused on my recovery. After six months of painful physical therapy, I reinjured my knee kicking a football in the park with friends. I was devastated!

I look back on it now and realize that God knew what He was doing. I found God in my darkest days. I identified how self-centered I was during this whole process. At first, I would have told you that grappling was my idol, but I have come to realize that I was my own idol. I did grappling for all the wrong reasons. I did it for my glory, not God's. So, I hung it up and let life take its course.

I pursued other forms of martial arts, but nothing felt the same. Deep down, I missed something. Pastor Randy, I remember taking your Bible study about the ten men of God and how failure struck every one of them. I realized that the only difference between them and me was that they never quit, and their pursuit was God centered. Today, I have identified my vision, pastor. I want to use grappling arts to preach to under-privileged kids and adults. Now, it is time to pursue something for God with the same tenacity as I had pursued my own glory.

> **GODFIDENCE LESSON**
> Godfidence is believing that when your dreams vanish, God has something better for you.

FAST-FORWARD FAITH

Many years ago, a young lady asked me my opinion

about her boyfriend. I said, “I don’t know him. He never comes to church.”

She answered, “Yeah, I know he doesn’t come to church, but he does believe in God.”

I asked, “Does he pray with you, lead you in Bible devotions, and tithe?”

She conceded, “No, he doesn’t, but I believe he will do that one day. He will change.” It sounded like this guy is one of the 42% of Americans who claim they are Christian but are not truly committed to the Lord.

Then I asked, “How serious are you guys?”

Excitedly, she responded, “Really serious. I think that, very soon, he will ask me to marry him. He is so cute, and he has a great sense of humor. Plus, he’s got a good job.”

I counseled her, “Ok. I know you. I see that you have a great relationship with the Lord. But yet, you want to be with someone who has faith but not real faith. Don’t expect him to change once you are married, because he probably won’t. Let’s suppose you two get married. Fast forward five years from now. Will you be ok going to church by yourself and serving God without him?”

An old joke goes like this: Have you ever noticed that women marry men with the expectations that they will change, but they don’t? And men marry women with the expectations that they won’t change, and they do?

That has some truth to it...at least the first part of that joke.

Many people, even Christ followers, make bad decisions in life because they simply don’t think ahead. They live for the here and now and forget that their life is a spiritual journey with God Almighty. They say, “I have faith in God,” but they still make their choices in life without God’s consultation or wisdom.

Faith is much more than a one-time decision at the point of salvation – it is the way we live. “Walk by faith and not by sight” (2 Corinthians 5:7 ESV).

GODFIDENCE LESSON

If you can trust God that your eternity is in heaven, then you can have Godfidence to trust Him with your everyday decisions in life.

WORDS OF LIFE

I have Godfidence! I refuse to give in to fear or worry. I believe in a big God. My faith in God is more than just words I say; it is revealed in the actions I take. When my faith is tested, I will pass the test! I have Godfidence!

GODFIDENCE CHECKUP

1) List two reasons why so many people in our world believe that we get to heaven based on being a good person.

____

____

____

____

____

____

2) List the things you are worried about and think about why you have trouble trusting God with them.

____

____

____

____

____

____

3) In response to Andy Stanley's story about the Chinese young lady, what would you say to her if she asked you, "Why doesn't everyone in America go to church?"

____

____

____

____

____

____

PRAYER FOCUS

Lord God Almighty, I come to You in the name of Jesus. Today, I reaffirm my faith in You. I have Godfidence to know that I am Your child and I will spend eternity in heaven with You. I also want to have faith for the here and now. May my everyday decisions reveal my faith in You. With each difficulty I have to deal with, I pray that my faith will grow stronger and stronger in You. May I have the faith and Godfidence to know that You always have the final Word. Amen. So be it.

CH. 3 REAL OVERCOMING POWER

Through him you have ***confidence*** *in God, who raised him from the dead and gave him glory, so that your faith and hope are in God.*
1 Peter 1:21 RSV

The 1981 movie *Chariots of Fire* portrays the true story of Eric Liddell, a man who represented Great Britain on the track in the 1924 Olympics before becoming a missionary. It was a tremendous story of faith and courage. But don't forget the showdown that happened a year before those Olympics. In 1923, Liddell ran in a meet between England, Ireland, and Scotland. In the 440-yard event, moments after the gun sounded, Liddell tangled his feet with J.J. Gillis of England, and he tumbled to the track. It appeared his dreams were shattered.

But instead, when Eric heard someone say, "Go on, go on!" he jumped to his feet and pursued the pack, even though they were a full twenty yards ahead of him. With forty yards to go, he pulled into third place, then second. Right at the tape he passed Gillis, stuck his chest out, and won the race, collapsing in total exhaustion.

The next day, the Scottish newspaper reported, "The circumstances in which Liddell won the race made it a miracle performance." Others said it was the greatest track performance they had ever seen. And without this performance, the gold at the upcoming Olympics would have never gone to Eric.

Perhaps you know what it is like to be knocked down. Some of you feel like you've been thrown to the side. How do you respond? Do you stay down? Or do you get up? The choice is yours.

GODFIDENCE LESSON

It doesn't matter when you start.
It matters if you finish.

Recently, Brenda and I decided to move into a new house. When we made our decision, I knew we had lots of work to do. I had accumulated years of belongings, and I needed to determine which items to keep and which items to throw away. The good news is that, although it was hard, I got rid of some things – like my old audio cassettes – but it was the right thing to do. Keeping those items would only take up space in our new house.

Spiritually speaking, many people hold on to "stuff" from their past and have a hard time letting go. But if they don't get rid of those hurts, habits, and strongholds, they are only taking up space in their hearts and minds...space that should be occupied by the Holy Spirit.

Emotional strongholds. Frustration. Discouragement. Fear. Inferiority complex. Anger. Depression. Lack of self-esteem. Unforgiveness. Rejection. And the list goes on.

GODFIDENCE LESSON

Godfidence turns obstacles
into opportunities.

Life is tough. The good news is God has a way of turning the negative into something good. Really good. Here is an example of this. In 1809, Simon Renee Braille and his wife Monique welcomed their fourth child into the world – a lively boy named Louis. They lived in a small stone house near Paris where Braille was the local harness maker. Leather working tools are dangerous, so the toddler had been instructed not to go into his father's shop alone.

But when Louis was still small, he slipped into the shop and, with curiosity, started to handle all the fascinating tools. As Louis was inspecting an awl, the sharp tool used to punch holes in leather, he slipped and punctured a part of his eye with the tool. The injured eye became infected. The little boy could not keep his hands from rubbing and scratching the wound, and soon the infection spread to his other eye as well. When Louis was only four, he became completely blind.

Louis was fortunate enough to study at the Royal Institution for Blind Youth in Paris. He excelled as an organist, and at twelve years old began asking the question "How can the blind read?" Over his summer break at home, Louis was determined to find the answer. As he moved and groped around his father's shop in search of the right tool for his task, the awl presented itself as perfect for the job. The awl would make the raised dots he had seen in the French military system of "night writing."

And with the very instrument that had blinded him, Louis worked and worked until he had created a system of dots whereby the blind could read and write, work math problems and compose music.

What is your awl? What is it that has crippled you, either by your own doing like young Louis or someone else's? Is it a divorce? Is it the death of someone you love? Is it a lost career? Let God take it and use it in your life for good – to reshape you or comfort others.

> "Disappointment is a place we pass through, not a place we stay. God wants us emotionally engaged in his purposes. Fully alive. He wants us to let him restore our hearts, so we can keep moving forward and fulfill his good purpose for our lives. Even when people – and life – fail us."
> – Christine Caine, Unexpected

The thief comes only to steal and kill and destroy; I have come that they may have life, and have it to the full.
John 10:10

Perhaps you are familiar with this passage. I would venture to say that you know what it is like to have the devil tempting you, attacking you, and trying to take you down. Let's look a bit deeper into his tactics.

The Greek word for "steal" in this passage is the word *klepto*, where we get the word kleptomania. An example of a kleptomaniac is a pickpocket, who takes your wallet or other valuables right in front of you. He didn't break in. He didn't wear a mask. He steals right in front of you.

That's what the devil does. He is sly. He will take something from you, e.g., your joy, your peace, your purpose for living, right in front of you. He may even disguise it in a pretty package. While you are distracted by the busyness of life, the devil will steal something from right under your nose.

HEAT AND PRESSURE

Do you enjoy ironing your clothes? Brenda knows how to get me to do some ironing: when she calls me Iron Man, I know that she is not only building up my self-esteem but she is also hinting that there is work to do. I've taken note of two things that happen to make a shirt nice and pressed. Heat and pressure. If both of these are not happening, then you are not going to get the results you want.

This is similar to what needs to happen when our pain and struggles need to get ironed out. We don't like to deal with the heat and the pressures of life, but we've got to realize that they serve a purpose, helping us get to the point of overcoming.

When someone has just experienced an open wound, one of the first things a first responder does is to place pressure on the wound. In the natural, this doesn't make sense. Pressure? Wouldn't that make the wound worse? It is my understanding that the pressure slows the blood flowing at the point of injury. It reduces the amount of blood loss and can save a life.

There are times that you have experienced a deep emotional or spiritual wound. Someone did something to you. Someone betrayed you. And you have been hurt deeply. Almost always, it seems as though other things take place to make matters worse. And you cry out to God with the questions, "Why, Lord?" Do you know what I'm talking about? In the middle of dealing with the pain, we don't always understand why the added pressures come against us as well, but they serve a purpose. These pressures result

> **GODFIDENCE LESSON**
> When others walk away from their problems, Godfidence gives you the ability to overcome.

in healing.

In Matthew 17:14–20, we are told of the story of how a man brought his demon-possessed son to the disciples, but the boy was not healed. Then, he took his son to Jesus, and the boy was delivered. Here is the dialogue that followed:

> Then the disciples came to Jesus in private and asked, "Why couldn't we drive it out?"
>
> He replied, "Because you have so little faith. Truly I tell you, if you have faith as small as a mustard seed, you can say to this mountain, 'Move from here to there,' and it will move. Nothing will be impossible for you." (Matthew 17:19–20)

Are you dealing with a mountain of a problem? If you are, then I've got some good news...you are a candidate for a miracle from God. The only way that we see the powerful, overcoming hand of God in our lives is if we are dealing with a problem. "Little faith"–believers get bent out of shape when a problem hits them. The Greek words for "little faith" here in verse 20 is *oligopistos*, which means "dull to hearing the voice of God; disinterested in walking intimately with Him."

LITTLE FAITH VERSUS OVERCOMING FAITH.

Why do so many of us fall into this trap of little faith? Is it because we worry way too much? Or we want to do things our own way? Maybe it's because God's way doesn't make sense. Or, as the Greek teaches, we are simply not listening to God's voice. A believer with little faith will say, "Oh, no, what am I going to do?"

A believer with overcoming faith will say, "God, I am giving you this problem, and I am not going to worry about it anymore. I don't know how You are going to solve this one, but I have faith that somehow, someway, You will. I believe that nothing is impossible with You."

> Faith does not operate in the realm of the possible. There is no glory for God in that which is humanly possible. Faith begins where man's power ends.
> – George Muller

When dealing with pain and struggles, it is so easy to give up. Then there are those who hang in there in tough times. They have stickituity. What, "stickituity"? Yes, this is another word I made up. You won't find it in Webster's dictionary, but you will find it in mine. Here is my definition:

> **STICKITUITY (N):**
> the relentless ability to keep on keeping on despite opposition

Thomas Edison is known as the genius who invented electricity. But he didn't succeed in his first try. One reporter asked him, "How does it feel to fail 1,000 times?" Edison responded by saying, "I didn't fail 1,000 times. The light bulb was an invention with 1,000 steps." Stickituity.

Everybody recognizes that Ludwig van Beethoven was a musical genius, but few realize the adversity he had to overcome to achieve greatness. In his twenties, Beethoven began to lose his hearing, but he refused to give up. He kept on playing music; he kept on writing music. He refused to quit. By the time he reached his fifties, Beethoven was completely deaf. His enemy was deafness. What made him a musical success was his relentless ability to overcome! Stickituity through the tough times.

GODFIDENCE LESSON

The devil says, "It's time to give up."
Godfidence says, "It's time to rise up!"

A lifeguard was on duty when he noticed a man in trouble. He dove into the water and stopped about three feet from him. The lifeguard recognized that this guy was a pretty big guy, and he was swinging his arms frantically, yelling for help. The lifeguard continued to tread water at a short distance, not because he didn't care but because he was waiting for the man to stop trying to save himself. He knew that he would be unable to save this drowning man as long as he continued to swing his arms, use his own strength, and rely on his own abilities.

Finally, the man's energy left him, and he had no more fight. When he stopped beating the water and stopped "leaning on his own understanding," the lifeguard took over. He came from behind, reached over his shoulder, cupped the man's chin under his hand, and put an elbow in the middle of his shoulder blade. This allowed the man's body to come closer to the surface of the water and rest on the hip of the lifeguard as he side-stroked to the edge of the pool.

There are times when you and I find ourselves in a troubling situation. We cry out for help, but we continue to frantically beat the things around us, panicking and try to use our own strength. And all the while, our Lord and Savior is just a few feet away...waiting for us to calm down, to stop throwing a fit, and to allow His strong and powerful hand to reach out and bring us to safety. Sometimes, God is waiting until we stop frantically trying to do things on our own strength so that He can step in and take care of the problem.

Overcoming faith says, "God, I am not going to try and handle this on my own any longer. I give it to you." That is faith. Overcoming faith!

GODFIDENCE LESSON

If you believe that your problems are too big, perhaps the problem is that your God is too small.

SPIRITUAL WARFARE

Much is said about spiritual warfare and the attempt by the devil to take you down. The enemy is for real, but greater is He who is in you than he that is in the world (cf. 1 John 4:4). It is my contention that the primary battleground is in the mind of the believer. Your flesh entices you to do what is wrong while your spirit convicts you to do what is right. And the battle is on.

This reminds me of the cartoon of the guy on the verge of making a choice between right and wrong. There is an angel with a halo on one shoulder trying to influence him to do right. Then there is a red devil with a pitchfork and pointy ears on the other shoulder tempting him to do what is wrong.

Spiritual warfare happens between your flesh and your spirit. It happens every day. Some are small battles and others are bigger ones. With each small victory, you gain strength to take on the bigger ones.

Here is the key to winning in spiritual warfare: have the Godfidence to make godly decisions. The principle is this: In the context of flesh versus spirit, whatever you feed will grow and whatever you starve will die. With every godly choice you make, you are starving your fleshly desires. But with every choice you make to sin, you are starving your spirit. The choice is yours. When you make the right choices, the victory is yours.

GODFIDENCE LESSON

Godfidence is the key to your victory over your fleshly desires.

Not every believer has overcoming power. Many try to

live life on their own strength. Remember, many believers talk the talk but don't walk the walk. Those who walk the walk give their cares and needs over to the Lord and then live with overcoming power!

GODFIDENCE TO OVERCOME

Your boyfriend drops you. Your boss fires you. Your best friend betrays you. Your health fails you. Your finances worry you. Your spouse disappoints you. Your family doesn't understand you. Your loved one passes away. The list goes on.

Life is tough. So, how do you respond? Where do you go for answers to get out of being down and out? Dr. Phil? Oprah? Nirvana? Your horoscope? I hope you don't turn to those options. You know where to go: God!

> **GODFIDENCE LESSON**
> Sometimes God places a Goliath in front of you to bring out the David within you.

You, dear children, are from God and have overcome them, because the one who is in you is greater than the one who is in the world.
I John 4:4

Over my years of life, I have faced my share of challenging situations that have tested my faith. I would like to give you the five steps I have learned that enable me to live with overcoming power.

1) Identify your enemy. "Put on the full armor of God, so that you can take your stand against the devil's schemes. For our struggle is not against flesh and blood, but against the rulers, against the authorities, against the powers of this dark world and against the spiritual forces of evil in the heavenly realms" (Ephesians 6:11–12).

Satan, our enemy, is the father of lies. He is the evil one who does everything to steal, kill, and destroy. He seeks to distract us from our faith and deceive us from the truth. He attacked Jesus, and he will attack you. But here is the good news: Jesus overcame him with the Word, and so can you and I.

Remember this: your boss is not your enemy. Neither is your spouse or family member. A political party is not your enemy. Neither is that news station. Satan is your enemy. And once we properly identify who the enemy is, we can take steps to overcome.

{ "The Christian life is a not a playground; it is a battleground." – Warren Wiersbe

2) Connect with other believers. Do you realize that connecting with the church (the people of God) sets you up to overcome the enemy? That's what Jesus told Peter, "And I tell you that you are Peter, and on this rock I will build my church, and the gates of Hades will not overcome it" (Matthew 16:18). I will discuss this further in the chapter "Real Community."

3) Go to the Word of God. Have you ever wondered why there are so many great stories in the Bible? One reason is to teach us lessons on how we can overcome. For example, Moses had to overcome a speech impediment. David had to overcome the death of his child. Noah had to overcome ridicule from the people. Job had to overcome tragic circumstances. Gideon had to overcome his lack of self-esteem. Joseph had to overcome the rejection of his brothers. Daniel had to overcome his boss's misunderstanding. Both Naomi and Ruth had to overcome the deaths of their husbands. Elijah had to overcome a spiritual battle against 450 prophets of Baal. Paul had to overcome a thorn in his flesh. The list goes on. These stories are terrific! And they serve to teach us that we can overcome as well. Do you have Godfidence in that?

GODFIDENCE LESSON

Your Godfidence won't grow unless it is tested.

Oh, and by the way, Matthew 4 tells us that Jesus Himself had to overcome temptations from the devil. And how did He overcome? By standing on the Word of God. Three times the devil temped Jesus. And three times Jesus responded with a Scripture, saying, "It is written."

For Scriptures that help us overcome specific issues in life, check out Appendix 1, "Scriptures of Life."

4) Pray intentionally. Yes, prayer is always involved in helping us overcome the enemy. But sometimes, we must be intentional about the way we pray.

a) Confess unbelief. Reject the mind games that the enemy is playing with you.

b) Ask God for his perspective. Perhaps there is a good reason why you are dealing with this issue.

c) Pray the promises of Scriptures over yourself.

5) Live with Godfidence. Know that God is in charge and that He has your back. As a child of God, you have faith for today and hope for tomorrow. Let's live like it.

"God stretches us to grow us. To stretch means to be capable of being made wider or longer without tearing or breaking. To spread out; to make capable. The key to effective stretching is pressing toward Jesus. He is going to pull you toward Himself. Anything that the Lord has allowed to come to you is not made to break you, but to grow you into [who] God wants you to be."
– Christine Caine

UNFORGIVENESS

One of the most challenging things to overcome is when someone does us wrong. Do we have the ability to forgive, especially when the hurt is so deep? Former San Antonio Spur Monty Williams is a committed believer in Jesus Christ. On the evening of February 9, 2016, Monty's faith was deeply tested when he received a phone call that he was not expecting. His wife of twenty-six years, Ingrid, was driving with three of their five children on a downtown street in Oklahoma City. Suzannah Donaldson was driving the opposite direction when she – going twice the speed limit and influenced by methamphetamine – swerved to avoid a car and ended up hitting Ingrid's car head on. That night, Ingrid went to be with the Lord, and Donaldson died as well.

At his wife's funeral, Monty said this in response to the Donaldson family, "In my house, we have a sign that says, 'As for me and my house, we will serve the Lord.' We cannot serve the Lord if we don't have a heart of forgiveness. Life is hard. It is very hard. And we hold no ill will toward the Donaldson family. God will work this out." This is forgiveness. This is being more like Christ. This is an example of someone who has Godfidence that things will work out.

> "Forgiven people become forgiving people."
> – Dr. Henry Cloud

Remember this: when you forgive a person, it doesn't mean that you have to trust them or that they must be your friend. It doesn't mean that you will be immediately healed, but it does mean that you are opening the door to your own healing.

Forgiveness. This is never easy to do. Peter thought he had it all figured out, but Jesus taught him a great lesson. It is found in Matthew 18:21–22:

> Peter came to Jesus and asked, "Lord, how many times shall I forgive my brother or sister who sins against me? Up to seven times?"
>
> Jesus answered, "I tell you, not seven times, but

seventy-seven times."

I have a feeling that Peter was trying to make himself look good in front of his peers and Jesus. You see, religious tradition taught that you must forgive someone three times. So, Peter must have thought, "I can do better than that. I am willing to forgive someone not just three times, but seven times." After all, seven is the number of completion. That should merit accolades from Jesus. But Jesus' response put Peter in his place when He said, "seventy-seven times," which implies: don't put a limit on your forgiveness.

> **GODFIDENCE LESSON**
> God doesn't give you the people you want. He gives you the people you need. To help you. To hurt you. To leave you. To love you. To make you the person you were meant to be.

When someone does you wrong, it is so easy to fall into the trap of responding in the wrong way. As we said earlier in this chapter, it is the devil who is our enemy, not another person. How would the enemy want you to respond? He wants you to react in anger, rehash the offense over and over again, replace God's voice with his voice, refocus your eyes on the problem, not on the solution, resent people instead of loving them, retaliate against those who hurt you and regress in your spiritual life. That is an ugly trap. Wouldn't it be better to forgive that person?

> "Forgiveness does not change the past, but it does enlarge the future." – Paul Lewis Boese

An Armenian nurse had been held captive along with her brother by the Turks. Her brother was slain by a Turkish soldier before her eyes. Somehow, she escaped and later became a nurse in a military hospital.

One day she was stunned to find that the same man who had killed her brother had been captured and brought wounded to the hospital where she worked. Something within her cried out "vengeance," but a stronger voice called for her to love. She nursed the man back to health. Finally, the recuperating soldier asked her, "Why didn't you let me die?"

Her answer was, "I am a follower of Him who said, 'Love your enemies, do good to them which hate you'" (Luke 6:27). Impressed with her answer, the young soldier replied, "I never heard such words before. Tell me more. I want this kind of religion."

Sometimes, God orchestrates the events of your life to get your attention. It's not bad luck. It's not karma. The word "oops" is not in God's vocabulary – because God doesn't make mistakes. He just waits for your response. Animosity or love? Retaliation or grace? Revenge or forgiveness? The choice is yours.

MIND GAMES

When Hank Aaron and Yogi Berra played baseball against each other, they had a playful rivalry. During one particular game, Hank stepped up to bat, and Yogi, who was the catcher tried his best to distract Hank. He said, "Hey Hank, you can't hit. Your mama can't hit. And did you notice that your name on back of your uniform is spelled wrong?"

Well, Yogi's attempt to distract Hank didn't work, as Hank hit the next pitch over the center-field fence. After he rounded the bases and touched home plate, he looked at Yogi and said, "Just thought you might want to know that I didn't come here to read, I came to win."

Yes, indeed, the enemy does all he can to distract you from reaching your spiritual goals. Distractions come in all shapes and sizes. Temptations. Busyness. People. Wrong motives. Culture. Media. Disappointments. Sin. People's opinions. And the list goes on...but God gives you the ability to overcome!

> "You will never reach your destination if you stop and throw stones at every dog that barks."
> – Winston Churchill

Distraction is one of many tactics of the enemy. He will use anything and everything he can to entice you or trap you to fall into his hands. If you set up a mouse trap to trap a mouse, you will probably use cheese, because that's what will attract the mouse. The cheese is the bait. An unwise mouse doesn't know that if he goes for the cheese, he will pay the price with his life. Likewise, Satan will try to entrap you by hiding the consequences. He doesn't want you to know that sin will cost you your life.

What are some of the other tactics of the enemy that we must be careful about? He will lie to you. He will tempt you. He will condemn you. He will place guilt on you. And he will bully you.

> "Advancement invites opposition."
> – Randall Sean Garcia

THE GIFT OF PAIN

Lora Batterson and her husband, Mark, pastor a great church in Washington, DC. In 2017, Lora was dealing with breast cancer. Her response to God was this, "God, what have you come to teach me?" And her statement to others is this, "Cancer has been a gift." This is Godfidence!

Beth Moore said, "Life shouldn't be a journey to the grave with the intention of arriving safely in a pretty and well preserved body, but rather to skid in broadside, thoroughly used up, worn out and loudly shouting, 'Wow! What a ride! Thank You, Lord!'"

> "Problems are a signal that you are on the right path." – Carly Fiorina

A twenty-two-year-old young man was looking for affirmation in life. He didn't find it at home, so he thought he could find it in a circle of friends who were ungodly. He got himself into trouble, one negative incident after another.

Finally, he and his dad had a heart-to-heart talk. When his dad realized what his son needed, he said, "Son, forgive me. I have not given you the affirmation you deserve. I am sorry. And I want you to know that I believe in you. You are a fantastic, gifted young man with great potential, even for the kingdom of God."

That's all that the young man needed to hear. After that conversation, he changed. He left that group of ungodly friends and pursued a close relationship with the Lord. Words of life made of world of difference.

WORDS OF LIFE

I am an overcomer. Discouragement will no longer get the best of me, because I am a child of the King. I have the power to overcome guilt, shame, condemnation, jealousy, unforgiveness, offenses, hatred, rejection, fear, grief, worry, temptation, pain, depression, anger, and anything else the devil tries to throw at me.

GODFIDENCE CHECKUP

1) In your opinion, what gave David the Godfidence to accept the challenge to fight Goliath? Hint: Look at 1 Samuel 17:32, 34–37, 41–47

____

____

____

____

____

____

2) Lisa Bevere said, "The attacks on your life have much more to do with who you might be in the future than who you have been in the past. The enemy fears you becoming who God has made you to be." What do you believe the enemy is trying to stop in you and your life?

____

____

____

____

____

____

3) Looking back on the challenges in life you have already dealt with, list the lessons you have learned because of those challenges:

____

____

____

____

____

____

PRAYER RESPONSE

Lord God Almighty, I come to you in the name of Jesus. I am so grateful that You give me the ability to overcome any obstacle, any temptation, any struggle, or any attack from the enemy. By the power of the Holy Spirit, I have Godfidence that You are in control and can turn any negative into a positive. May I receive my victory, and may You receive the glory. Amen. So be it.

CH. 4 REAL LOVE

Dear friends, let us love one another, for love comes from God. Everyone who loves has been born of God and knows God. Whoever does not love does not know God, because God is love.
1 John 4:7–8

Marie broke her boyfriend's heart when she told him, "It's over." Then, a month later, she had a change of heart and texted the following words to him, "Johnny, my Love, I can't tell you how much I love you and miss you. Breaking up with you was the biggest mistake of my life. Please tell me that you will take me back. I am sorry. I will make it up to you. Love, Marie. P.S. Congrats on winning the state lottery!"

That is not an example of real love. We live in a world of superficial love. Many people say "I love you!" even when they don't mean it. Our world today is looking for real love. A love that goes deep. A Jesus kind of love.

If you were given the opportunity to spend five minutes one-on-one with anyone in the history of mankind, who would it be and what would you ask them? There are a few sports stars that come to my mind, or perhaps a famous singer or musician. But, because I am writing this book, it's best if I get spiritual and say that I would use my opportunity to speak with Jesus. Actually, there will come a time when I get to spend time face-to-face time with the Lord in heaven, and it will be a lot more than just five minutes. And today, although I don't see Jesus physically, I do get to speak with Him every day.

In Matthew 22, we are told that a teacher of the law had an opportunity to speak with Jesus face to face. What question did he ask? On his mind were the 613 commandments of the Torah (the original Hebrew Scriptures). That's a lot to keep up. So, he asks a very good question...which is most important?

> One of them, an expert in the law, tested him with this question: "Teacher, which is the greatest commandment in the Law?"
>
> Jesus replied: "'Love the Lord your God with all your heart and with all your soul and with all your mind.' This is the first and greatest commandment. And the second is like it: 'Love your neighbor as yourself.'" (Matthew 22:35–39)

The two greatest commandments are summarized with "Love God and love people." Where did Jesus get this from? In His answer to this question, Jesus references the Shema, which is the standard of Hebrew prayer, much like Christians recite the Lord's Prayer. The Shema (Deuteronomy 6:4–5) is a prayer that focuses on our need to love God, the one and only God.

Jesus' answer is classic. He doesn't do away with the Law (the Torah). Instead, Jesus quotes it. But then, He takes it to another level. He tells this expert of the law that not only should we love God, but we should also love people. Wow! This is known as "The Great Commandment."

It's all about love. Christ's reference to the Shema is a reminder of the depth of love we must have for God. It tells us that we are to love the Lord our God not just any ol' way, but with all of our heart, all of our mind, and all our strength. That's lots of love. "Hear, O Israel: The LORD our God, the LORD is one. Love the LORD your God with all your heart and with all your soul and with all your strength" (Deuteronomy 6:4–5).

What is most important to the Lord? Loving God and loving people. When I came to understand this, it changed my life. It changed the way I looked at people. No more judgment. No more expectations of others. Simply loving them, the way Jesus would.

REAL LOVE - AHAVAH

In the Old Testament, the word "love" comes from the Hebrew word *aheb* or *ahavah*, which means "I give" and "love." The idea is simple: true love is giving. It is a picture of a deep relationship between two people; not superficial, which focuses on getting. True love for God is expressed in how you give to Him. Your time. Your resources. Your abilities. Your mind. Your heart. Everything. This is real love.

There is another meaning to this Hebrew word *ahavah*, as it goes even deeper than just love and giving. It is connected with the Hebrew word *echad*, which means "one." Both of these Hebrew words are part of the Shema. True love (*ahavah*) means that you are one (*echad*) with that person, whether it means you are one with God or one with the individual you love.

> "The Great Commission is hindered when the Great Commandment is disregarded."
> – Timothy Simpson

Can this same deep love that we have for God be translated to people as well? Yes. It can. In fact, it is the kind of love we are *supposed* to have for people, but loving people is much more difficult. God never lets you down, but people do. God never turns His back on you, but people do. Perhaps that is why we hold back when it comes to loving people. We don't want to get burned. Loving people is a greater test of whether or not we have real love.

It's a bit easier to love someone who loves you. You simply love them back. But how about loving someone who clearly doesn't love you. That is a test. Remember, to love God and love people is the Great Commandment, not the Great Suggestion.

GODFIDENCE LESSON

When a person truly loves God, they are empowered to love people.

All this was a huge mind shift for the teachers of the law, because they were taught to be law-abiding, religious men. We must understand that the Great Commandment principle is not bashing the importance of the law. Not at all. The focus is to understand how we interpret the law. When we fully understand the depth of the Word of God (the law), then we can live it out. Many of the religious teachers of the law had lots of head knowledge but not very much heart knowledge. Jesus never spoke against the Old Testament Torah – instead, He emphasized the need to live it out.

One of the Jewish traditions is to place the Shema prayer on a parchment in a mezuzah, which is a small decorative case that is attached to the doorframe of a front door. Both in my current home and my previous home, I placed a mezuzah on my front doorframe. I didn't place it there for the sake of tradition. I did it for two reasons: (1) to remind me that I am blessed coming, and blessed going out, and (2) to remind me that I need to love God and love people in practical ways when I enter my house and when I leave my house, which is ALL the time.

When Brenda and I sold our house in 2019, I handed the keys over to the new owner and then told her, "I just wanted to let you know that when I had this home built, I had Scriptures, prayers, and blessings written on the wood frame before the sheetrock was installed. Then, I placed this mezuzah right here (I pointed to the doorframe) as a reminder that we are blessed coming in and blessed going out. This is a Hebraic/Biblical blessing from Scripture. Let me know if you want me to remove it or leave it up. This is a blessed home."

With tears in her eyes, she said, "I want you to leave it there."

With the busyness of life, we need a daily reminder of the love of God. The basis of a real *ahavah* love for God gives you a real ahavah love for people. You cannot love your neighbor until you first love God. Even the New Testament verse 1 John 4:19 emphasized this point, "We love because he first loved us." Our love for people is a response to the way God loves us. This is easy to say, but difficult to do.

> "More people have been brought to Christ by the kindness of real Christian love than by all the theological arguments in the world."
> – William Barclay

REAL LOVE EXPRESSED

A group of children were asked the question, "What is real love?" Here are a few of their responses:

- Real love is when a little old lady and a little old man still love each other after they know each other so good.
- Real love is when mommy sees daddy all smelly and sweaty and still says that he is handsomer than Matthew McConaughey.
- Real love is when your puppy licks your face even after you left him home alone all day.
- Real love is when my grandma got arthritis and can't bend over to paint her toenails. So, my grandpa does it for her, even though he's got arthritis too.
- Real love is when somebody hurts you and makes you so mad, but you don't yell at them because you know it would hurt their feelings.

> "If you are weak in faith, it means that your love is also weak. No love, no faith. Weak love, weak faith. Strong love, strong faith." – Chris Hayward

A frail old man went to live with his son, daughter-in-law, and four-year-old grandson. The old man's hands trembled, his eyesight was blurred, and his step faltered. The family ate together at the table, but the elderly grandfather's shaky hands and failing eyesight made eating difficult. Peas rolled off his spoon onto the floor. When he grasped his glass, milk spilled on the tablecloth.

The son and daughter-in-law became irritated with the mess. "We must do something about Father," said the son. "I've had enough of his spilled milk, noisy eating, and food on the floor."

So, the husband and wife set a small table in the corner. There, Grandfather ate alone while the rest of the family enjoyed dinner. Since Grandfather had broken a dish or two, his food was served in a wooden bowl. When the family glanced in Grandfather's direction, sometimes he had a tear in his eye as he sat alone.

Still, the only words the couple had for him were sharp admonitions when he dropped a fork or spilled food. The four-year-old watched it all in silence.

One evening before supper, the father noticed his son playing with wood scraps on the floor. He asked the child sweetly, "What are you making?"

Just as sweetly, the boy responded, "Oh, I am making a little bowl for you and Mama to eat your food in when I grow up." The four-year-old smiled and went back to work.

The words so struck the parents that they were speechless. Then tears started to stream down their cheeks. Though no word was spoken, both knew what must be done. That evening the husband took Grandfather's hand and gently led him back to the family table. For the remainder of his days, he ate every meal with the family. And for some reason, neither husband nor wife seemed to care any longer when a fork was dropped, milk spilled, or the tablecloth soiled. Their four-year-old son taught them a lesson about real love.

"The Christian life is far more than a list of rules God has given us to follow. He has given us himself. Love inspires us to please the One who has proven His love by giving His life for us." – Dennis Rouse

LOVING DESPITE DIFFERENCES

Have you noticed that each of us is different? In fact, life would be quite boring if everyone was exactly like you. And because we are different, we often disagree. Here's the question: Can you love someone, even if they disagree with you? Can you love someone, even if they have opinions different than yours?

Some say, "Ford trucks are better!" Others say, "Chevy trucks are better!" Some say, "I'm a Republican!" Others say, "I'm a Democrat!" Can we still love each other?

Some say, "Hook 'em Horns!" Others say, "Gig 'em Aggies!" Some say, "Blue Bell Ice Cream is the best!" Others say, "Breyers Ice Cream is the best!" (Author's note: I like both brands of ice cream.)

> **GODFIDENCE LESSON**
> Real love means giving people a piece of your heart rather than giving them a piece of your mind.

On several occasions in the New Testament, the Apostle Paul wrote about a major disagreement among the people in that time: Can we eat meat that was sacrificed to idols? Some believed such meat was spiritually contaminated. Others believed that as long as God blesses that meat, it is ok to eat. This was a big issue. Many were tempted to do what they thought was right in their own eyes, even if it offended others.

In Romans 14:21, Paul gives us some great advice, "Don't eat or say or do things that might interfere with the free exchange of love" (MSG). Love. Real love is a much better option.

Brenda and I enjoy doing devotions together from Christian books on the topic of marriage. In their book *Saving Your Marriage Before It Starts*, Dr. Les and Leslie Parrott teach a communication lesson that can be applied not only in a marriage but in other relationships as well. "Rather than evaluating or requiring change, you simply accept the thoughts, feelings and actions of the person you love." I confess that I used to be more focused on changing a person's mind than loving them. Now I see no need to debate over differences. No need to prove my point. I now focus on loving God and loving people.

Today, there are over 1,000 denominations. Why?

Because so many Christians disagree about doctrine. Someone once complained to me that church is not the way it used to be. He said, "I don't like the way Christians today disagree about so many things. We need to do church the way it was for the early church in the book of Acts."

I responded by saying, "Ok. As long as you realize that there were many disagreements in the early church." Here is a list of conflicts that Paul had:

- Paul had a disagreement with Peter (Galatians 2:11).
- Paul had a conflict with Elymus the sorcerer (Acts 13:8–12).
- Paul had a conflict with the Judaizers (Acts 15:1–21).
- The church of Corinth attacked Paul (Acts 18:12).
- Paul had a disagreement with Demus (2 Timothy 4:10).
- Paul had a disagreement with John Mark (Acts 15:37–38).
- Paul had a disagreement with Barnabas (Acts 15:39–41).
- Paul had a disagreement with Alexander the coppersmith (2 Timothy 4:14).

Disagreements are inevitable, but we can still love each other. I have noticed that most of our differences center around personal opinions. Not facts but opinions.

One man tried his best to convince me that Steven Furtick is a false Bible teacher. He had no proof. No facts. It was just his opinion. He was trying to force his opinion on me. When I didn't agree with him, he got angry. Very angry. I responded, "It's fine if you have your opinions, but when you try to force your religious opinions on others, that becomes legalism. I love you, my brother."

In 2 Timothy 4:11, we read that Paul reconciled with John Mark. "Only Luke is with me. Get Mark and bring him with you, because he is helpful to me in my ministry." We have a great ending to this story.

GODFIDENCE LESSON

Godfidence gives you the ability to love someone whom you disagree with.

PROVE IT

A man and his wife were driving on the highway when they got into a heated argument. It was getting bad. The husband's anger got a hold of him so much that he lost control of the car and crashed into a tree. Immediately, the wife passed away and went to heaven. She was greeted by St. Peter (he's always there to greet people in these heaven jokes), who said, "Welcome to heaven. In order to gain entrance, all you have to do is spell the word love."

She said, "That's easy. L – O – V – E."

Pete said, "That is correct. Welcome to heaven! Oh, by the way, I've got to run to a quick meeting. Can you monitor the entrance gate here?"

She said, "Sure."

Ten minutes later, her husband, who she had been arguing with, arrives at the pearly gates and asks, "What are you doing here and what do I need to do to get past these gates?"

She said, "St. Peter left me in charge, and all you have to do is spell a word."

He said, "What word do I need to spell?"

She said, "Czechoslovakia!"

It's easy to love someone when they are treating you right. But real love happens when you have to look beyond their faults. It's easy to tell someone, "I love you!" It's not as easy to prove it.

Here are ten ways and ten Scriptures we can use to prove our love to others in a practical way:

1) Listen before you speak (James 1:19).
2) Speak words of life (Proverbs 18:21).
3) Restore with gentleness (Galatians 6:1).
4) Encourage and lift up (Colossians 2:2).
5) Withhold judgment (Matthew 7:1-2, Deut. 32:35–36).
6) Give with a generous spirit (1 John 3:17–18).
7) Pray for others consistently (1 Thessalonians 1:2).
8) Be patient with everyone (1 Thessalonians 5:14).
9) Forgive unconditionally (Matthew 6:14).

10) Go the extra mile with compassion (Luke 10:30–37).

REAL LOVE - *AGAPE*

In the English language, the word "love" is a broad term. I can say, "I love my wife, Brenda," and I may also say, "I love pecan praline ice cream." It's obvious that those are two different kinds of love. The Greek language, on the other hand, has four words to describe what we call "love." To understand the Jesus kind of love, it's best to understand this conversation in the Greek language that this was written.

The Greek word *agape* is the highest level of love, where someone would even give their life for another. I call this "Real Love." The Greek word *phileo* is a brotherly type of love. The Greek word *storge* is a family kind of love. And the Greek word *eros* is a romantic and sensual kind of love. I've noticed that when anyone focuses on the *agape* kind of love, everything else falls into place.

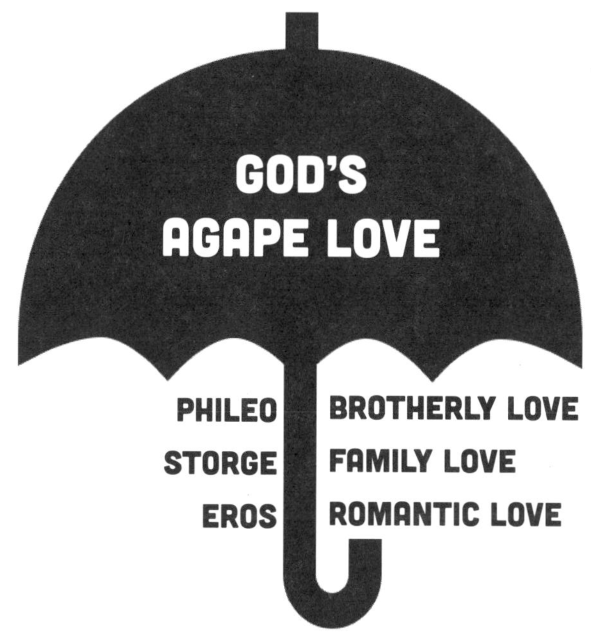

GOD'S UMBRELLA OF LOVE
FOUR GREEK WORDS FOR LOVE

In this diagram, we see that this *agape* (real love) is the standard by which all types of love are to flow. Wouldn't you like to have the Godfidence that every area of your life is blessed by God's covering? This can happen when we strategically place ourselves under God's umbrella of agape love. Unfortunately, many people have chosen to get out from under God's love.

What happens when we step out from under the will of God and away from the love of God? A host of problems. Here are some examples:

- When we remove the *phileo* brotherly kind of love out from under God's Real Love, we fall into the trap of racism and bullying (no brotherly love).
- When we remove the *storge* family kind of love out from under the will of God, one trap we can easily fall into is abortion (no love for the soon-to-be-born baby).
- When we remove the *eros* romantic/sensual kind of love out from under the will of God, we are susceptible to fall into the trap of fornication or homosexuality (no romantic love the way God intended it).

Racism. Abortion. Homosexuality. Three issues of our day that have come about because we have stepped out from under the umbrella of God's love.

I believe we in America are dealing with so many moral issues today because so many individuals have redefined love to suit their own preferences rather than living out God's love the way He intended us to live.

> **GODFIDENCE LESSON**
> The solution to today's cultural and moral issues is love but not any kind of love – a Jesus kind of love.

I drove up to my mailbox at the end of my block. There was an elderly lady with a handful of mail and a box. She had her hands full. I offered to help her place her items in her car. She looked at me and said, "I know who you are. You are the technology whiz who opens and closes my garage door while sitting in your house. Sometimes, I can't even sleep because of you."

I was in shock. No, I'm not a technology geek. No, I don't sit around my house all day opening and closing other people's garage doors. No, I don't have any hatred toward this lady. Unfortunately, she prejudged me, and it wasn't pretty.

That's what happens with many people today. They misidentify their enemy. Your enemy is not that guy with a different skin color. Your enemy is not your boss or your co-worker or cousin or your husband. Your enemy is the devil himself. So, don't lose sleep because of the mind games the devil plays with you. Love people even when our culture disagrees.

THE LOVE GOD HATES

Do not love the world or anything in the world. If anyone loves the world, love for the Father is not in them. For everything in the world – the lust of the flesh, the lust of the eyes, and the pride of life – comes not from the Father but from the world. The world and its desires pass away, but whoever does the will of God lives forever.

1 John 2:15–17

It would be totally absurd for a man to tell his wife, "Honey, I love you, but I am also in love with someone else." That's not real love.

Many people have this kind of conversation with God. They love God but also have another love on the side. The Scripture above is referring to the love of the world. This is the kind of love that God hates. A marriage with a double-minded husband won't work and neither will a relationship with the double-minded Christian.

Temptation to pull away from our love for God is always a challenge. This is spiritual warfare. You may be tempted to sin in ways that are different than the ways I am tempted, but we are all tempted. When I am tempted, I often meditate on the cross of Calvary. I picture Jesus suffering and dying for the sake of my sins and my forgiveness. When I sin, I picture picking up a hammer and putting another nail through one of Jesus' hands. Do I really want to cause Him more pain, to abuse the grace of God? If my relationship with God is based on real love, I will choose not to sin. I will choose to overcome temptation.

> **GODFIDENCE LESSON**
> Lust can't wait for opportunities to get.
> Love can't wait for opportunities to give.

Here are seven common excuses we often use to compromise our love for God:

- Everybody else is doing it.
- The principles of the Bible are so old fashioned.
- The devil made me do it. (Truth reminder: The devil can't make you do anything. It is always your choice.)
- I had a temporary lapse of judgment.
- I've been through so much. I deserve a pass.
- It's just a little sin, nothing big. (Truth reminder: Sin is sin.)
- This is fine, because it won't hurt anyone. (Truth reminder: Sin hurts you and it hurts God.)

During the 2020 coronavirus pandemic, we were given clear instructions to wash our hands well, not just haphazardly but for at least twenty seconds. I never sang the "Happy Birthday" song more in my life. Why were we going through these measures? To keep clean of any virus. Or we can say it this way: we love health and hate germs. There is a similar spiritual approach to sin. Love God, hate sin.

WITHOUT LOVE, YOU ARE BANKRUPT

Read at many wedding ceremonies, 1 Corinthians 13 is known as the Love Chapter because it describes a true *agape* kind of love. The Message version of the Bible expresses this Scripture in a contemporary language. Here are a few verses of it:

I'm bankrupt without love.
Love never gives up.
Love cares more for others than for self.
Love doesn't want what it doesn't have.
Love doesn't strut,
Doesn't have a swelled head,
Doesn't force itself on others,
Isn't always "me first,"
Doesn't fly off the handle,
Doesn't keep score of the sins of others,
Doesn't revel when others grovel,
Takes pleasure in the flowering of truth,
Puts up with anything,
Trusts God always,
Always looks for the best,
Never looks back,
But keeps going to the end.

That's a pretty powerful synopsis of what real love is. Now read Ephesians 3:16–19. What does it say we can be filled with?

> I pray that out of his glorious riches he may strengthen you with power through his Spirit in your inner being, so that Christ may dwell in your hearts through faith. And I pray that you, being rooted and established in love, may have power, together with all the Lord's holy people, to grasp how wide and long and high and deep is the love of Christ, and to know this love that surpasses knowledge – that you may be filled to the measure of all the fullness of God.

Does this Scripture say that we can be filled with God? Actually, it says more. Does this Scripture say that we can be filled with the measure of God? Actually, it says more. Does this Scripture say that we can be filled with the measure of the fullness of God? Actually, it says more. It says, "that you may be filled to the measure of all the fullness of God." That is a lot of love!

{"It's the Holy Spirit's job to convict, God's job to judge and my job to love." – Billy Graham

A JESUS KIND OF LOVE

Who does God love? He loves that annoying kid down the street. He loves that lady who lets her dog poop on your lawn. He loves that unfriendly checkout clerk. He loves that jerk you work with. He loves that weird guy at the grocery store. He loves the foul-mouthed dad at the Little League baseball game. He loves that show-off at the gym. He loves your self-centered sister. He loves your nosy neighbor. He loves your bossy boss. He loves your verbally abusive family member. He loves that crazy driver who cut you off on the I-10. He loves that crook who took you for money. God loves them, and so should we.

Why must we love them? Because behind every jerk, every show-off, and every narcissist is a hurting soul who needs to know that God loves them. And that you love them as well. Behind every foul-mouthed, verbally abusive, nosy, bossy, annoying, grumpy individual is a person who Christ died for. That is love! Real love.

GODFIDENCE LESSON

Never allow religious activity to take the place of your love for the heart of God.

A volunteer at Stanford Hospital was present when a little boy decided to give the ultimate sacrifice because he loved his sister, Liza. The volunteer says the little girl was dying of a rare disease, with only one chance for survival – a blood transfusion from her five-year-old brother. After the doctor explained what would happen during the transfusion, the little boy agreed to give his blood to save his sister.

He peacefully laid still during the transfusion. After a while, he asked the doctor a question that gave great insight into his character, "Will I start to die right away?" Apparently, the boy thought he would have to give all his blood but was willing to do so to save his sister. That is real love.

PERSONAL RIGHTS

Have you noticed that we live in a world that is constantly fighting for their rights? Some will say, "I have a right to freedom of speech!" Yes, you do. "I have a right to push my agenda!" Yes, you may. I've noticed that when people focus on fighting for their rights, it often leads to dissention and revolution. On the other hand, when people focus on love, it leads to reconciliation and unity.

Think about Jesus. He endured a crown of thorns on His head, whippings on His body, nails in His hands and feet, and even a spear in His side. But He didn't *have to* deal with all of that because He is indeed the Son of God. He had "the right" to call 10,000 angels to come to His rescue and take Him back to the Father so that He wouldn't have to suffer so much. He could have commanded the angels in heaven to come and strike down those evil Roman soldiers who were delivering so much pain to Him, but He didn't do that. Why? Jesus Christ laid down His personal rights because of His love for you. Yes, indeed, His love for you is far more important to Him than His personal rights. That, my friend, is real love.

> ### GODFIDENCE LESSON
> Every time you lay down your rights in order to love others, you are being more and more like Jesus.

Back in 2010, my son Randy Sean and his buddies competed in a 3-on-3 basketball tournament. In the third round of competition, their game ended in a bit of controversy. As regulation time was ending, Randy shot the ball and it went in, but there was a question about whether the shot happened before or after the final buzzer. The referee said that the shot counted, which meant that the game went into overtime. In overtime, my son's team won the game.

A few minutes after the game, Randy Sean, Dario, Caleb, and Joshua all agreed that there are things in life, like godly character, that are more important than winning a basketball game. They had the Godfidence to give the win to the other team, even though they had the *right* to receive the trophy.

One of the players from the other team could not understand why they would give away the win. Randy Sean used the opportunity to sow seeds of faith in this young man's life. This is what can happen when we lay down our rights and show some love.

THE MINISTRY OF RECONCILIATION

Therefore, if anyone is in Christ, the new creation has come: The old has gone, the new is here! All this is from God, who reconciled us to himself through Christ and gave us the ministry of reconciliation.

2 Corinthians 5:17–18

If you have made the decision to be a Christ follower, I have some good news for you: You are a new creation. The old life is gone, and the new is here! Your relationship with God has been reconciled. Praise God! But don't stop on verse 17. In verse 18, Paul says that you have been given a ministry. Now that you have been reconciled back to God, you have the ministry of reconciliation to help others connect with God as well.

Does the Scripture here say that we now have the right to judge others? No. Does it say that now we can disagree with others who disagree with our opinions? No. Does it say that we can now condemn others who are not Christ followers? No. Not at all. The ministry of reconciliation teaches us that instead of taking sides, we bring two sides together. And how do we reconcile? With God's *agape* love. Real love.

> "True love is an act of the will – a conscious decision to do what is best for the other person instead of ourselves." – Billy Graham

On June 17, 2015, in Charleston, South Carolina, Dylann Roof made a horrible decision and killed nine people. Shortly afterwards, the daughter of one of the victims, Nadine Collier said this, "I forgive you. You took something very precious from me. I will never talk to her again. I will never, ever hold her again. But I forgive you. And have mercy on your soul."[6]

The natural response was animosity. The supernatural response was love. What made Nadine choose love over animosity? I believe it was her strong desire to love God and love people. Do you have that kind of Godfidence?

GODFIDENCE LESSON

Loving people is a reflection of spiritual maturity.

WORDS OF LIFE

I choose to love the way Jesus loves. I will love the hard-to-love people in my life. I will love the hurting people, the sinners, the arrogant, the needy, and the lost. I choose to love them both with words and with action. God is love and so am I.

GODFIDENCE CHECKUP

1) Think of a hard-to-love individual. Write down how you can love that person.

____

____

____

____

____

____

2) When Jesus had his "Do you love me" conversation with Peter in John 21, what was His point? How would you respond to that question from Jesus? How would you explain your love to Him?

____

____

____

____

____

____

3) In reference to the "God's Umbrella of Love" diagram, list ways you can stay under God's covering of love when you are tempted to get out from under it.

Phileo (brotherly love) ______________________

____

____

____

Storge (family love) _________________________

____

____

____

Eros (romantic love) ________________________

____

____

____

PRAYER FOCUS

Lord God Almighty, I thank You for loving me first. You have proven your love for me time and time again, even while I was in sin. Today, I respond by giving You my heart and promising to love You for eternity. Teach me how to love my brothers, my family and my spouse with an agape kind of love, placing others before me and giving without expecting anything back. Help me love hard-to-love people the way You taught me. May I always go the extra mile to love people. And like King David, may I always be an individual after Your heart. Amen. So be it.

CH. 5 REAL GRACE

Let us then approach God's throne of grace with confidence, so that we may receive mercy and find grace to help us in our time of need.
Hebrews 4:16

A college professor passed out his final exam in his class and said, "Read through the test all the way before beginning to answer it." This caution was written on the exam as well. As the students read the test, it became unquestionably clear that they had not studied nearly enough.

The further the students read, the worse it became. About halfway through, audible groans could be heard throughout the lecture hall. On the last page, however, was a note that read, "You have a choice. You can either complete the exam as given or sign your name at the bottom and in so doing receive an A for this assignment."

"Was he serious? Just sign it and get an A?" Slowly, the point dawned on the students, and one by one, they turned in their tests and silently filed out of the room.

Some students began to take the exam without reading it all the way through, and they would sweat it out for the entire two hours of class time before reaching the last page.

Others read the first two pages, became angry, turned the test in blank, and stormed out of the room without signing it. They never realized what was available.

One fellow, however, read the entire test, including the note at the end, but decided to take the exam anyway. He did not want any gifts; he wanted to earn his grade. And he did. He made a C+, but he could easily have had an A.

This story illustrates differing reactions people have to God's solution for sin. Some people look at God's standard – moral and ethical perfection – and throw their hands up in surrender. Why even try? They tell themselves, "I could never live up to all that stuff."

Others are like the student who read the test through and was aware of the professor's offer but took the test anyway. Unwilling to simply receive God's gift of forgiveness, they set about to rack up enough points with God to earn it.

But God's grace truly is like the professor's offer. It may seem unbelievable, but if we accept it, like the stunned students who accepted the professor's offer, we too will discover that, yes, God's grace truly is free. All we have to do is accept it. God's message to you and me has always been and always will be a message of "grace."

Like many Americans, I was taught that the key to success in life is a hard work ethic. Perhaps you are familiar with these clichés: Give it all you've got. No pain, no gain. We make money the old-fashioned way, we earn it. Be the first to get there and the last to leave. Give 110%. Nothing worth having comes easy.

I'm not saying that these clichés about hard work are wrong, because they are not. But we must learn not to bring this work ethic into our salvation experience. If we do, we end up trying to earn our way to eternal life, which is the wrong approach.

Grace is a gift. It is a gift that some people have a difficult time receiving, perhaps because we are accustomed to working hard for the nice things in life. Grace has a way of saying: No matter what you've done or where you've been, you are welcomed to the family of God.

> **GODFIDENCE LESSON**
> When you live by the grace of God, the impossible becomes possible.

A number of years ago, a poll was done among 5,000 born-again Christ followers asking them to define the word "grace." Most of the answers were accurate, e.g., salvation, free gift, forgiveness of sins. The greatest percentage of people in the study knew that we are saved by grace and that it is a gift of God. We cannot earn it. Praise God!

Then, they were asked a follow-up question in this poll that didn't go so well. "Does grace help you live your everyday life?" Only 2% said "yes" to this question. Here is the good news: God not only gives us grace to enter into our relationship with Him, but He also gives us His grace to live for Him every day.

The Bible is filled with references to the God-ordained concept of grace:

Acts 13:43 says we keep going by grace.
Romans 11:5 says we are chosen by grace.
2 Corinthians 12:9 says we are empowered by grace.
Galatians 1:15 says we are called by grace.
Ephesians 1:7 says we are forgiven by grace.
Ephesians 2:8–9 says we are saved by grace.
Colossians 4:6 says we speak with wisdom by grace.
2 Timothy 1:9 says we are called to a holy life by grace.
Titus 3:7 says we are justified by grace.
Hebrews 13:9 says we are strengthened by grace.
1 Peter 4:10 says we serve others by grace.
2 Peter 3:18 says we can grow in grace.

GODFIDENCE LESSON

The more you understand the depth of God's grace, the more Godfidence you will have to live by God's grace.

I once heard a Bible teacher say this phrase: "The Old Testament is all about the Law and the New Testament is all about grace." I understand that he was trying to distinguish that the Old Testament is about the commandments and the New Testament is about Jesus coming to earth. But I disagree with that assessment because when I read the Old Testament, I see God's hand of grace all over the place. Noah found grace in the eyes of the Lord (Genesis 6:8 KJV). David was given a second chance (2 Samuel 12; Psalm 51). Abraham lied and still was the father of faith (Genesis 12, 20; Hebrews 11). And the list goes on. God loves to extend grace. Always has. Always will.

UNMERITED FAVOR OF GOD

A few years ago, I was having fun at Peter Piper Pizza when I decided to put two tokens in a race car simulator. I figured, "This is for kids, so this should be easy." I pressed "Go" and off I went.

As I pressed my right foot on the gas pedal, the simulated race car was going faster and faster. I was having fun until I lost control of the race car and crashed into the wall. How embarrassing! But then, about five seconds later, I saw that my race car was back in one piece and on the track ready to go again. Yes! I was given a second chance, even though I didn't deserve it.

This is a picture of God's grace. There are times when you get involved in a spiritual wreck. It may have been your fault, or it may not have been. Either way, God gives you a second chance. In Hebrew, this is the word *chesed*, which takes our understanding of grace to another level. *Chesed* means "God's grace, mercy, and lovingkindness." God blesses me with his unmerited favor (grace) by withholding punishment that I deserve (mercy) and by showing me a deep committed love (lovingkindness). Because God is a God of second chances, I can get back on track on my journey toward eternal life.

Some people open God's gift of grace, and others do not. When the Bible speaks of Peter and Judas, one opened God's gift of grace, the other did not. As Jesus was arrested and preparing to go to the cross, Peter denied Christ three times. He failed, but his story didn't end there. In fact, it was only just beginning.

A few days after Christ's crucifixion and resurrection, Jesus has an interesting conversation with Peter on the seashore. He forgave Peter when He asked, "Peter, do you love me?" (John 21:15–19). Peter opened God's gift of grace and responded affirmatively. He was reinstated. Shortly thereafter, Peter preached a sermon, and 3,000 came to faith in Christ. His kingdom ministry was just beginning. Because of the grace of God, Peter reached his potential in life.

On the other hand, Judas betrayed Christ. Like Peter, Judas failed the Lord, but he did not hang in there like Peter did. Judas gave up. He failed to open God's gift of grace. He went and hung himself. So much promise, but no longer.

CHARISMATIC

It took me a long time to learn about real grace. Early on, I thought grace was what we said before we ate a meal, the first name of a young lady, or that amazing thing we sing about in a hymn. I didn't have the Godfidence yet to live by grace.

As we have learned, the Hebrew word *chesed* actually means the fullness of grace, mercy, and lovingkindness. That's powerful. The Biblical Greek word for grace is *charis*. It is where we get the word "charismatic".

Many times, people use the word charismatic, or someone with charisma, to describe someone with an outgoing, vivacious personality that many people are drawn to. There is nothing wrong with using the word in that manner. Still others use the word charismatic to describe someone who is filled with the Holy Spirit and speaks in tongues. Likewise, there is nothing wrong with using the word in this manner.

I used to think that God was up in heaven with a clipboard in His hands, keeping track of every little thing I did wrong and writing down every sin I committed. I thought that, at any moment, I might be zapped into eternal torment when I did something wrong. I was told that going to a movie theatre was a sin, and if Jesus came back to earth while I was in the theatre, I would be left behind. Then, I studied Ephesians 2:8–10: "For it is by grace you have been saved, through faith – and this is not from yourselves, it is the gift of God – not by works, so that no one can boast."

Can you imagine the conversations that would take place in heaven if we were saved by works, not grace?

"Hi buddy, I got here to heaven because I never cheated on my wife. How did you get here?"

"Well, I made it to heaven because I gave $500 to a needy family once."

Get the picture? Comparing notes about our goodness would lead to crazy, self-serving conversations. If we did that, the glory would be ours, not God's. Does this mean that once I accept Jesus Christ as Lord, I can live a life of sin? No, not at all. We are warned against this assumption in Romans 5:20–21 and Hebrews 10:26. Rather, grace gives you the Godfidence to live for Christ.

"For we are his workmanship, created in Christ Jesus for good works, which God prepared beforehand, that we should walk in them" (Ephesians 2:10 ESV). In this passage, Paul continues this "grace" principle by reminding us that, because of God's grace, not only are we saved but we are also created to do good works. Is doing good works our ticket to heaven? No, that's not what he is saying. Good works come out of our salvation experience. In other words, the way we live changes.

The greatest thing you can do in life is to place your faith in God and receive salvation by His grace. Many people say a prayer asking the Lord to forgive them of their sins and asking Him to come into their heart, but not everyone who says this prayer changes the way they live. Transformation is what happens when an individual sincerely repents of sin, makes Jesus Lord of their life, and lives their life to please the Lord. Will they live a perfect life with no more sinning? Nope. Each of us is a work in progress. My friend, you are God's workmanship. His masterpiece. You have charisma. You are filled with God's grace.

> **GODFIDENCE LESSON**
> Grace is the gift that gives you Godfidence for your eternal life in heaven and the Godfidence to live for Christ here on earth.

FILL IN THE BLANKS

Pop quiz time. The answer to the following fill-in-the-blank questions is the same word, has five letters, rhymes with race, and is defined as "God's unmerited favor."

Question 1: Kyle has been born again for fourteen years. He loves the Lord. But lately, he has lost his joy. He finds himself going through the motions of Christianity but still lacking spiritual life. He doesn't know what to do or where to turn. As he begins to earnestly seek the Lord, he now receives a powerful sense of purpose and direction for life. He has been blessed with God's __________.

Question 2: The morals and convictions of the people of the United States of America continue to decline as we make decisions apart from the Word of God. The only reason we are still a blessed nation is because of God's __________.

> **GODFIDENCE LESSON**
> The worst of your deeds are never so bad that you are beyond the reach of God's grace, and the best of your deeds are never so good that you are beyond the need of God's grace.

Question 3: Margaret's world has been falling apart. The doctors found a tumor in her, and she doesn't know the extent of it. Her boss let her know that her position is being eliminated in a few months. Also, her son was caught with some drugs. And her car needs a new transmission that she cannot afford. With all that she is dealing with, the one thing that is sustaining her during these difficult times is God's __________.

Question 4: Holly is ready to give up on life. She has been dealing with rejection from friends, frustration with her job, and discouragement from life. She feels defeated. She doesn't have much hope left. She doesn't know if she can make it any longer. Then, her friend takes the time to connect with her, encourage her, and pray over her. Holly now determines not to give up but rather overcome her challenges in life. She is now moving forward because of God's __________.

> "I am not what I ought to be. I am not what I want to be. I am not what I hope to be. But still, I am not what I used to be. And by the grace of God, I am what I am." – John Newton

THE TRAP OF LEGALISM

I've noticed that some Christ followers forget about applying grace to other areas of their Christian faith. Peter, for example, loved the Lord. He was discipled by Jesus. He was preaching the Word. But...he had some issues. One of his issues was legalism. Legalism is living by a set of standards based on tradition and man-made rules rather than the Bible. Legalism is the mentality that rules and regulations are more important than a relationship with the Lord. There is nothing wrong with tradition – unless it supersedes what God's Word says.

When I was a teenager, someone at church told me, "Do you see that couple over there? They are divorced and remarried. God cannot use them." Overcoming legalistic perspectives oftentimes means that we have to "unlearn" some traditions based on religion but not on the Word of God. Not all traditions are bad, but it is a good idea to distinguish between biblically based traditions and religion-based traditions.

Peter needed to unlearn some religious traditions as well. He had this mentality that the gospel of Jesus was intended for the Jews only. He was limiting God. So, God wanted to teach Peter a lesson. Let's read about his vision in Acts 10:

> *...he fell into a trance and saw the heavens opened and something like a great sheet descending, being let down by its four corners upon the earth. In it were all kinds of animals and reptiles and birds of the air. And there came a voice to him: "Rise, Peter; kill and eat." But Peter said, "By no means, Lord; for I have never eaten anything that is common or unclean." And the voice came to him again a second time, "What God has made clean, do not call common." (Acts 10:11–15 ESV)*

Just because Peter was saved and born again and going to heaven didn't mean that he was perfect. No, he was far from it. God is always challenging you and me to learn, grow, serve, and reach out. Peter needed to make some attitude adjustments to get out of the trap of legalism and better understand real grace. We read in this passage above that Peter was placing certain people (non-Jews) in a spiritual box. Legalism has a way of doing that. He had been calling certain people unclean whom God had cleaned up. Many Christ followers fall into this trap as well. Maybe it's because they sin differently than we do. Just sayin'.

Then, there are those who have the nostalgia blues. These legalists will make comments like, "Churches today are not like churches of years ago." "Back in the day, this is how we did church." "We can only worship with the gospel hymns." "The pastor must wear a coat and tie." "We only use the King James Version of the Bible." They limit people, and they limit God. The legalism list is long.

A SECOND CHANCE

When I read the stories of many of the great spiritual leaders in the Bible, I noticed that many of them made big mistakes, but God used them anyway. God gave them a second chance. That second chance is called grace.

Abraham stepped out of God's perfect will by having a child with his maidservant but still fulfilled God's call on his life to be the father of the nation of the people of God. God's grace gives you Godfidence to fulfill your calling.

Moses murdered an Egyptian and disobeyed God but was still given the responsibility of leading God's people out of Egypt because of God's grace. God's grace gives you Godfidence to overcome your past.

David experienced the grace of God as well. He committed adultery and arranged to have a man killed but still fulfilled his calling to be king and was known as a man after God's own heart. God's grace gives you Godfidence to get back on track. Peter denied Christ but was still used of God to preach the gospel message and work miracles. God's grace gives you the Godfidence to make the best of your second chance.

> **GODFIDENCE LESSON**
> The grace of God is ready
> to take you to your potential.

GRACE AND FORGIVENESS

One evening, when I was a fifteen-year-old learning how to drive, my dad said, "Let's go get dinner. You are driving." I got in the driver's seat. He sat in the passenger seat.

We headed over to Church's Fried Chicken. As we approached the parking lot, I saw an open parking spot. As I drove into it, I mishandled the car, and it veered into the car on the right and hit the parked car. Most dads would have been extremely upset, but my dad did not yell. He had self-control. I felt terrible. He calmly "took the wheel," went into the restaurant to find the owner, and told me, "I've got it covered."

He extended grace. A father's grace. And this is what our heavenly Father extends to you as well. God has a way of picking us up, embracing us through our failures, and placing us back on track.

> "My sin was deep, but His grace was deeper."
> – Shane Pruitt

On October 2, 2006, a man entered an Amish schoolhouse in Pennsylvania and killed five girls and then himself. This was a horrible tragedy. In a display of Amish love, the families of the victims invited the widow of the killer to the funerals. In his book *Amish Grace: How Forgiveness Transcended Tragedy*, Steve Nolt says,

> Their understanding of forgiveness is embedded in their culture and their history – their 500-year history that includes martyrs that did not seek revenge but asked for forgiveness for their persecutors. In one sense, this is part of their cultural DNA.
>
> Their understanding of forgiveness is that it is a long process, that it is difficult, that it is painful, that replacing bitter feelings toward someone is something that takes time, and they would say that happens only through God's grace. But they begin with expressing their intention to forgive, with the faith that the emotional forgiveness will follow over months and years. They don't begin with trying to blame someone or something.

GODFIDENCE LESSON

Because of God's grace, you are forgiven. Because of God's grace, you can forgive others.

Hannah is thirty-five years old and loves the Lord, who has transformed her life tremendously. She used to be depressed day and night. Now, she lives in joy. She used to be so negative, but now she has a positive view of life here on earth and eternally. But once in a while, she finds herself haunted with something she did many years ago. She had an affair with an old flame outside the boundaries of marriage. Every so often, the enemy puts these thoughts in her mind, "Remember what you did in 2003? How can you call yourself a Christian?"

How does Hannah respond when those thoughts flood her mind? She stands on the grace of God. You see, because she no longer lives in sin, she is no longer condemned. The blood of Christ has forgiven her. The grace of God sustains her. This is Godfidence.

> "The grace of God is not merely a cover-up. Yes, it covers, but it goes beyond that. It enables and empowers us to live a life of obedience."
> – John Bevere

GRACE IS ALWAYS THE BEST CHOICE

If a drunk driver lost control of his car and crashed into the car driven by your daughter, leaving her dead, you would be dealing with pain, grief, anger and much more. How do you think you would respond? Here are three possible responses:

1) Revenge. You could choose to do all you can to pay the drunk driver back for what he did. You may even resort to killing him. This is revenge.
2) Justice. You could choose to pursue legal action and make sure that our justice system applies the appropriate consequences to this guilty man.
3) Grace. You could choose to forgive this drunk driver, hold nothing against him, and not legally charge him with anything.

Life isn't fair. We live in an imperfect world with imperfect people. This is not heaven. Life is not about fairness. Evil people do evil deeds. And if you don't understand grace, you could very well end up bitter. You are called to forgive not just because it is God's will but also because it will keep you from falling into the trap of deeper issues, such as bitterness, anger, and hatred. Unforgiveness and its consequences can even open the door to addictions and pain. Would you have enough Godfidence to leave the justice to God?

One of my favorite Scriptures is found in James 2:13, "Mercy triumphs over judgment." I love this principle.

Earlier in this chapter, we learned that the Hebrew word *chesed* pulls together the meanings of grace, mercy, and lovingkindness. This is God's way of pulling everything together, including the way He expresses His love to you. Grace is the answer.

GRACE OVERCOMES FEAR AND DOUBT

Sometimes, life gets the best of you. That's when God extends His grace to you. When the devil is constantly on your back or people test your patience, God extends His grace to you. When Peter walked on water, he not only conquered fear, but he also got a taste of what it means to walk in the grace of God.

> **GODFIDENCE LESSON**
> Grace means that all of your mistakes now serve a purpose instead of serving shame.

GRACE IS THE ANSWER OVER RELIGION

But grow in the grace and knowledge of our Lord and Savior Jesus Christ.
2 Peter 3:18

In the chapter "Real Doctrine," we will review details of what many of the cults believe and how they differ from Christianity. One of the primary differences is that most cults adhere to the doctrine of works (earning your way to salvation and eternal life) instead of the Christian doctrine of grace. God's message to you has been and will always be a message of grace.

> **GODFIDENCE LESSON**
> The more we learn about God,
> the more we understand God's grace.

GRACE WINS, HANDS DOWN

All that passing laws against sin did was produce more lawbreakers. But sin didn't, and doesn't, have a chance in competition with the aggressive forgiveness we call grace. When it's sin versus grace, ***grace wins hands down****. All sin can do is threaten us with death, and that's the end of it. Grace, because God is putting everything together again through the Messiah, invites us into life – a life that goes on and on and on, world without end.*

Romans 5:20–21 MSG

Do you enjoy receiving birthday gifts? I have a feeling you do. When you were a kid, wouldn't it be a shame if your parents had said, "You don't deserve any gifts, because you were born eight years ago. Your birthday already happened. You don't deserve to open any more gifts."

Aren't you glad God doesn't tell you, "My child, you were born again eight years ago, so you don't deserve the gift of grace any longer." No, God doesn't do that. He remembers the day you first experienced grace, and He extends grace to you again and again. We needed grace then, and we need it now! We needed His unmerited favor then, and we need His favor now!

GODFIDENCE LESSON

Godfidence gives you the ability to live by grace, even though you are imperfect.

YOUR INVITATION IS WAITING

The following anonymous story helps us understand God's grace.

I shook my head in disbelief. This couldn't be the right place. After all, I couldn't possibly be welcome here. I had been given an invitation several times, by several different people, and had finally decided to see what this place was all about. But this just couldn't be the right place. I peered through the window again and saw a room of people whose faces seemed to glow with joy. All were neatly dressed and appeared strangely clean as they dined at this exquisite restaurant.

Ashamed, I looked down at my own tattered and torn clothing, covered in stains. I was dirty – in fact, I was filthy. A foul smell seemed to consume me, and I couldn't shake the grime that hung to my body. As I turned around to leave, the words from the invitation seemed to leap out at me – "Come as you are. No jacket required."

I decided to give it a shot. Mustering up every bit of courage I could find, I opened the door to this restaurant and walked up to a man standing behind a podium. "Your name, sir?" he asked me with a smile.

"Jimmy D. Brown," I mumbled without looking up. I thrust my hands deep into my pockets, hoping to conceal their stains.

He didn't seem to notice the filth that I was covered in, and he continued, "Very good, sir. A table is reserved in your name. Would you like to be seated?"

I couldn't believe what I heard! A grin broke out on my face and I said, "Yes, of course!"

He led me to a table and, sure enough, there was a placard with my name written on it in a deep, dark red. As I browsed over a menu, I saw many delightful items listed. There were things like, "peace," "joy," "blessings," "assurance," "hope," "love," "faith," "mercy," and "[Godfidence]." I realized that this was no ordinary restaurant! I flipped the menu back to the front in order to see where I was. The name of this place was God's Grace.

The man returned and said, "I recommend the 'Special of the Day.' With it, you are entitled to heaping portions of everything on this menu."

I thought to myself, *You've got to be kidding! You mean, I can have ALL of this?* "What is the 'Special of the Day'?" I asked with excitement ringing in my voice.

"Salvation," he replied.

"I'll take it," I practically cried out. A sick, painful ache jerked through my stomach, and tears filled my eyes. Between my sobs, I said "Mister, look at me. I'm dirty and nasty. I'm unclean and unworthy of such things. I'd love to have all of this, but I just can't afford it."

Undaunted, the man smiled again. "Sir, your check has already been taken care of by that gentleman over there," he said as he pointed. "His name is Jesus."

Turning, I saw a man whose very presence seemed to light the room. He was almost too much to look at. I found myself walking towards Him; and in a shaking voice, I whispered, "Sir, I'll wash the dishes or sweep the floors or take out the trash. I'll do anything I can do to repay you for all of this."

He opened His arms and said with a smile, "Son, all of this is yours if you just come unto me. Ask me to clean you up, and I will. Ask me to take away the stains, and consider it done. Ask me to allow you to feast at my table, and you will eat. Remember, the table is reserved in your name. All you must do is accept this gift of grace that I offer you."

Astonished, I fell at his feet and said, "Please, Jesus. Even though I don't deserve it, please forgive me. Change me and give me a new life."

Immediately, I heard the words, "Your sins are forgiven. Welcome to the family."

I looked down, and my clothes were clean. I felt new, like a weight had been lifted.

"The 'Special of the Day' has been served," the Lord said to me. "Salvation is yours."

We sat and talked for a great while, and I so enjoyed the time that I spent with Him. He told me, me of all people, that He would like for me to come back as often as I liked for another helping from God's Grace. He made it clear that He wanted me to spend as much time with Him as possible.

Then, He said something to me that I will never forget. He said, "My child, do you see these empty tables throughout this room? The individuals whose names are on each placard have not accepted their invitations to dine. Would you be so kind as to hand out these invitations to those who have not joined us yet?"

"Of course," I said with excitement as I picked up the invitations. I walked into God's Grace dirty and hungry. Stained in sin. And Jesus cleaned me up. I walked out with eternal life and the Godfidence to live to my potential in life.

So, I ask you, Have you responded to your invitation? There's a table reserved in your name: "Grace, because God is putting everything together again through the Messiah, invites us into life – a life that goes on and on and on, world without end" (Romans 5:21 MSG).

This is a great invitation. An invitation to eternal life. How do we receive this invitation? By the grace of God. That's the way we are called to live. Have you RSVP'd?

WORDS OF LIFE

I am a recipient of the grace of God. I am forgiven. My sins are washed away. I am now a child of God. I live by the grace of God. I am empowered by the grace of God. I am called by the grace of God. I have God's unmerited favor. Yes, I am blessed.

GODFIDENCE CHECKUP

1) In your opinion, why do so many people today believe in the gospel of works rather than the gospel of grace?

____

____

____

____

____

____

2) Legalism is one example of how we must unlearn some traditions that are not biblically based. What are one or two examples of things you needed to unlearn?

____

____

____

____

____

____

3) Suppose you were sharing your faith with someone and they say, "I've committed so many sins, I don't believe God could ever forgive me for everything." What would you say in response?

____

____

____

____

____

____

PRAYER FOCUS

Lord God Almighty, I come to You in the name of Jesus. I receive your gift of grace. Thank You for accepting me just as I am. I ask you to forgive me of my sins. Today, I open this gift and approach Your throne of grace with confidence. I don't deserve Your favor, but I receive it with joy and gratitude. I need Your grace to take my spiritual life to another level. I need your favor to help me overcome the challenging situations I am dealing with. I need the Holy Spirit to empower me to be an overcomer. I am ready to live by grace from this day forward. Amen. So be it.

CH. 6 REAL PRAYER

This is the confidence we have in approaching God: that if we ask anything according to his will, he hears us. And if we know that he hears us – whatever we ask – we know that we have what we asked of him.

1 John 5:14–15

A middle-aged lady was a tremendous and faithful prayer warrior. Every day, she would spend time seeking God. She and her son lived alone. When she prayed, she would often open the windows in her living room. This would greatly perturb her next-door neighbor, who was an atheist.

On one particular day, her funds were totally dry, and she wasn't expecting a check for another week. There was no food left in the house, but as usual, she began to pray. Her prayer on this day went something like this, "Oh, Lord, You know that my son and I don't have any food in the house. We don't have any money, but I know that You are my Jehovah Jireh, my Provider. I am asking for a miracle. Could You provide our daily bread?" She prayed with Godfidence!

Her atheist neighbor happened to be doing some lawn work, and he heard her praying. He thought to himself, "I am going to teach her a lesson. I will prove to her that there is no God. I will bring her groceries and make her think that it was her God."

He got in his car, went to the grocery store, purchased two big bags of groceries, and quietly placed them on this lady's doorstep. He rang the doorbell and ran to hide behind the shrubs. The praying lady opened the door and saw no one. When she looked down and saw the two big bags of groceries, she began to rejoice, "Praise God! Praise God! He has answered my prayers again!"

At that point, her atheist neighbor jumped out from behind the shrubs and shouted, "No, you have it all wrong. God didn't bring you these groceries. I did!"

She continued to rejoice and shouted, "Praise God! God

has supplied my needs! It wasn't you – it was God who came through."

This enraged the man all the more as he said, "Lady, there is no God, and I will prove it to you. I have the receipt from the grocery store. I am the one who provided this food for you. There is no God." He showed her the receipt.

She looked at him and then looked at the receipt and began to shout even louder, "This is a bigger miracle than I thought. God has not only provided for my needs, but He made the devil pay the bill!"

GODFIDENCE LESSON

When you pray with Godfidence, you know that somehow, someway, God will come through for you.

I have a clear memory of hearing something most every night of my teenage years. My bedroom was across the hall from my parent's bedroom. When I walked down the hallway to my room, I would hear both my parents crying out to God from their bedroom, interceding for my siblings and me, for the church, and for those in need of healing or a miracle. That's when I learned about real prayer!

Any healthy relationship needs good communication. If there are any issues in communication between two people, then the entire relationship is in jeopardy. This is especially true of our relationship with the Lord.

Our prayer life reflects the health of our relationship with God. I can't emphasize enough the importance of your prayer life. Speaking to God has great significance, but listening to God is even more vital to your spiritual life. Prayer is our two-way dialogue with Almighty God. You can't have a relationship with God without prayer.

> "Prayer is a disinfectant and a preventative. It purifies the air; it destroys the contagion of evil."
> – E. M. Bounds

How important is prayer to Jesus? Let's take a look at just a few examples of when Jesus prayed to the Father...

He prayed often (Luke 5:16).

He prayed early in the morning (Mark 1:35): "Very early in the morning, while it was still dark, Jesus got up, left the house and went off to a solitary place, where he prayed."

He prayed late at night: "One of those days Jesus went out to a mountainside to pray, and spent the night praying to God" (Luke 6:12).

He prayed at the beginning of His ministry (Luke 3:21–22): "When all the people were being baptized, Jesus was baptized too. And as he was praying, heaven was opened and the Holy Spirit descended on him in bodily form like a dove. And a voice came from heaven: 'You are my Son, whom I love; with you I am well pleased.'"

He prayed before He chose His twelve disciples (Luke 6:12–13).

He prayed before the confession that He was the Christ (Luke 9:18–20).

He prayed before His transfiguration (Luke 9:28–29): "About eight days after Jesus said this, he took Peter, John and James with him and went up onto a mountain to pray. As he was praying, the appearance of his face changed, and his clothes became as bright as a flash of lightning."

He prayed before He taught His followers (Luke 11:1): "One day Jesus was praying in a certain place. When he finished, one of his disciples said to him, 'Lord, teach us to pray, just as John taught his disciples.'"

He prayed while He was teaching others (Matthew 11:25–26): "At that time Jesus said, 'I praise you, Father, Lord of heaven and earth, because you have hidden these things from the wise and learned, and revealed them to little children. Yes, Father, for this is what you were pleased to do.'"

He prayed after He ministered to others (Matthew 14:23).

He prayed before healing the crowds (Mark 1:35).

He prayed before feeding the 5,000 (Mark 6:41).

He prayed before healing the man who was deaf and mute (Mark 7:34).

He prayed before bringing the dead back to life (John 11:41–43).

He prayed for His friends (Luke 22:32).

He prayed for His disciples (John 17:9–19).

He prayed for all Christians (John 17:20–21).

He prayed before the cross (Luke 22:39–42): "Jesus went out as usual to the Mount of Olives, and his disciples followed him. On reaching the place, he said to them, 'Pray that you will not fall into temptation.' He withdrew about a stone's throw beyond them, knelt down and prayed, 'Father, if you are willing, take this cup from me; yet not my will, but yours be done.'"

He prayed on the cross (Luke 23:34): "Jesus said, 'Father, forgive them, for they do not know what they are doing.' And they divided up his clothes by casting lots."

And today, He is constantly interceding for you (Hebrews 7:25).

> "If you are not a praying person, you must carry your faith. If you are a praying person, your faith carries you." – Ravi Zacharias

PRAYING WITH GODFIDENCE

Real prayer isn't a superficial, skin-deep collection of words that don't rise above the ceiling. Real prayer is about a heart-to-heart conversation with the Creator of the Universe. When an individual has a true relationship with the King of Kings, they pray with Godfidence. Here are seven Biblical examples of what Godfident prayer can do.

1) Godfident prayer catches the ear of God.

Joshua led the people of God to many victories. In Joshua 10, we read about their battle with the Amorites when he prayed to God with a huge ask. He asked the Lord to stop the sun and moon in the sky so that they can have light to finished off their enemy. Here is what happened after

Joshua prayed: “The sun stopped in the middle of the sky and delayed going down about a full day. There has never been a day like it before or since, a day when the LORD listened to a human being. Surely the LORD was fighting for Israel!”(Joshua 10:13–14).

This was a Godfident prayer, and not only did God listen but it led to victory over the Amorites.

2) Godfident prayer changes lives.

1 Kings 18 gives us the account of when Elijah was up against 450 prophets of Baal. Indeed, the odds were against him. The challenge was on. The prophets of Baal would pray to their god to consume the altar with fire. And Elijah would pray to his God (Jehovah), asking Him to consume the altar with fire. The prophets of Baal prayed, and nothing happened. Then, Elijah came up to bat. He prayed to the Lord with Godfidence and, sure enough the Lord answered him by consuming the altar.

But that wasn’t the only miracle that day. The details of the story tell us how these idol worshippers responded. “When all the people saw this, they fell prostrate and cried, “The LORD – he is God! The LORD – he is God!” (1 Kings 18:39). These people experienced a greater miracle: their lives were changed. Now, they were no longer idol worshippers, but instead, worshippers of the Lord God Jehovah. And it all came about because Elijah prayed with Godfidence.

GODFIDENCE LESSON

Praying with Godfidence makes the impossible possible.

3) Godfident prayer can change the course of history.

The book of Esther is a great story of what God can do when people pray. The Jewish people living in Persia were on the verge of annihilation. Their only hope was for someone to step up and change the heart of King Xerxes.

That someone was Esther. As she prepared to petition the king, she gave the people specific instructions. "Go, gather together all the Jews who are in Susa, and fast for me" (Esther 4:16).

What happened when the people prayed and fasted with Godfidence? God gave Esther favor, and the people of God were saved. It changed the course of history.

GODFIDENCE LESSON

Godfident prayer brings God into the picture.

4) Godfident prayer can get you out of trouble.

Acts 12 tells how Peter was thrown into prison for preaching the gospel. Verse 5 tells us that the church responded with prayer, believing for Peter's release: "So Peter was kept in prison, but the church was earnestly praying to God for him."

What happened when the people prayed with Godfidence? An angel appeared on the scene, and the chains fell off of Peter's wrists. Yes, God answered the prayer of the church, as the angel led him out of prison. Remember this: circumstances change when the people of God pray with Godfidence.

5) Godfident prayer can defeat your enemy.

In 2 Kings 6, Elisha and his servant found themselves surrounded by the enemy. They had no chance of survival, unless God stepped in. Elisha had Godfidence, but his servant did not...he was scared. So, Elisha made this Godfident statement to his servant: "Those who are with us are more than those who are with them" (2 Kings 6:16). He knew that God was in control.

Then, Elisha prayed a simple prayer. "Open his eyes. LORD, so that he may see." (2 Kings 6:17). Remember, your prayers don't need to be all that fancy. They just need to come from your heart.

God answered that prayer. The servant's eyes were opened, and the army was struck with blindness. Elisha and his servant had the victory. The enemy was defeated. The great worship song by Elyssa Smith, "Surrounded," borrows this image, declaring, "It may look like I'm surrounded, but I'm surrounded by You."[7] We defeat our enemy with Godfidence!

{"Prayer is a strong wall and fortress of the church; it is a goodly Christian weapon." – Martin Luther

6) Godfident prayer can give you the ability to move on.

King David sinned. He committed adultery. Could God ever forgive him? The nineteen verses of Psalm 51 record David's prayer to God, asking for forgiveness. He uses phrases like, "have mercy on me O God"; "blot out my transgressions"; "cleanse me from my sin"; "create in me a pure heart"; and "my sacrifice, O God, is a broken spirit." God took note of David's genuine, heart-felt prayer, and He forgave David.

Perhaps many of us need to learn this lesson that David learned: there is no sin too great that God cannot forgive. All it takes is a repentant heart and Godfident trust in God. Then, we can move on.

7) Godfident prayer opens the door to the glory of God.

In Exodus 33, we read that Moses found himself having an intimate conversation with God, which illustrates a truly Godfident prayer. When the Lord told Moses that He was pleased with him, Moses had the boldness to ask, "Now show me Your glory" (Exodus 33:18).

Wow! What a bold request! What was it that Moses had that many of us do not have? Godfidence. Here's the rest of the Exodus 33 story: God gave Moses what he requested. Moses experienced the glory of God, and so can you.

April, the administrative assistant at our church office wrote this testimony: "On Tuesday, August 20, 2019, as I was preparing coffee in our supply room. Something on the monitor from the security cameras caught my eye. I was thinking to myself, 'No, it can't be what I am seeing.' I was seeing multiple beings that were very bright and transparent walking back and forth in the CrossWalk area of our property. I could see the outline of their faces but couldn't really make out their features. They were about fifteen feet tall. I was in awe because I could not believe that the cameras were actually capturing them. I just had to praise the Lord at that moment, because I knew He had sent His angels to guard our church."

POWER IN AGREEMENT

If two of you on earth agree about anything they ask for, it will be done for them by my Father in heaven.
Matthew 18:19

In a Peanuts cartoon, Lucy demands that Linus change TV channels and then threatens him with her fist if he doesn't. "What makes you think you can walk right in here and take over?" asks Linus.

"These five fingers," says Lucy. "Individually they are nothing, but when I curl them together like this into a single unit, they form a weapon that is terrible to behold."

"What channel do you want?" asks Linus. Turning away, he looks at his fingers and says, "Why can't you guys get organized like that?"

One of my favorite prayer principles is the power of agreement. God has a way of bringing certain individuals together for the purpose of great things. I love the time I spend alone with God in prayer, but there is a special dynamic that takes place when I pray with others. This is called the power of agreement.

> "God is looking for people through whom He can do the impossible. What a pity that we plan only the things we can do by ourselves." – A.W. Tozer

Marriage is another great place to activate the power

of agreement. On the day I took my vows with Brenda, the power of agreement was activated. As we communicate together, our relationship becomes better. As we plan together, our future becomes brighter. As we hurt together, our bond becomes tighter. As we laugh together, our joy becomes livelier. As we spend time together, our love tanks fill fuller. As we stick together, our commitment becomes stronger. As we pray together, our potential raises higher. This is the power of agreement.

There are two Hebrew words for prayer that describe this principle of the power of agreement. First there is the Hebrew word *palal* that means "intercession." This comes from the word intersection. When situations are at a crossroads and people are wondering which direction to take, that is your cue to intercede.

A second Hebrew word that captures the secret of prayer is the term that combines purpose with prayer, *kavanah*, which means, "directing one's heart to God." It is the idea that prayer must be heartfelt.

> **GODFIDENCE LESSON**
>
> The most dangerous weapon you have against the enemy is your prayer to our Almighty God!

For fifteen years, I was blessed to have John Murphy as my prayer partner. He was an introverted, scheduled, humble, elderly man who loved to communicate with God. Four weekday mornings a week, I would spend about twenty minutes with him. I loved it. I felt so secure to share anything I was dealing with in life and in ministry.

Countless times, I would be bent out of shape over something I was dealing with. When I shared it with John, he would smile and, very calmly say, "Let's pray about it." Nothing ruffled his feathers. He always kept his cool. He fully trusted God with every situation. After praying with him, I would walk away with the assurance that God was in control.

He never preached a sermon. He never taught a class. But yet, I learned so much from him about prayer. He was very intentional about his prayer life.

A friend was telling me how he didn't consider himself a praying person because he didn't spend two hours a day in prayer. I assured him that he is indeed a prayer warrior, but his focus is a little different than those who do spend two hours a day on their knees. I led him to a discussion on the nine types of prayer warriors based on the teaching "Prayer Force" by Pastor Chris Hodges. He was excited to find out that he was a Crisis Warrior. (Note: These details are written in my book To Another Level.)

THE DISCIPLE'S PRAYER

"This, then, is how you should pray:
"'Our Father in heaven, hallowed be your name, your kingdom come, your will be done, on earth as it is in heaven. Give us today our daily bread. And forgive us our debts, as we also have forgiven our debtors. And lead us not into temptation, but deliver us from the evil one.'"
Matthew 6:9–13

Here in Matthew 6, Jesus taught us to pray with Godfidence. Most people refer to this as the Lord's Prayer. I refer to this as the Disciple's Prayer, because this is the way Jesus taught His disciples to pray.

In fact, in Luke's version of this account, he points out that the disciples had a desire to learn how to pray. "Lord, teach us to pray" (Luke 11:1). They didn't say, "Lord, pray for us." They said, "Lord, teach us to pray." They knew the value of learning how to pray themselves.

It reminds me of that old proverb that says, "If I give you a fish, you'll eat for a day. If I teach you to fish, you'll eat for a lifetime." Here are a few lessons we can learn from the prayer strategy Jesus taught in the Disciple's Prayer.

YOU CAN PRAY WITH GODFIDENCE...

1) When you have a relationship with God, your Father.

"Our Father, who art in heaven…"

Have you ever been stood up? Perhaps someone you cared about was supposed to meet you at a certain restaurant at a certain time. You arrived and waited. And waited. And waited. Until you finally realized that he was not going to show up. Then you began to experience an array of feelings. From anger to doubt. From "Wait 'til I talk to him again," to "I'll never talk to him again." It's not a good feeling.

Every day, you have a date with God. He wants to meet with you and chat. He wants to get to know you. He wants to share His heart with you. He wants to spend time with you. Every day. He calls this time with you "prayer." The Lord looks forward to His date with you.

For some of you, your standing daily date with God is at 6:00 a.m. For others, it's at 11:00 p.m. There, He waits for you. The table is set. Your chair is waiting. He's dressed in righteousness. Ready to listen. Ready to talk. Ready to give you His full attention. Ready to be there for you. Ready to pay the bill. Don't disappoint Him. Don't stand Him up.

GODFIDENCE LESSON

You are as close to God as you choose to be.

2) When you desire to worship God.

"Hallowed be your name…"

Most of the time, I begin my prayer time with thanksgiving and worship to God. I want to always have an attitude of gratitude; thanking God for all that He has done for me. I also like integrating worship and praise, whether it is sung or spoken. "Lord, I worship You. You are my Savior, my God, my Redeemer, my Prince of Peace, my Rock, my Fortress, and my Deliverer. And Lord, I praise You because You have saved me, healed me, restored me. I praise You because when other people leave me, You do not."

There was a group of people on an ocean liner, and it

wasn't a fancy cruise like many of us experience today. An atheist had two oranges in his pocket as he walked around on the deck. There on the deck, he was passing by an elderly lady who perturbed him because she had her hands raised in worship to God. He thought he'd play a joke on her and make fun of her faith in God, so as she had her hands raised to God and palms opened, this atheist placed an orange in each of her hands. He laughed and walked off.

Later that evening, many of the people on the ocean liner had gathered together to fellowship, and he walked over to see what was going on. As he got closer, he noticed this elderly woman stood up and began to tell people about the Lord.

She said, "God answers prayer. He is so good to me. I've been seasick for days. I was asking God to send me an orange. I was worshipping God with my hands raised and my eyes closed, and then I felt something. I opened my eyes and there was an orange in each of my hands. I had asked God for one orange and He gave me two."

> **GODFIDENCE LESSON**
>
> The Lord listens to those who take time to pray, and He speaks to those who take time to listen.

3) When your priorities in life are in order.

"Your kingdom come…"

A heart-broken little girl began to kneel and pour out her heart to God in the altar at her local church. She did not know what to say. As she wept speechless, she began to remember what her Father had told her, "God knows your needs even before you pray, and He can answer when you don't even know what to ask." So she began to say her alphabet.

A concerned adult from that church knelt beside her and heard her sobbing and saying her ABCs and inquired what exactly she was trying to do. The little girl told this caring adult, “I’m praying to God from my heart.”

But the adult answered, “It sounds to me more like you are saying the alphabet!”

“Yes,” she said, “But God knows more about what I need than I do, and he can take all these letters and arrange them in just the right way to hear and answer my prayers!”

GODFIDENCE LESSON

The key to worrying less is praying more.

4) When you are willing to submit to God

“Your will be done, on earth as it is in heaven.”

In the summer of 1876, grasshoppers nearly destroyed the crops in Minnesota. So in the spring of 1877, the farmers were worried. They believed that the dreadful plague would once again visit them and again destroy the rich wheat crop, bringing ruin to thousands of people.

The situation was so serious that Governor John S. Pillsbury proclaimed April 26 as a day of prayer and fasting. He urged every man, woman and child to ask God to prevent the terrible scourge. On that day, all schools, shops, stores and offices were closed. There was a reverent, quite hush over all the state.

The next day dawned bright and clear. The temperature soared to what they ordinary were in midsummer, which was very unusual for April. Minnesotans were devastated as they discovered billions of grasshopper larvae wiggling to life. For three days, the unusual heat persisted, and the larvae hatched. It appeared that it wouldn’t be long before they started feeding and destroying the wheat crop.

On the fourth day, however, the temperature suddenly dropped, and that night frost covered the entire state. As a result, it killed every one of those creeping, crawling pests as surely as if poison or fire had been used. It went down in the history of Minnesota as the day God answered the prayers of the people.[8] Sometimes, we just need to trust God with what He is doing.

GODFIDENCE LESSON

The primary focus of prayer is not to change a situation but rather to change you.

5) When you trust God to meet your needs.

"Give us today our daily bread."

If, today, you are dealing with a challenging issue, I would like to suggest that you present your need to God and trust Him. Really trust Him. God's response will go something like this:

> My child, now that you have given me your troubled situation, remember that I won't need your help. You don't need to worry or be troubled with it any longer. Do not attempt to take it back from Me. If you choose to take it back, it will only delay the answer. I will handle it in My timing.
>
> Do not assume that I will handle your situation the way you think I will. I know what is best. And I may answer your prayer in a different way that you anticipate. You have my favor.
>
> Instead of being a worrier, I want you to be a warrior. I am only a prayer away. No need to lose any sleep. You can rest, knowing that the answer is on the way. Because I always have the final Word! Have Godfidence.

"Is prayer your steering wheel or your spare tire?"
– Corrie ten Boom

6) When you need to forgive someone.

"And forgive us our debts,
as we also have forgiven our debtors."

Nora experienced something that no woman should ever have to go through, domestic abuse. She walked away depleted, discouraged, and depressed. Her self-esteem was gone, and her hope was lost. How could she ever forgive her ex-husband for such horrific acts?

One day, she decided to give God a try. As she drew

closer to God, she realized that, as hard as it was, she had to forgive her ex. She thought about how Jesus forgave those who crucified him and had no animosity. But that doesn't mean it is easy.

The day came when she surrendered everything in her life to the Lord, including the past abuse. It was then that she gained the Godfidence to forgive her ex. She learned that we are called to forgive people, even if we don't trust them. When she did that, she was set free! It was like a new lease on life.

GODFIDENCE LESSON

Forgiveness doesn't excuse their behavior. Forgiveness prevents their behavior from destroying your heart.

7) When you need power to overcome the enemy

"And lead us not into temptation,
but deliver us from the evil one."

My car has these red dashboard indicator lights that go on when something is about to go wrong in the engine. They are warning signals. When one of those lights goes on, I have a choice. Do I pay attention to that warning and do something about it, or do I ignore it and face the consequences?

When you are led by the Holy Spirit, He has the tendency to give you a warning that something bad is about to go down. The enemy is trying to put a halt to your spiritual journey. Do you do something about that temptation (warning) or just ignore it? If you ignore His warnings, the consequences will be great. But the choice is yours.

Jesus knows what it's like to be tempted. In Matthew 4, He had to deal with the devil, and He overcame! Do you have the Godfidence to overcome the temptations of the evil one?

GODFIDENCE LESSON

When the prayers go up,
the blessings come down.

"Prayer does change things, all kinds of things. But the most important thing it changes is us. As we engage in this communion with God more deeply and come to know the One with whom we are speaking more intimately, that growing knowledge of God reveals to us all the more brilliantly who we are and our need to change in conformity to Him. Prayer changes us profoundly."
– R.C. Sproul

After they prayed, the place where they were meeting was shaken. And they were all filled with the Holy Spirit and spoke the word of God boldly.
Acts 4:31

BY YOUR SIDE

A young lady asked her pastor to come to her home and pray over her father. When the pastor arrived, he found the man lying in bed with his head propped up on two pillows and an empty chair beside his bed.

The pastor assumed that the old fellow had been informed of his visit. "I guess you were expecting me," he said.

"No, who are you?" answered the man.

"I'm the new pastor at your local church," the pastor replied. "When I saw the empty chair, I figured you knew I was going to show up."

"Oh yeah, the chair," said the bedridden man. "I've never told anyone this, not even my daughter. All of my life I have never known how to pray. Until one day about four years ago my best friend said to me, 'Joe, prayer is just a simple matter of having a conversation with Jesus. Here's what I suggest. Sit down on a chair, place an empty chair in front of you, and in faith see Jesus on the chair. It's not spooky because He promised, "I'll be with you always." Then just speak to him and listen in the same way you're doing with me right now.'

"So, I tried it and I've liked it so much that I do it a couple of hours every day. I'm careful, though. If my daughter saw me talking to an empty chair, she'd either have a nervous breakdown or send me off to the funny farm."

The pastor was deeply moved by the story and spent some time praying with him. Two nights later, the daughter called to tell the pastor that her daddy had died that afternoon.

"Did he seem to die in peace?" he asked.

"Yes, when I left the house around two o'clock, he called me over to his bedside, told me one of his corny jokes, and kissed me on the cheek. When I got back from the store an hour later, I found him dead. But there was something strange. Apparently, just before Daddy died, he leaned over and rested his head on a chair beside the bed."

PRAYING SCRIPTURE

One of my favorite ways to pray is combining it with the power of the Word of God. This is a dynamic duo. The pattern of prayer not only makes the Scriptures come alive but also makes it personally relevant. The Psalms are a great resource to pray Scripture. First, let's read Psalm 91.

Whoever dwells in the shelter of the Most High
    will rest in the shadow of the Almighty.
I will say of the LORD, "He is my refuge and my fortress,
    my God, in whom I trust."
Surely he will save you
    from the fowler's snare
    and from the deadly pestilence.
He will cover you with his feathers,
    and under his wings you will find refuge;
    his faithfulness will be your shield and rampart.
You will not fear the terror of night,
    nor the arrow that flies by day,
    nor the pestilence that stalks in the darkness,

nor the plague that destroys at midday.
A thousand may fall at your side,
ten thousand at your right hand,
but it will not come near you.
You will only observe with your eyes
and see the punishment of the wicked.
If you say, "The LORD is my refuge,"
and you make the Most High your dwelling,
no harm will overtake you,
no disaster will come near your tent.
For he will command his angels concerning you
to guard you in all your ways;
they will lift you up in their hands,
so that you will not strike your foot against a stone.
You will tread on the lion and the cobra;
you will trample the great lion and the serpent.
"Because he loves me," says the LORD, "I will rescue him;
I will protect him, for he acknowledges my name.
He will call on me, and I will answer him;
I will be with him in trouble,
I will deliver him and honor him.
With long life I will satisfy him
and show him my salvation."

Now, let's pray this Scripture and make it personal...

Lord God Almighty, I place myself in Your shelter with the Godfidence to know that my rest is in You. You are my Refuge and my Fortress, the One I can always trust in. In Your presence, I am safe.

I am so blessed to know that You will save me from the attacks of the enemy and protect me from harmful evil. I know that in Your Presence, I am safe. It is there that I am sheltered from harm. And Your faithfulness to me is something I never question.

Thank You for taking away my fears of the night and protecting me from the attacks during the day. With You,

I know that I am safe from terrible viruses and deadly diseases.

Thousands of times, I have experienced the hedge of Your protection over me to the point that I don't have to fight because You are dealing with my enemies.

With Godfidence, I proudly say, "The Lord is my Refuge." And when I make this my mantra, I receive Your promise that no harm or disaster will destroy me. With great faith, I believe that You have sent your angels to protect and cover me, so that I won't be tripped up by the enemy. Even if my enemy is intimidating, You have my back.

When I declare that I am a Christ Follower, then I am blessed to receive Your words of love and your promise of protection. When I call on You, I have no doubt that You will answer me and see me through anything I face. My relationship with You is filled with satisfaction and eternal life. I am truly blessed!

What are you praying for right now? A family member to come to faith in Christ? A loved one battling cancer? Victory over a stubborn habit? Deliverance from a critical spirit? Physical healing? Wisdom to make a difficult decision? A prodigal son or daughter? A deeper walk with God? Courage to not give up? Grace to forgive someone who has wronged you? Hope for the future? A marriage on the rocks? Money to pay your bills? Boldness to share Christ? Don't give up. You can have Godfidence that God has the final Word!

WORDS OF LIFE

I am a warrior! I am a prayer warrior! I have the privilege of having daily conversations with the Maker of the Universe. When I have a need, I can take it to the Lord and have the Godfidence that He will answer my prayer. He has answered me before, and He will do it again! I know that my prayers go up, and His glory comes down!

GODFIDENCE CHECKUP

1) Assess your current commitment to prayer. Are you satisfied? Is it time to take your prayer life to another level? If so, then what specifically will you commit to do to make that happen?

____

____

____

____

____

____

2) Based on the quote from R.C. Sproul, the most important thing that prayer changes is us. How has God changed you, your ways, or your attitudes instead of changing your situation?

____

____

____

____

____

____

3) Moses asked God for His glory. Solomon asked God for wisdom. David asked God for forgiveness. Jonah asked God for a second chance. Hannah asked God for a son. If you had one big ask from God, what would it be? Why?

____

____

____

____

____

____

Lord God Almighty, I come to You in the name of Jesus. I am so grateful that You desire to speak with me on a daily basis. In much the same way that the disciples asked of You, I ask as well: teach me to pray. I'm not satisfied with a superficial relationship with You. I want to go deeper. Any material blessings You send my way is secondary to Your Presence. I simply want more of You. Amen. So be it.

CH. 7 REAL DOCTRINE

Then we will no longer be infants, tossed back and forth by the waves, and blown here and there by every wind of teaching and by the cunning and craftiness of people in their deceitful scheming.
Ephesians 4:14–15

My phone rang, and I was hesitant to answer it. My caller ID could not identify the caller, but I answered it anyway.

PHILIP: Hello, my name is Philip, and I would like to mail you a brochure about faith in God. If I mail it to you, will you promise to read it?

ME: Well, what organization do you represent?

PHILIP: The Watchtower.

Note: Because I am aware that the Watchtower publications are associated with the Jehovah's Witness religion, I realized that I just entered an interesting conversation.

ME: Before I say "yes" to receive your paraphernalia, can you answer three questions for me?

PHILIP: Yes, I will.

ME: Question 1. The Jehovah's Witnesses believe that Michael the Archangel and Jesus are one and the same person. Can you show me a Scripture to back this up?

PHILIP: Yes, Michael the Archangel and Jesus are the same person. There is no Scripture that says this, but this is a fact because of church tradition.

ME: Hmm. Ok. Question 2. The Jehovah's Witnesses say that Jesus returned to earth back in 1914. Do you believe that this happened?

PHILIP: Oh, yes, Jesus did come back to earth.

ME: Oh, He did? How come there is no reports of that happening?

PHILIP: That's because He came invisibly.

ME: Interesting. One more question. The Jehovah's Witnesses say that only 144,000 people will have the privilege of spending eternity in heaven, but that number was reached back in 1935. So, why should I even consider joining your church. I won't go to heaven. Is that right?

PHILIP: Well, you won't go to heaven, but you will be able to be part of the Great Crowd who experience heaven on earth.

ME: Because everything you have stated to me has no Scriptural basis, I am going to pray for you. Lord God Almighty, I come to You in the name of Jesus. I ask You to open the spiritual eyes of my friend, Philip. I pray that You would help him see the truth and begin to live in the truth. I pray that...

Then I heard the line go dead as other phone hung up.

Why are so many Christians being misled today by false doctrine? The number one reason is because they don't have Godfidence in what they believe. Most of the time, when I have a conversation with someone who is involved in a cult or false religion, they come across as being sincere, but they are sincerely wrong. This chapter is designed to help you develop Godfidence in what you believe.

THE ESSENTIALS OF OUR FAITH

But there were also false prophets among the people, just as there will be false teachers among you. They will secretly introduce destructive heresies, even denying the sovereign Lord who bought them – bringing swift destruction on themselves. Many will follow their shameful ways and will bring the way of truth into disrepute. In their greed these teachers will exploit you with stories they have made up. Their condemnation has long been hanging over them, and their destruction has not been sleeping.

2 Peter 2:1–3

When Peter wrote these words about 2,000 years ago, there was a problem of false doctrine, also called heresy. Today, we still deal with the problems of false Bible teaching.

HERESY (N.):

opinion or doctrine at variance with the orthodox or accepted doctrine [9]

Many years ago, I was told the way a bank would train their tellers to identify counterfeit bills was to require the teller to handle thousands of authentic bills. In this way, the teller would be so familiar with the real thing, that when a counterfeit bill comes across their fingers, they would be able to quickly identify it. Similarly, the more you familiarize yourself with the Word of God, the easier it will be for you to identify heresy.

How can we properly identify a Bible teaching as heresy or a church as a cult? The easiest way is to apply the six Jesus questions, because a true Christian church's doctrine centers on the deity of Christ.

DEITY (N.):

divine character or nature [10]

When each of these six questions are answered "yes," the belief system embraces the divine character (deity) of Christ Jesus. If any of these six questions are answered with a "no," then you are dealing with false teachings that deny who Jesus is. Here are the six essentials of Christianity:

Is Jesus Christ the Son of God?
Is Jesus Christ Lord?
Was Jesus born of a virgin?
Did Jesus die on a cross for the forgiveness of our sins?
Did Jesus rise from the grave?
Is Jesus the only way to salvation and eternal life?

Being that the Christian faith is based on these six statements, there is no negotiating around them or agreeing to just most of these statements. Real Christianity is based on who Jesus is and what Jesus has done. Saying "no" to any of these statements is saying "no" to Christianity.

Concerning the coming of our Lord Jesus Christ and our being gathered to him, we ask you, brothers and sisters, not to become easily unsettled or alarmed by the teaching allegedly from us – whether by a prophecy or by word of mouth or by letter – asserting that the day of the Lord has already come. Don't let anyone deceive you in any way, for that day will not come until the rebellion occurs and the man of lawlessness is revealed, the man doomed to destruction. (2 Thessalonians 2:1–3)

The Thessalonian church was being bombarded with false teachings, and Paul needed to address this issue. He wanted to make sure the church was standing strong and not being swayed by false doctrine. The essentials of their faith were important to them, and it is important to us today as well.

If you are going to build a doghouse, you don't need a foundation. If you are going to build a house, you need a good foundation. If you are going to build a high-rise structure, you need a very strong foundation. Your belief system forms your spiritual foundation. How tall and strong do you want to build your spiritual life?

GODFIDENCE LESSON

The more Godfidence you have in your doctrine, the better you will be able to stand strong in what you believe.

CENTRAL THEOLOGY VERSUS PERIPHERAL THEOLOGY

To help us understand the six essentials of the faith, we can look at the difference between central theology and peripheral theology. Theology is the study of God and His attributes. Central theology pertains to essential doctrines of the Christian faith. In other words, the portions of your faith that determine your salvation and eternal life. The six essentials of the faith comprise central theology.

Peripheral theology deals with doctrines not related to salvation or eternal life. For example, the doctrine of speaking in tongues (glossolalia) is a great benefit to the believer in the world we live in today, but speaking in tongues is not your ticket to heaven. It is an example of peripheral theology. Another example of peripheral theology is eschatology – the study of end-time events. When you believe Jesus will return in relation to the Tribulation – the beginning, the middle, or the end – doesn't affect your salvation as long as you believe that Jesus is coming back again.

CULTS

For the time will come when people will not put up with sound doctrine. Instead, to suit their own desires, they will gather around them a great number of teachers to say what their itching ears want to hear.

2 Timothy 4:3

On September 3, 2012, I read a news report that Sun Myung Moon had died. Who was he? He was the self-proclaimed leader of the Unification Church, a cult also known as the Moonies. Years ago, Sun Myung Moon began teaching that Jesus Christ failed to complete what God the Father sent Him to do here on earth. So, God sent him (Moon) to complete the mission. In other words, Moon was proclaiming himself to be the Messiah.

So, when I read that Moon had died, I thought to myself, "Ok, let's wait three days and see if he rises from the dead. After all, he claims to be the Messiah." Well, it's been a number of years, and Sun Myung Moon is still in the grave. No, he was not the Messiah. Jesus is the only one who has conquered death, hell, and the grave. Jesus is the Messiah, and that is the absolute truth.

What is a cult? Simply put, a cult is a religious group that denies one or more of the essentials of Christianity. Any time a person follows the teachings of a cult, they are headed in the wrong spiritual direction, and their eternity is at stake.

GOSPEL OF WORKS VERSUS GOSPEL OF GRACE

Not too long ago, I struck up a conversation with someone who is part of the Church of Latter-Day Saints, aka Mormons. He was trying to convince me to join his religion. After I asked him why he was going door to door, he responded by saying, "I believe doing this fulfills my requirements for salvation and eternal life."

What he was describing to me was the gospel of works. Those who adhere to the gospel of works believe that they can "work" their way to heaven.

Ephesians 2:8–9 says, "For by grace you have been saved through faith. And this is not your own doing; it is the gift of God, not a result of works, so that no one may boast" (ESV). Scripture is clear. We are saved by grace. What is grace? Grace is God's unmerited favor. We don't deserve it, but God offers it to us anyway.

Can you imagine what the conversations in heaven would be like if we got there by the gospel of works?

"Hey, buddy, what did you do to earn your way to heaven? I knocked on 2,455 doors during my lifetime."

His buddy tries to top that, saying, "Well, I sang on my church worship team for twelve years, and I am sure that God was pleased with me."

Those who believe in the gospel of works are focused on they need to "do," whereas those who believe in the gospel of grace focus on what Christ has "done." It's time to believe in what Christ has done rather than "earning" your way to salvation.

On the evening of September 10, 2001, nineteen young men read a prayer-laden letter regarding their last night on earth. "Be obedient on this night, because you will be facing situations that are the ultimate and that would not be done except with full obedience. When you engage in battle, strike as the heroes would strike. As god says, strike above the necks and strike from everywhere...and then you will know all the heavens are decorated in the best way to meet you."[11]

The "god" referred to in this letter is not the same Jehovah God Who is the Creator of the world. The "god" referred to in this letter is Allah, who is the god of the Islamic religion.

The next morning, on Sept. 11, 2001, those nineteen men gave their lives for what they believed. They were trying to earn their way to heaven. These terrorists had deep convictions, deep beliefs, but they were deeply wrong. The truth was far from them.

In April of 2017, Kori Ali Muhammad shot and killed three people in Fresno, California. As he was arrested, he shouted out "Allahu Akbar," which is an Arabic phrase meaning, "Our God Allah is greater." Terrible things take place in the name of god. Unfortunately, the god they worship doesn't even exist.

TRUTH VERSUS HERESY

An eight-year-old girl asked her mom, "How did the human race begin?" Mom said, "Well, according to the Bible, God created mankind on the sixth day."

The girl went over to her dad and asked the same question. He said, "Well, as Darwin says, we were first monkeys and then, over thousands of years, we became human beings."

The girl went back to her mom and said, "Mom, I'm confused. You and dad have different answers to where we come from. Why?"

Mom said, "Well, I've told you where my family came from, and he told you where his family came from."

Ok. After a little laugh, let's ask some serious questions.

Question 1: Who is God? The truth is that there is one God – Jehovah – and He is Triune in nature, God the Father, God the Son, and God the Holy Spirit. This answer is simple and true, but many get this wrong. Here are a few examples of how those outside of Christianity answer this important question:

Mormon heresy: God was a human who progressed to Godhood.
Islamic heresy: God is not Jehovah but another god, Allah.
New Age heresy: Every human being is God.
Buddhism heresy: God is an unnecessary concept.

Question 2: Who is Jesus? The truth is that Jesus is God. The second person of the Trinity. He is fully God and fully man. He is the only way to the Father, salvation, and eternal life. He died on a cross as full sacrifice and payment for our sin.

Jehovah's Witnesses heresy: Jesus is Michael, the archangel.
Mormon heresy: Jesus is Lucifer's brother.
Islamic heresy: Jesus is one of Allah's prophets.
New Age heresy: Jesus is a guru and ascended master.
The Unification Church (Moonies) heresy: Jesus was not God. He was the son of Zechariah and not born of a virgin. His mission failed.
Judaism heresy: Jesus is not the Messiah.

Question 3: How are we saved? The truth is that salvation is by God's grace, not by our works. Salvation must be received by faith. People must believe in their hearts that Jesus died for their sins and physically rose again, and they must develop a personal relationship with Christ Jesus.

Buddhist heresy: We are saved by reaching Nirvana and achieving nonexistence.
Mormon heresy: Entering eternal life requires secret temple rituals.
Hindu heresy: We are saved by being released from the cycle of reincarnation through yoga and meditation.
Scientologist heresy: We have not sinned and therefore

do not need to repent. Salvation is freedom from reincarnation.

Christian Science heresy: All of us are already saved. Sin, evil, sickness, and death are not real.

Question 4: What do you consider truth? The Bible, God's Holy Word, is the Truth.

Islamic heresy: The Quran (Koran)

Mormon heresy: The Bible plus the Book of Mormon.

Jehovah's Witnesses heresy: New World Translation of the Bible and the Watchtower Publications.

Here's an example of how the Scriptures in the New World Version twists the truth. In John 1:1, my Bible says, "In the beginning was the Word, and the Word was with God and the Word was God" (ESV). The capitalization of "Word" is a reference to Jesus. He is the Word. The New World Translation adds one little word ("a") that changes the entire meaning of the Scripture. Instead of reading, "and the Word was God," this version reads, "and the Word was a God," implying that Jesus is one of many gods.

Question 5: What do you believe about eternal life and heaven? The Jehovah's Witnesses' heresy teaches that Jesus already returned to earth in 1914 and only 144,000 Jehovah's Witnesses will make it to heaven, a number that has already been reached.

A HERESY CUT SHORT

Like many little girls, Lisa Brockman earnestly believed that someday she would grow up to be a mommy. She also believed that someday she would be a god.

Lisa, a fifth-generation Mormon, said, "Every Mormon boy and girl wants a temple marriage, because that is the only way you can get into the Celestial Kingdom. There you enter into an eternal family and become a god or goddess."

In college, Lisa began dating a Christian baseball player

named Gary. In the ensuing months, they debated the differences between Christianity and Mormonism. One of the more difficult issues that confronted Lisa was the notion that she was sinful and in need of divine forgiveness – a Christian teaching that sharply contradicts Mormon doctrine. The significance behind this philosophy is rooted in the Mormon worldview. "As man now is, God once was; as God now is, man may become."

"For the first time, I began to see how sinful I was and how holy God is," Lisa said. She finally accepted the truth and invited Christ into her life.

RED FLAGS

In addition to the five important doctrinal questions we just covered, we must be aware of other doctrinal heresies that are prevalent around us today. The enemy is very subtle in his ways to attempt to lead us astray.

Church Tradition

There are some churches which claim to be Christian churches but have created religious traditions that are not from the Bible. For example, some churches will teach their followers to pray to a saint or to the Mother Mary, even though the Bible makes it clear that we pray to the Father through the Son, Jesus (John 14:6, 13–14).

In another example, I was attending a funeral when the minister said, "This man received his entrance into eternal life when he was baptized at the church as an infant." Hmmm. How does an infant have the capability to ask Christ to forgive them of their sins and consciously place their faith in the Lord Jesus Christ? Not possible. Then there is a teaching in a church that says God chooses who He wants to be saved and who He doesn't want to be saved. In other words, man does not have free will to make a choice to be a Christ follower.

Would you rather base your doctrines of faith on religious traditions or on what the Word of God (the Bible) says? Just because a church says that they are "Christian" doesn't mean that its doctrines are based on the Bible. Acts 17:10–12 tells us that the Bereans examined the Scriptures to see if what Paul was teaching was indeed true. When you and I do the same, we will develop real doctrine.

Karma

Sadly, I've heard many people use this term – even Christians. This is a term from Buddhism meaning what goes around, comes around. In other words, if something bad happens to you, it's because you've done something wrong and you are simply paying the price. There is a word for these thoughts: baloney!

For example, we know that Jesus had to deal with a crown of thorns, thirty-nine lashes on his back, nails in his hands and feet, etc. So, according to karma, Jesus was beaten and nailed to a cross because He sinned and did wrong. What goes around comes around, and He was simply paying the price. Not true. Totally not true. He was the sinless Lamb of God and taking punishment for sins he had not committed.

Reincarnation

Another popular false doctrine is reincarnation – the belief that after death, a soul comes back to earth in the form of another body or form. Drew Barrymore said this, "Either I am the reincarnation of my grandfather, or he is in spiritual limbo and won't pass on 'til he knows I'm okay."

A popular 2017 movie entitled, *A Dog's Purpose* is all about how a dog dies and gets reincarnated. Then dies again and gets reincarnated again, and on, and on. Who is Hollywood's target audience for these types of movies? Children. The percentage of Americans who believe in reincarnation has risen to 25%.[12]

Prayer

Let's consider the word "pray." Prayer is a terrific thing.

Unless it is directed to someone other than our God, Jehovah. In conversations with individuals in cults, they will often talk about how much they pray. They sound godly. A few years ago, I heard about a Julia Roberts movie called *Eat, Pray, Love*. It sounded like a good movie, until I read a review that describes how the main character chants and learns meditation before a shrine erected for the guru. Then, she spends quite a bit of time practicing her newfound mysticism, trying to fill the void she feels in her soul, revealing an ungodly, cultish theme hidden behind the theme of "pray." Just because someone says they pray, doesn't mean their prayers are going to the Lord our God.

Here's another example. You may hear a Jehovah's Witness say, "I believe in Jesus," but their interpretation of the person of Jesus is quite different than Christianity's. Not only do they believe that Jesus is Michael, the archangel but they also believe that Jesus was merely human as He walked the face of the earth. They do not believe that he rose from the dead either – a denial of one of the primary essentials of our faith in Christ Jesus.

> Many cults refer to themselves as Christians. They often use the same terminology that Christians use, but their definitions are often different.

Let's consider the word "salvation." In my conversations with individuals associated with cults, I've noticed that they often use the word "salvation" too. At first glance, it sounds good, but after talking more, I realize that their definition of salvation is different than the Bible's definition. Their concept of eternal life cannot be backed up with Scripture. I've learned to be careful about accepting their terminology at face value.

Syncretism

Syncretism is the union of different or opposing principles

or practices as in philosophy or religion. Many people today syncretize Christianity with other beliefs. For example, a person who would call himself a Christian and yet reads his horoscope is syncretizing his beliefs. Horoscopes are the prediction of future events or advice based on the positions of the planets and the signs of the zodiac. In essence, the person who believes in their horoscope is saying, "I am not going trust God with my future, I would rather trust the zodiac signs." This is a form of astrology.

What does the Bible say about astrology, zodiac signs, and horoscopes? Leviticus 19:26 says, "Do not practice divination or seek omens." Unfortunately, the percentage of Americans who believe in astrology has grown to 29%.[13] It does not necessarily mean that most of these people deny Christianity. Most of them embrace Christianity and also embrace astrology. This is syncretism.

Then, there are many people today who get caught up in demonic activity, like Ouija boards, palm reading, tarot cards, curanderas, white magic, psychic hotlines, crystal balls, etc. Don't play with fire.

YOU HAVE A CHOICE

While Brenda and I were taking a few days off in Chicago, I scheduled an Uber to take us back to our hotel. As we got into the back seat, I noticed that our driver was Middle Eastern. I decided to chat with him about his faith. We talked about the country of Jordan – where he was from. We talked about fasting (it was the month of Ramadan). And then I asked him, "What in the Islamic religion brings you joy?" He thought and thought and thought. I could see that he didn't have a definite answer to my question. Finally, he said, "Well, I don't know any other religion. I was born into it, and I will always be a Muslim."

Sadness filled my heart as this man was communicating to me that he felt that he had no other choice in life. Even though I told him that Jesus is the way, the truth, and the life, and no one goes to the Father except through Him, it was obvious that he felt he was not allowed to believe that.

Many cults do not embrace God's free gift of grace. Buddhists, for example, follow an eight-fold path to enlightenment. It's not a free ride. Hindus believe in karma, that your actions continually affect the way the world will treat you; that there is nothing that comes to you not set in motion by your actions.

In Islam, god is a god of judgment not a god of love. You live to appease him. In Mormonism, you have to work for your salvation. Only Christianity dares to proclaim God's love is unconditional. An unconditional love that we call grace, not based on what you have to "do" but rather based on what Christ has "done."

A Muslim became a Christian and one of his friends asked him why. He said, "Well, it is like this. Suppose you were going down a road, and suddenly the road forked in two directions, and you didn't know which way to go. Then, you met two men at the fork – one dead and one alive – which one would you ask to show you the way?"

Muslims and other cults serve a dead god...but we, as Christians, serve a risen Savior! Do you have Godfidence that the doctrine you follow is based on our Risen Savior?

WORDS OF LIFE

I believe that Jesus Christ is Lord. My past is forgiven. My present is blessed, and my future is promised. I purpose to stand on God's grace and live by God's power. I refuse to be brought down by false teachings. I have Godfidence in what I believe!

GODFIDENCE CHECKUP

1) Review the six essentials of the Christian faith. Can you personally say "yes" to each of these six questions? Why would one answer of "no" to any of these six questions place you outside of the Christian faith?

---

2) In your opinion, why are some cults attracting such a large number of people?

3) A popular belief today is, "I will make it to heaven because I am a good person." Why is this doctrine false?

PRAYER FOCUS

Lord God Almighty, I come to you in the name of Jesus. I believe that You, Lord Jesus, are the Way, the Truth, and the Life, and no one goes to the Father except through You. Open my spiritual eyes to be able to identify false spiritual doctrines that are so prevalent in our world today. Now that I have a solid doctrine for my faith, I pray that I can work to build my spiritual life stronger and stronger every day. Amen. So be it.

CH. 8 REAL TRUTH

"Then you will know the truth, and the truth will set you free."
John 8:32

It was a Monday morning, and I had the privilege of driving my three-year-old grandson, Cam, to daycare. Because I was in the singing mood, I started to sing a song I learned as a child, "Jesus loves me this I know, for the Bible tells me so. Little ones to Him belong. They are weak but He is strong. Yes, Jesus loves me. Yes, Jesus loves me. Yes, Jesus love me, the Bible tells me so."

On Tuesday's drive to daycare, I sang the song again. And for the next twelve trips or so to daycare, I sang the song. Then one day, as my daughter, Shalyse, was driving around with Cam, he started to sing "Jesus Loves Me." It caught her totally off guard. When she texted me a video of Cam singing, I texted her back, letting her know that I taught him that song.

I didn't realize that my grandson was soaking in the words and melody to the "Jesus Loves Me" song, but he was. This simple lesson he learned is a lesson that will stick in his mind for the rest of his life. "Jesus loves me." How do you know that? "The Bible tells me so."

There are thousands and thousands more Bible lessons waiting for you and me to learn and promises waiting for us to claim. Are you ready to receive them? This is Godfidence. God has a purpose for my life. How do I know that? Godfidence. The Bible tells me so. God is ready to make you more than a conqueror! How do I know that? The Bible tells me so.

The Bible is an amazing book. It was the world's first printed book and has been translated fully into more than 2,000 languages and into many more partial translations like the Gospel of John. Despite attempts to discredit it and destroy it over the centuries, it remains the best-loved, best-selling book of all time.

Some people claim that archeology proves the Bible wrong. That was a popular belief in the nineteenth century, but it doesn't hold up anymore. In fact, as archeological discoveries increase, the more support the Bible gains. Jewish archeologist Nelson Glueck made over 1,500 archeological discoveries, using the Bible as a guide. He stated that no archeological discovery has ever been made that contradicts the historical content of the Bible.

The Bible is made up of sixty-six books, written over 1,500 years by forty human authors in three languages, making its unity truly remarkable. As you search through the chapters of the Bible, you will find one plan of redemption for mankind: salvation through the Son of God. This is true because each one of the human authors was anointed by one Divine Author. Here's the bottom line: It's easy to believe that the Bible is a fine piece of literature, an accurate historical account, and even spiritually significant, but do you really believe that the Bible is indeed the Word of God?

GODFIDENCE QUESTION

Is the Word of God your source for Godfidence?

Teri, a single mom, worked a full-time job, and life was tough. Everything seemed to be spiraling downward, and she was convinced that her life was meaningless. She found herself sitting in a dark closet with a pistol, planning to end her life. In desperation she cried out loud to God, "If for some reason I should not end my life right here, right now, you need to do something."

Just then, her son burst through the front door of their home, shouting, "Momma, Momma, come look what I have."

Teri put the pistol away, composed herself as much as possible, and walked out to meet her son. He was waving a New Testament he had received from the Gideons

International after school that day. She and her son opened God's Word together and began their journey of faith. The Bible gave her the Godfidence to live.

BIBLICAL WORLDVIEW VERSUS SECULAR WORLDVIEW

What is truth to you? A worldview is simply a framework that defines what an individual assumes to be true based on how they see the world we live in. In today's era, we are influenced by the people around us, the media that speaks to us and the culture that impacts us. Individuals who form their philosophies based on worldly influences are known to have a secular worldview.

Then there are individuals who have created their framework through the eyes of the Word of God. They make decisions based on God's perspective. They have a Biblical or Christian worldview. Do you believe that the Bible is truth and that the choices you make in life are based on what God says? There are many hot topics today, such as abortion, same-sex marriage, racism and cohabitation, and most everyone has their opinion. Do you hold a Biblical worldview?

> ### GODFIDENCE LESSON
> Godfidence in the Word of God is reflected when your daily decisions are based on your Biblical worldview.

Josh McDowell has done extensive research on this topic of teenagers and a Biblical worldview. His research shows that teenagers who do not possess a Biblical worldview are…

36% more likely to lie to a friend
48% more likely to cheat on an exam
200% more likely to steal
200% more likely physically hurt someone

300% more likely to use illegal drugs
600% more likely to commit suicide [14]
Yes, a Biblical worldview makes a difference.

ABSOLUTE TRUTH

In mathematics, absolute truth says that 2 plus 2 equals 4. There is no room to debate whether there is a different answer than 4. In a spiritual sense, Jesus said, "I am the Way, the Truth and the Life, and no one comes to the Father except through me." That is spiritual absolute truth.

In recent years, more and more people no longer believe in absolute truth. One popular philosophy is "You believe what you want to believe, I'll believe what I want to believe, and we will meet up on heaven." This statement is inaccurate because it leaves out what God's Word says.

> **GODFIDENCE LESSON**
> As I put my faith in the Lord Jesus Christ, I have the Godfidence that I will spend eternity in heaven.

Suppose your son just turned sixteen years old and wants to start driving. He hasn't taken driver's ed and has no experience behind the wheel of a car. Would you hand him the keys to your car? Who needs driver's ed or a permit anyway? Your teenager doesn't need that. He can be guided by his instincts and whims. No rules. No regulations. No absolutes.

I have a feeling you would not turn your car keys over to your son until he learns the rules of the road. There are speed limits. There are restrictions and laws. And there are consequences to the person who does not follow those rules.

> "Our kids have been conditioned to believe that truth is not true for them until they choose to believe it." – Josh McDowell

In today's culture, many famous athletes, actors, singers, and celebrities have a great influence on others, especially young people. And many times, they lead the younger generation down the wrong path. Here is a quote from one celebrity, Oprah Winfrey, who just doesn't get it, "One of the biggest mistakes we make is to believe there is only one way. There are many diverse paths leading to God."

CONVICTIONS

Perhaps you can identify with Manny's story. He was happy because he had a good position in his company and was making some good money. One day, his boss asked him to do something that was illegal, and Manny had a decision to make. Would he choose to say "no" to his boss and have the Godfidence to stand on his convictions from his Biblical worldview? He did. And it cost him his job.

He was distraught and asked God why this had happened if he did what was right. After a month or so, God opened up a new door for Manny, and it was his dream job. Shortly thereafter, he heard that his old company had folded because of impropriety in the management. In retrospect, God did have Manny's back, and he learned that living by godly convictions does pay off.

A conviction goes beyond having a personal preference or a strong opinion. When someone has a conviction, they are willing to stand for it despite any consequences that may result. That's what many people – even Christians – lack in today's world.

> "A belief is something you'll argue about. But a conviction is something you'll die for." – Howard Hendricks

WHAT IS YOUR STANDARD?

The United States of America is blessed to have a strong spiritual foundation. Many of our founding fathers were strong in the faith. Abraham Lincoln was quoted as saying, "I do not rely on the patriotism of our people, but the God of our Fathers, who raised up this country...that this nation, under God, shall have a new birth of freedom."

Patrick Henry was known for his famous words, "Give me liberty or give me death!" But he also didn't hold back when it came to his faith: "It cannot be emphasized too strongly or too often that this great nation was founded, not by religionists, but by Christians, not on religion, but on the Gospel of Jesus Christ."

David Barton reports that the political-science professors at the University of Houston collected and cataloged 15,000 writings by our founding fathers. Their goal was to determine the primary source of ideas behind the Constitution by identifying the sources quoted most often by them. Can you guess what that primary source was? Yes, it was the Bible. 94% of the quotes of the founders of our nation were based upon the Bible.

The list of examples of great faith by our founding fathers is long. They went to great lengths to establish this great nation with a Biblical worldview. But over the years, our standards have been compromised. Our core values have changed, and it is not for the better.

Biblical Core Values: Standards that dictate our lifestyle based on our faith in the Son of God, our devotion to the Word of God, and our dependence on the Spirit of God.

On the morning of April 20, 1999, a sixteen-year-old girl named Cassie Bernall, a student at Columbine High School in Colorado, handed her friend, Amanda Meyer, a note that read, "Honestly, I totally want to live my life completely for

God. It's hard and scary, but totally worth it."

Later that day, she was shot to death. Another teenager who was shot and killed that day was Rachel Scott, who had written these words in her diary, "I'm not going to apologize for speaking the Name of Jesus. I'm not going to hide the light God has put in me." With guns pointed at them, these two young ladies were asked, "Do you believe in God?" They chose to stand strong on their Biblical convictions, and it cost them their lives.[15]

GODFIDENCE LESSON

When the influences of the world try to sway you away from the ways of the Lord, you can have the Godfidence to stand strong on your convictions.

Raising three children who love the game of basketball was a treat. In fact, I had a half-court sized concrete slab poured in our backyard. Perhaps it was because I wanted less lawn to mow. I remember the day we lowered the basket from the regular ten feet height to eight feet. Dunking the basketball was so much fun! We took pictures and enjoyed the moments. Here's what I learned that day: Dunking a basketball is so much easier when you lower the standard.

God has His standards. They are laid out in His Word. Living life according to God's standards is not the easiest thing to do – but it is the most rewarding. When it comes to morality, the world we live in tends to lower their standards. That leaves us with a choice. Do we follow the ways of the world, or do we follow the standards of God? This is real truth.

"For my thoughts are not your thoughts,
neither are your ways my ways," declares the LORD.
"As the heavens are higher than the earth,
so are my ways higher than your ways
and my thoughts than your thoughts." (Isaiah 55:8–9)

GODFIDENCE LESSON

News articles may inform you, music may inspire you, stories may capture you, but only God's Word can transform you.

GOD'S WORD IS TRUTH

In September of 1994, I was struggling with my calling to ministry. I was asking the Lord to show me His will for me. I knew that God had a calling on my life, but I needed a job to support the family. I had interviewed for two positions in the accounting field and got turned down. There was also an opportunity for me to plant a new church. I wanted to make sure it was God. I told the Lord that I didn't want advice from this person or that person, I wanted to hear from Him.

One night, I was up most of the night. Reading the Word. Praying. Crying out to God. About 6:00 a.m., I received a phone call from Trini Guerrero. She said, "Pastor, God gave me a Word for you from Revelation 3:7–8. The Lord has closed certain doors for you, but he is also opening a big door for you. Now, it is time to lead your people." God's written Word (from Revelation 3) opened the door to God's revealed Word. Real Truth. All I needed was Godfidence to step into God's will.

GODFIDENCE LESSON

Real Godfidence gives you the ability to step into God's will.

GODFIDENCE SCRIPTURES

When You Are	God's Word Encourages
Facing Financial Challenges	My God will meet all your needs according to the riches of his glory in Christ Jesus. (Philippians 4:19)
Battling With Fear	The LORD is my light and my salvation – whom shall I fear? The LORD is the stronghold of my life – of whom shall I be afraid? (Psalm 27:1)
Losing Hope	For everything that was written in the past was written to teach us, so that through the endurance taught in the Scriptures and the encouragement they provide we might have hope. (Romans 15:4)
Weighed down with troubles	For our light and momentary troubles are achieving for us an eternal glory that far outweighs them all. So we fix our eyes not on what is seen, but on what is unseen, since what is seen is temporary, but what is unseen is eternal. (2 Corinthians 4:17–18)
Under persecution	Blessed are you when people insult you, persecute you and falsely say all kinds of evil against you because of me. Rejoice and be glad, because great is your reward in heaven. (Matthew 5:11–12)
Praying for someone's salvation	The LORD is not slow in keeping his promise, as some understand slowness. Instead he is patient with you, not wanting anyone to perish, but everyone to come to repentance. (2 Peter 3:9)

A BASIS FOR SPIRITUAL GROWTH

For the word of God is living and powerful, and sharper than any two-edged sword, piercing even to the division of soul and spirit, and of joints and marrow, and is a discerner of the thoughts and intents of the heart.
Hebrews 4:12 NKJV

Without question, the best resource for spiritual growth is the Bible. It is the primary way God speaks to you. The more you get into the Word of God, the more you get to know God. Here are four ways the Bible can help your spiritual life grow.

1) Read the Bible.

Your word is a lamp for my feet, a light on my path.
Psalm 119:105

Developing the discipline of reading the Word of God is the foundation of your spiritual life. Does it take time? Yes, it does. While some people will make the excuse that they don't have time to dedicate to reading the Bible, the truth is that each of us makes time for what we value the most. In fact, with today's technology, listening to the Bible on audio is a great way to read on the go.

2) Listen to Bible messages.

So, faith comes from hearing,
and hearing through the word of Christ.
Romans 10:17 ESV

One of the primary ways in which I am inspired is listening to a good Bible teaching. I love the preaching and the teaching of the Word. Because of that, I often listen to Bible teachings on podcasts. While I drive in my car or while I walk through my neighborhood for exercise, I enjoy listening to the Bible being taught. Not too long ago, I had a four-hour drive to an important meeting. I used those eight hours of drive time to listen to an audio Bible study book and half of a second one. I felt I made best use of my time and was so enriched spiritually. I will expound on this topic in the next section, "What are you listening to?"

3) Study the Bible.

Study to shew thyself approved unto God, a workman that needeth not to be ashamed, rightly dividing the word of truth.

2 Timothy 2:15 KJV

The depth of your understanding of the Bible comes with intentional study. Good Bible study methods will help you analyze verses, research wording, ask questions, determine key meanings of words, and learn how to apply the principles to your life. I have also learned not to be in a rush to read through chapters of the Bible just for the sake of reaching a "reading" goal. I would rather read shorter segments and study them closely for better understanding.

4) Meditate on and memorize the Bible.

Oh, how I love your law! I meditate on it all day long.

Psalm 119:97

Recently, I was going through a difficult time and the enemy was trying his best to convince me that God had let me down. I was starting to feel lonely. Then, I remembered Hebrews 13:5 which says, "I will never leave you nor forsake you." In just a few minutes, I had my Godfidence back. Memorizing that Scripture years ago gave me the reminder I needed.

And why is Scripture meditation important? In a world where you and I are bombarded by negative thoughts, fake news, opinionated friends, and ungodly people, meditating on the Word of God keeps your mind on what is true, what is noble, what is right, what is pure, what is lovely, as Paul encouraged in Philippians 4:8.

Michael Billester visited a small village in Poland shortly before World War II. He gave a Bible to a villager, who read it and placed his faith in the Lord. The new believer then passed that same Bible on to others. The cycle of conversions to faith on Christ continued until 200 people had become believers through that one Bible.

When Billester returned a short while later, he met with this group of Christians and suggested that several in the audience recite verses of Scripture. One man stood and said, "Perhaps we have misunderstood. Do you want us to quote verses or chapters?" These villagers had not memorized a few select verses of the Bible, but whole chapters and books. Thirteen people knew Matthew, Luke, and half of Genesis. Another person had committed to memory the Psalms. That single copy of the Bible given by Billester had done its work. It transformed lives and bore witness to the power of the Word.[16]

WHAT ARE YOU LISTENING TO?

An elderly man was greatly concerned that his wife was losing her hearing, so he sought advice from his friend, who came up with a plan to test the wife's hearing. The next time the man entered his house, he stopped at the front door and yelled, "Honey, I'm home. What's for dinner?" No response. So, he took about eight steps and said, "Honey, I'm home. What's for dinner?" No response. Then, he walked about eight feet from his wife and said, "Honey, I'm home. What's for dinner?"

She said, "Babe, for the third time, I heard you, and we are having meatloaf for dinner." Yes. You guessed it. He was the one with the hearing problem.

That's the way it is with so many of us. We pray and ask, "God, why aren't you listening to me. Are you hard of hearing?" When all the time, we are the ones who are not listening to God intently.

God speaks to you every day, primarily through the Bible. But sometimes, we are not listening. Today's technology makes it quite easy to stay "in tune" with God. At our fingertips, we have access to Bible teaching podcasts and videos, Christian audio books, godly music, online Bible studies, Zoom small groups, and so much more. I wish I had all this when I was a young man.

> **GODFIDENCE LESSON**
> What God has to say to you is far more important than what you have to say.

SIX WAYS TO TUNE IN TO GOD'S VOICE

I am the good shepherd; I know my sheep and my sheep know me – just as the Father knows me and I know the Father – and I lay down my life for the sheep. I have other sheep that are not of this sheep pen. I must bring them also. They too will listen to my voice, and there shall be one flock and one shepherd.

John 10:14–16

"It's real simple. The more you know God, the more clearly you can hear God." – Henry Blackaby

Love the Shepherd. Remember that the deeper your personal relationship with God goes, the more you know His heart.

Long to spend time in prayer. Set daily time aside to pray. Put it on your calendar. The Lord longs to hear from you, and He also desires to speak to you.

Learn the Scriptures. God has already spoken. Check it out. It's in the Bible.

Listen to godly sources. Godly music. Godly teachings. These are two great menu items you should consider when it comes to feeding your spirit.

Look for godly confirmation. Have you ever heard the

phrase, "Consider the source"? Make sure what you hear can be tied back to what God has said.

Linger in God's presence. Each of us makes time in our busy schedule for what is important to us. Consider spending time in God's presence a priority.

"I know the Lord is speaking to me when I have an impression during prayer that is consistent with His Word and supported by wise counsel."
– Christine Caine

A Colombian man was upset when he found his daughter reading a copy of the New Testament. He told her not to read it anymore because it was full of lies and fantasy. He grabbed it from her hands and put it in his pocket. Then, he went off to work where he was a mining engineer.

Several hours later, sirens went off in the community. There had been a cave-in at the mine. This man was trapped in the mine. The rescue workers took five days to finally reach the men, but it was too late. All thirty-one men died, including the father of this little girl.

Curiously, workers found the man clutching the New Testament between his praying hands. When they opened the front cover, they read a note that said, "To my daughter, keep reading this Bible. It is true and right, and I will see you one day in heaven." Then they turned to the back page where the father had signed the commitment card after having said the sinner's prayer. But that was not the end of the story – turning the page, there were signed names of the other thirty workers.[17]

GODFIDENCE LESSON
When you find yourself in a life or death situation, you can find Godfidence in God's Word.

IMPERFECT PEOPLE

One of the many distinguishing attributes of the Bible is relatability. It tells stories of imperfect people who have done imperfect things. This gives me hope and should give you hope as well. Noah was a drunk. Abraham lied. Sarah laughed at God's promises. Isaac was a daydreamer. Jacob was a trickster. Joseph was mistreated. Moses had a stuttering problem. Miriam was a gossip. Gideon lacked Godfidence. Samson was a womanizer. Jeremiah and Timothy were too young. Naomi was a widow. Job went bankrupt. David had an affair. Solomon had way too many wives. Elijah was suicidal. Jeremiah dealt with depression. Jonah ran from God. Hosea's wife was a prostitute.

When we get to the New Testament, John the Baptist ate bugs. Martha worried about everything. The Samaritan woman was divorced – more than once. Peter denied Christ. The disciples fell asleep while praying. Thomas doubted. Zaccheus was too small. John Mark was rejected by Paul. Paul was a murderer, as were Moses and David. And of course, Lazarus was dead! Which of these people became overcomers and were used of God? All of them. You, too, qualify to be used of God. This is real truth.

> "Put your nose in the Bible every day.
> It is your spiritual food. And then share it.
> Make a vow not to become a lukewarm Christian."
> – Kirk Cameron

WORDS OF LIFE

I love God's Word. Its principles are holy, its history is true, and its stories are inspiring. I read it to be wise, believe it to be safe, and practice it to be real. The Bible is light to direct me, food to nourish me, and comfort to cheer me. It is real Truth. And for me, it is always the final Word.

GODFIDENCE CHECKUP

1) If someone were to say, "I don't believe in the Bible. It was written so long ago that it is no longer relevant." How would you respond?

2) In what specific ways are you willing to make the reading and the studying of the Bible more prominent in your spiritual life?

3) Biblical worldview versus secular worldview. Which do you adhere to, and why?

PRAYER FOCUS

Lord God Almighty, I come to You in the name of Jesus. Today, I purpose to base my beliefs, values, and decisions on the Bible. I know that Your Word is real Truth. It is Your voice speaking to me, and I receive it. I believe that You will reveal Your will to me through Your Word. Thank You for Your Word. May I always have a hunger to learn from it. Amen. So be it.

CH. 9 REAL DISCIPLESHIP

Jesus called out to them, "Come, follow me, and I will show you how to fish for people!" And they left their nets at once and followed him.
Matthew 4:19–20 NLT

It was on the shore of the Sea of Galilee that Jesus called Simon Peter and Andrew to follow Him. What was their response? Verse 20 says that they left their nets at once and followed him. Then, Jesus called James and John to follow him. "Going on from there, he saw two other brothers, James son of Zebedee and his brother John. They were in a boat with their father Zebedee, preparing their nets. Jesus called them, and immediately they left the boat and their father and followed him" (Matthew 4:21–22).

How long did it take for James and John to make their decision to follow Rabbi Jesus? The Bible says "immediately."

Then, Jesus gave the very same "come follow me" invitation to Philip and Nathaneal. John 1:43–45 says this:

> The next day Jesus decided to leave for Galilee. Finding Philip, he said to him, "Follow me."
>
> Philip, like Andrew and Peter, was from the town of Bethsaida. Philip found Nathanael and told him, "We have found the one Moses wrote about in the Law, and about whom the prophets also wrote – Jesus of Nazareth, the son of Joseph."

This "Come, follow me" invitation that Jesus gave to these men and their immediate responses intrigued me. What was it that caused these six Jewish men to drop their nets, leave their families and their jobs, and follow this Rabbi? The answer to this question is found in understanding the Hebrew traditions of that time.

GODFIDENCE LESSON

Rabbi Jesus believes in your potential. He believes in you!

During their beginning years of education (ages six to twelve or so), young Hebrew boys would be taught by rabbis in the synagogues in what was referred to as *beit sefer* (House of Books). The primary textbook was the Torah (the Word of God). How I wish the Bible was still our primary textbook.

The students who excelled would learn and even memorize the books of Moses (referred to as the Pentateuch in Greek and Latin), earning an invitation to the next level of education. Those who didn't make the cut would nicely be told that it was time for them to go help their dad in the family trade. They were not the best of the best.

In the second level of education which was *beit midrash* (House of Learning), students would learn and even memorize the entire Old Testament (Hebrew: *tanak*), from Genesis to Malachi. Of course, only a few exceptional students were able to complete this level and graduate to the next level. Those who did not make the cut were kindly asked to go help their dad in the family trade. Again, they were not the best of the best.

Those who excelled would advance to the highest level of learning called *beit talmud* (House of Oral Law), which focused on joining the rabbi as he traveled from synagogue to synagogue and village to village to teach and minister to people. They would qualify for this highest level of learning only after a rabbi would drill each with a series of tests and approve his promotion.

If a student was indeed approved, the rabbi would often say, "Come, follow me." It was at this point that the student became a disciple of the rabbi. A true disciple just doesn't want to know what a rabbi knows, he wants to be like the rabbi and wants to do what the rabbi does.

Imagine this pack of young men following their rabbi

on a hot, dusty, dirty road. In fact, the highest compliment attributed to these young men stated, "May you be covered in the dust of the rabbi." Only the best of the best were told that. This group of disciples were called *talmidim*, which in Hebrew means disciples/students.

Now, think about what happened in Matthew 4. Peter and Andrew were in the family fishing business. James and John were net menders with their dad, Zebedee. They were never told that they were the best of the best. But then, Rabbi Yeshua (Jesus) told them, "Come, follow me." For the first time in their lives, a spiritual leader spoke words of life to them.

We are often told, and rightly so, that we must have faith in God. But today, I also remind you that God has faith in you! With God's Spirit in you, you are the best of the best! You have been invited to be a disciple of Rabbi Jesus.

> **GODFIDENCE LESSON**
> You are often told that you must have faith in God. And this is correct. But today, I also remind you that God has faith in you!

Talmidim were not just any disciples, their commitment went deeper. Historian Ray Vander Lann said, "in the days of Jesus, there were two types of followers: students and disciples. A student wanted to know what a rabbi knew; but a disciple wanted to be who their rabbi was."[18]

THE JESUS WAY

In my years of ministry, I have read and heard many individuals share their perspective of discipleship. Many of them have terrific ideas. For example, I've heard a few people formalize it: "We will be having discipleship in Room 101 every Tuesday at 7 p.m." Classroom instruction is a great idea, but that is not all there is to discipleship.

Let's take a closer look at how Jesus did discipleship. He not only told us to go and make disciples, but He gave us a great model to do it. One reason why we often don't understand His model for discipleship is because we don't fully connect with the Hebrew culture. The primary characteristic of Hebrew discipleship is that most of it happened outside the classroom setting. If you were to read through the four gospels and take note of each scenario that Jesus was with His disciples, you will find that at least 70% of the time, discipleship was done outside the realm of classroom instruction.

> **GODFIDENCE LESSON**
> Spiritual growth and maturity doesn't happen overnight. Staying the course takes Godfidence.

A few years ago, a sixty-three-year-old man passed away with a very unique claim to fame: he never worked a day in his entire life. When he was a young boy, his rich uncle passed away and left him a very large inheritance that would result in a very hefty monthly sum of money as long as he stayed in school. So, he stayed in school all of his life. He ended up with multiple degrees to decorate his walls but never really made any significant impact during the years of his life. Why? Because, although he had obtained much knowledge, he never applied what he learned.

Many Christians fall into that same trap. They hear hundreds of sermons and sit in on hundreds of Bible classes and obtain lots of knowledge, but they don't make the effort to put what they learn into action. In the New Testament, the word "Christian" occurs three times, whereas the word "disciple" occurs over 260 times. Jesus placed his focus on discipleship.

Most of us would think if Jesus were choosing twelve men to be on His leadership team, He would have chosen the most intelligent, the most spiritual, the most talented, the wealthiest, or those with the highest positions in the community, but He didn't do it in this way. God's ways are not our ways. He chose twelve ordinary men who were previously overlooked and perhaps even rejected. These men ended up turning the world upside down...or rather, right side up.

Have you ever been rejected? It's not a good feeling. Sometimes, people can be cruel, and life can be difficult, but God never rejects you and never will. He created you in a unique and wonderful way. He chose you.

> **GODFIDENCE LESSON**
> You are chosen. You are invited to join Jesus in the journey of a lifetime. Welcome!

THE DISCIPLESHIP JOURNEY

Marie had just graduated from college and was getting settled in her new job as an elementary school teacher. With her education behind her and a new season ahead of her, she began to ponder about life. She met up with her friend, Rhonda, who she looked up to as someone who has her life together. Marie told Rhonda that she was tired of the partying and broken relationships of life and was ready to make changes. Rhonda told her that the difference in her life was her personal relationship with Christ Jesus.

At first, Marie was resistant to Rhonda's message because she had a negative experience at church when she was thirteen years old. A judgmental lady in the church condemned her for listening to non-Christian music. From that time, Marie didn't want to have anything to do with the church or even with God. But now, Rhonda explains to her that real Christianity is not like that. After thirty minutes of talking together, Marie made a decision to place her faith in Christ! She was now born again! Her discipleship journey was just beginning.

Three weeks later, Marie acted out her new faith in water baptism and testified what God had done in her life. Rhonda made a commitment to spend every Monday evening for two years to disciple Marie. Yes, Marie needed it, because she was dealing with temptations to fall back into her old way of living. With Rhonda's help, Marie got spiritually stronger and stronger every day.

> **GODFIDENCE LESSON**
> A true disciple of Christ has the Godfidence to take the steps necessary toward spiritual maturity.

Marie joined a church and got involved in a weekly small group. Is her life perfect? No, it is not. She still deals with different struggles and challenging situations here and there. But with her growing faith in God, she is learning how to overcome the trials of life. One example of her growing maturity is when she made a difficult decision to break up with her non-Christian boyfriend. The good news is that, a few months later, a godly young man began to pursue her, and they ended up getting married.

Today, Marie and her husband serve the Lord together and lead a small group of young married couples. Because Rhonda invested two years to disciple Marie, now Marie has made the choice to disciple other young ladies. This is discipleship. Real discipleship.

THE BIG THREE

As we learn how Jesus did discipleship, we see in the book of John, that Jesus describes real discipleship in three ways. His perspective of real discipleship is (1) doing what Jesus taught, (2) loving others, and (3) bearing spiritual fruit. Let's take a look at what Jesus said.

(1) Doing what Jesus taught

"Jesus said, 'If you hold to my teaching, you are really my disciples.'" (John 8:31). Jesus taught an obedience-based form of discipleship. He said that true discipleship consists of doing what Jesus teaches. Perhaps that is why 42% of those claiming to be Christian are not committed. They have a wrong concept of discipleship and commitment. Doing what Jesus taught is far different than just listening to what He has said.

(2) Loving others

"'A new command I give you: Love one another. As I have loved you, so you must love one another. By this everyone will know that you are my disciples, if you love one another'" (John 13:34–35).

In Luke 10:25–37, we read the story of a man who was robbed and beaten and left on the side of the road. A priest went by and didn't even stop. A Levite was walking by and didn't even stop. But a man who was not even accepted by these religious men, a good Samaritan, was walking by. He stopped, bandaged up the man, and took him to an inn. This is a great example of love and compassion. Not all religious people have it. In John 13:34–35, Jesus says that loving others is a trait of true disciples.

(3) Bearing spiritual fruit

"'This is to my Father's glory, that you bear much fruit, showing yourselves to be my disciples'" (John 15:8). Bearing spiritual fruit is the third characteristic of true discipleship that Jesus used in the book of John. There are various ways to produce spiritual fruit. Many people have their opinions about what exactly spiritual fruit is. Some say it is (1) evangelism – bringing people to Christ, (2) discipleship – both being discipled and discipling others, (3) tithing/giving – trusting God with your finances, (4) serving – being active in doing the work of the ministry, (5) daily time with God – praying and reading the Bible, (6) Christian character – living our life with Biblical principles, and (7) connection – showing up to church and living life with the Body of Christ.

In my opinion, it is a balance of each of those items. They are all important. They all show some sort of spiritual maturity. Paul says that the fruit of the Spirit is love, joy, peace, patience, kindness, goodness, faithfulness, gentleness, and self-control. Our attitude should not be, "Well, I'm good at seven of these nine fruits of the Spirit. I must be doing pretty good." No. That's not the way it works. Scripture says that the fruit of the Spirit "is." It is all or nothing. If the Holy Spirit is in you, your life will show all nine aspects of the Fruit of the Spirit. This is real discipleship.

"The fruit revealed is the heart concealed."
– Matt Garcia

I love the following story Frances Chan shares as it refers to bearing fruit.

> Perhaps you, as a parent, tell your daughter, "Go clean your room." How happy would you be if an hour later, your daughter comes to you and says, "Dad, you said, 'Go clean your room.' Well, during the last hour, I took time to study those words and I have even memorized these words of yours, 'Go clean your room.'"
>
> She continues to say, "I can even say this statement in Greek. In fact, tomorrow, my friends are coming over and we are going to do a study of what it would be like to clean my room." I don't think dad would be happy with this response. And neither will our Heavenly Father. If there is no spiritual fruit in your life, then true discipleship is not happening.[19]

"Some who profess faith in Christ have the erroneous belief that just because they went through a Christian ritual at some point that they are 'set for life.' Others think showing up at a church service once in a while is all they need." – Mike Jordahl

BEING MORE LIKE CHRIST

As a grandfather, I've received a few videos of my grandchildren taking their first steps. This is an exciting time. But when I see that video, I know there were some challenges along the way. First the child began to crawl.

Then, pull herself up. Next, stand unsupported. Then, a step or two and a fall. The child will probably cry along the way. Then, some encouragement from dad and mom, "C'mon, baby, you can do it!" Then, more falling to the ground. Getting a bump on the head from the coffee table. More getting up. More encouragement. Then, finally, the video showing their first ten steps. Yes! She is walking!

This is a spiritual picture of discipleship. After you've been born again, you needed someone to show you how to walk the walk. Even though there were times you fell. Times you got frustrated. Crawling. Standing. Falling. Tears. Bumps. Encouragement. And finally, you begin to walk. It takes work.

Becoming more like Christ doesn't happen overnight, and it never ends. Salvation deals with birth. Discipleship deals with growth. Salvation is free to you and I. Discipleship is costly. Salvation is instantaneous. Discipleship is an on-going process. Salvation is the impartation of life. Discipleship is the development of that life. Salvation is the beginning of the journey. Discipleship is the journey itself.

Andrew and Peter left their fishing business to take the journey. James and John left their net-mending business to take their journey. Matthew left his tax collecting position to begin his journey. They believed. They entrusted their lives to Yeshua (Jesus). And their lives would never be the same again. It was the best decision they could ever make.

> **GODFIDENCE LESSON**
> Real discipleship is not an easy journey, but it is the best decision you could ever make.

The word "disciple" means "follower, student or apprentice." But discipleship is sometimes hard to define. Here are a few phrases that are used to describe discipleship:

- Becoming more Christ-like

- Learning to trust God more
- Spiritual transformation
- Spiritual formation
- Spiritual growth and maturity

Each of these phrases are very good at identifying what discipleship is. My personal expanded definition of discipleship is this...

> Discipleship is the process of spiritual development that occurs in a community of loving accountability as the believer progressively rises to spiritual maturity and then brings others along the same journey.

On Rising Higher Radio, I had the privilege of an interview with Chip Ingram, and I asked him the question, "What is discipleship to you?"

Chip responded, "Discipleship is following Jesus – it's about listening, learning, and following Him so that I become like Him more every day. Now, I communicate His words, and I give a hug in the name of Christ, and I give my time and my money to love people the way He did. What matters most is our relationship. He wants me to experience His love, and He wants me to love Him and love others."

When Pablo Casals reached ninety-five years of age, a young reporter threw him a question, "Mr. Casals, you are ninety-five years old and the greatest cellist that ever lived. Why do you still practice six hours a day?"

Mr. Casals answered, "Because I am making progress." This is the mentality of a true disciple. We will always be a work in progress.

> **GODFIDENCE LESSON**
> Don't be afraid of taking steps toward spiritual growth. Be afraid of what might happen if you stay standing still.

THE RIGHT QUESTIONS

My friend, Mike Bingaman, is a minister as well as

licensed counselor. I once asked him, “What is the key to good counseling?” He answered me by saying, “The secret to better counseling is better questions.” Mike helped me understand this principle by explaining to me that when we tell someone to do something, it is our statement to them. But if we ask the right question, they own the answer, because it becomes their statement. This is how Jesus did discipleship.

- To help His followers be cautious about judging others, Jesus asked, “Why do you look at the speck of sawdust in your brother’s eye and pay no attention to the plank in your own eye?” (Matthew 7:3).
- To challenge the disciples to increase their faith, Jesus asked them, “You of little faith, why are you so afraid?” (Matthew 8:26).
- To the blind men who needed to be healed, Jesus asked, “Do you believe that I am able to do this?” (Matthew 9:28).
- To help the disciples come to grips with who Jesus was, He asked the question, “Who do you say I am?” (Matthew 16:15).
- To help the disciples understand the importance of obedience, Jesus asked them the question, “Why do you call me, ‘Lord, Lord,’ and do not do what I say?” (Luke 6:46).
- To challenge Simon Peter to love people, Jesus asked him, “Simon son of John, do you love me?” (John 21:17).

The list of questions Jesus asked goes on and on.

70/20/10 PRINCIPLE

Earlier in this chapter, I mentioned that about 70% of how Jesus did discipleship was outside of the classroom. When I understood this, I had to adjust my approach to discipleship. In his book *The Adult’s Learning Projects*, Dr. Allen Tough introduces the 70/20/10 Principle, which states that 70 percent of our learning comes by doing. This is informal, on-the-job development that comes through trial and error and growing in experience. Secondly, 20 percent of our learning is through receiving informal feedback from others, or through more formal coaching and mentoring relationships. This is primarily development through interacting with others. Last of all, 10 percent of our learning is through conferences, seminars, and courses. This is structured formal education. If the 70/20/10 principle holds true, then many of us need to make a shift in the way we do discipleship.

For more than ten years, I have had the privilege of teaching at Christ Mission College. One of the things I like about CMC is the way Dr. Monte Madsen and his staff disciple the students. While many colleges and universities focus primarily on classroom instruction, CMC requires the students to (1) attend chapel every weekday, (2) do two missions trips a year, (3) serve in a local church twice a week, (4) attend morning prayer, (5) stack chairs, (6) serve campus duty periodically, (7) do outreach projects, and much more. So much happens outside the classroom. This is discipleship.

GODLY HABITS

I am blessed to be in a covenant relationship with my wife, Brenda. We know each other so well that we often laugh at how much we can read each other's minds and hearts. For much of my life, my primary love language was words of affirmation, but since I married Brenda, my primary love language has been quality time. I love spending time with her, even if it is simply sitting on the couch and shooting the breeze. My love for her has changed many things in my life – for the better. Brenda and I would not have a deep relationship with each other if we only talked to each other once a week, but that's the way many believers treat their relationship with the Lord.

In 2006, I read a statistic from the Billy Graham Evangelistic Association that said only 50% of Americans who refer to themselves as Christians have consistent daily time with God (daily devotions). Sad statistic. This goes against the premise that Christianity is about a personal relationship with Jesus Christ. For many Christians, quality time is just not a priority. So, I decided to be intentional about helping Christ followers go deeper with God. Experts say that when someone does something every day, consistently for at least twenty-one days (some say thirty days), then it becomes a habit. Each of us have certain good habits and certain bad habits. Life would be so much better if we could get rid of the bad habits and focus on the good ones.

I thought, "It would be terrific if I can help others develop the godly habit of spending daily time with God." So, I wrote a thirty-day devotional, called Kingdom Keys and put it in the hands of the people in my church. Did everyone participate? No. But a good percentage did. And after the thirty days, most of us continued to spend daily time with God.

> "Discipline is consciously uncomfortable for a time, but habits are unconsciously maintained for life."
> – Randall Sean Garcia

One of the keys to effective *discipleship* is developing spiritual *disciplines*. In fact, the word discipleship and the word discipline come from the same root word. Discipleship takes discipline. Spiritual disciplines are "instructions and practices designed to develop spiritual conduct or spiritual growth." Or, in my simple concise terms, I refer to spiritual disciplines as "godly habits."

Examples of spiritual disciplines are prayer, fasting, Bible study, journaling, personal worship, service, solitude, submission, and meditation. Although the list is greater than this, these are a good start.

> "Discipleship is not a vocation prescribed only for minsters and other full-time staff members in the church. Discipleship is the full-time spiritual vocation of all God's people...the calling to be a disciple all the time in every place of life."
> – Robert Webber

If working out is important to you, you find time to work out. If going to the movies is important to you, then you will make time to go to the movies. If spending time on Facebook is important to you, then you will find time to spend on Facebook. You get the picture. You make time for what is important to you.

If daily devotions are important to you, then you will find time to have your daily devos. If small group Bible studies are important to you, then you will find time for small group Bible studies. What you do builds your daily and weekly habits.

TIME TO PUMP SOME IRON

Continue to work out your salvation with fear and trembling.

Philippians 2:12

Many people struggle with what this passage means. Does it mean that we must work for our salvation? No. Salvation is not something we earn. So, what does this Scripture really mean?

Each one of us have been blessed with a physical body, and it is up to us to take care of it. Some people work out and exercise. Others do not. Those who do work out strengthen their bodies and become healthier. They increase their chances of living longer.

In a similar fashion, when you come to faith in God, you are given a new spiritual being, and you choose whether or not you will "work out" your spiritual life. If you choose to "work out" on a regular basis, your spiritual muscles will grow, and you will become stronger. Hence, the advice from Paul is this: You've been blessed with this gift of salvation. Now, work out.

In essence, "work out" is another term for discipleship. It takes work. It is costly. Let's get it done! This is real discipleship.

WORDS OF LIFE

The decision has been made, and I've stepped over the line. I won't look back, let up, slow down, or back away. My past is redeemed, my present makes sense, and my future is secure. I am chosen. I am called. I believe that Jesus has faith in me.

I am a disciple of Christ Jesus!

GODFIDENCE CHECKUP

1) List some specific examples of how you have spiritually matured over the years.

____

____

____

____

____

____

2) In response to Jesus' discussion on spiritual fruit as a disciple, list the top five ways you show spiritual fruit today.

____

____

____

____

____

____

3) List the spiritual disciplines you believe are your strengths as well as your weaknesses.

Spiritual Disciplines – Strengths

____

____

Spiritual Disciplines – Weaknesses

PRAYER FOCUS

Lord God Almighty, I come to You in the name of Jesus. I thank You for choosing me and believing in me. Thank You for having confidence in me. Now, I place my Godfidence in You! I pray that You would, by the power of the Holy Spirit, help me grow to be a healthy disciple and a healthy disciple-maker. It is my desire to bear much spiritual fruit. It is my desire to be more like You. I consider it a privilege to be called a disciple of Jesus Christ. Today, I speak life into my discipleship role as I take the initiative to pour myself into others. Amen. So be it.

CH. 10 REAL WISDOM

Get wisdom; get insight;
do not forget, and do not turn away
from the words of my mouth.
Do not forsake her, and she will keep you;
love her, and she will guard you.
The beginning of wisdom is this: Get wisdom,
and whatever you get, get insight.
Prize her highly, and she will exalt you;
she will honor you if you embrace her.
She will place on your head a graceful garland;
she will bestow on you a beautiful crown.
Proverbs 4:5–9 ESV

A question was asked to a group of children, “What advice can you give adults?” Here is a sample of their responses...

- “When your dad asks you, ‘Do I look stupid?’ Don’t answer him.” – Michael, age 9
- “Never trust a dog to watch your food.” – Patrick, age 10
- “Never pick on your sister when she’s holding a baseball bat.” – Joel, age 10
- “When your mom is mad at your dad, don’t let her brush your hair.” – Taylia, age 11
- “You can’t hide a piece of broccoli in your milk.” – Mitchell, age 8
- “Puppies still have bad breath, even after you give him a breath mint.” – Andrew, age 9
- “Never tell your mom that her diet is not working.” – Tiffany, age 8

Looking back on my younger years, I did some crazy and even stupid things. Why did I do that? Why did I make that dumb decision? Life would be different if we had do-overs. But we don’t. We have to live with the decisions we make and the actions we have done. But as we mature, we also get smarter and wiser...at least, we should.

Life experiences teach us things. Do you believe you make better decisions today than you did ten years ago? Then, do you believe you will make better decisions in the next ten years? Hopefully so. As much as I would like to say that the older we get, the wiser we get, it's not always true.

> **GODFIDENCE LESSON**
> If you want to know God's will, get to know God.

Life is filled with decisions. Some of those decisions are menial, and others are quite important. When you are in school, you have decisions like... "Do I attend college?" If so, "What college do I attend?" And, if you go to college, "What is my major?" "What electives should I take?" And then, after a year, you change your mind about your major and ask, "Now what should I major in?"

Decisions. What kind of car should I buy? Do I go to graduate school? What career path should I pursue? Lord, I need wisdom. Where should I work? What city should I live in? Do I rent an apartment or buy a house? Lord, I need wisdom.

Who should I date? Who should I marry? When you are married, you ask, should we have kids? If so, how many kids. Then, when your kids are in junior high, you ask, Should I trade my kids for someone else's kids? Many ladies decide whether to work or be a stay-at-home mom.

Then, there are spiritual decisions. Am I ready to be a follower of Jesus Christ? Should I be baptized? Should I go deeper with God? Should I have daily devotions with God? Do I attend church? Do I become a member of a church? Do I serve in the church? Do I give? Do I tithe? Do I join a connect group? Lord, I need wisdom.

I find it intriguing that the words "philosophy" and "wisdom" are connected. The word philosophy is a combination of the word *philo* (Greek: love), and *sophia* (Greek: wisdom). Love of wisdom. Your philosophy of life is tied into your love for wisdom.

ANOINTED COMMON SENSE

Wisdom is one of the most important ingredients of your spiritual life. As Christ followers, are we automatically zapped with a dose of godly wisdom? No. Not necessarily. In James 1:5, Scripture teaches us to ask for wisdom. So, what is wisdom and why is it so important?

> **WISDOM (N.):**
> having the power of discerning and judging properly as to what is true or right; possessing discernment; judgment, or discretion.[20]

The Bible is filled with lessons on the topic of wisdom. A great place to go for godly wisdom is the book of Proverbs, which has thirty-one power-packed chapters of practical wisdom. Perhaps one chapter for each of the thirty-one days of the month. Just sayin'. Every time I read a chapter in Proverbs, God equips me with Godfidence to make godly choices and live to my potential.

> **WISDOM (N.):**
> anointed common sense
> (Randy's definition)

CAN WE GET PRACTICAL?

- Randy makes a trip to the grocery store while he is very hungry. Wise choice or unwise choice?
- Peggy gives her three-year-old son a highly caffeinated soft drink thirty minutes before his bedtime. Wise choice or unwise choice?
- Lawrence is twenty-nine years old and has some major

decisions coming up. A career decision, a relationship decision, and a possible relocation decision. He wants to make wise decisions. So, he gets online to check his horoscope. Is he turning to worldly wisdom or godly wisdom?

- Tammy is twenty-seven years old and having some financial struggles. Her boyfriend suggests that she moves in with him – to save money. Tammy struggles with a decision to please her boyfriend or please God. She seeks godly counsel and makes a decision NOT to move in with her boyfriend. Is she using worldly wisdom or godly wisdom?
- Frank has been praying for a promotion at work. The promotion would come with a very slight raise in salary and a nice title. But it also would come with extra work hours that would keep him away from his wife and kids and away from church on Sundays. He is offered the position and accepts. Has he made a decision based on worldly wisdom or godly wisdom?
- Gayle has been Fran's best friend since junior high. For over twenty years, they've stayed close – spending much time together. But lately, Gayle has turned against Fran. She has been speaking about her behind her back. She's been sharing certain things with others that Fran shared with her in confidence. And now, she's been verbally abusive to Fran.
- Fran is hurt. Very hurt. She wants to respond with a spirit of revenge, but as she prays and asks God how to respond, the Word of God impresses on her heart to forgive and respond with love. That's exactly what she does. Is she responding with worldly wisdom or godly wisdom?
- Mike, a famous athlete, earned over $400 million as a professional boxer but still had to file bankruptcy for being $27 million in debt. He once spent $179,000 on a gold chain for himself and $410,000 on a birthday party. Owing the IRS over $13 million, he said as he filed for

bankruptcy, “I’ve been under financial distress.” Did Mike use worldly wisdom or godly wisdom?

GODFIDENCE LESSON

Living with Godfidence will lead you to make decisions in life that you won’t regret.

WISDOM, KNOWLEDGE, AND UNDERSTANDING

The fear of the LORD is the beginning of wisdom and knowledge of the Holy One is understanding.
Proverbs 9:10

I love the way this proverb ties together knowledge, understanding, and wisdom. What is the correlation between these three attributes? Let’s start with knowledge. Knowledge is good. Knowledge is education. We need it. But what good is education if you don’t have common sense? Have you ever met someone who had lots of knowledge but very little wisdom? I admired a friend of mine because he had four degrees, but I noticed that he would often make some dumb choices in life. I noticed that he had lots of knowledge, but very little wisdom. Once again, the Word says that *wisdom* is supreme!

Knowledge is the acquiring of facts, *understanding* is the ability to make sense of the facts, and *wisdom* is the action that results from or the trait that enables one to respond with knowledge and understanding.

One man told me, “Pray for me, I am under attack.” After finding out some details of what he was dealing with, I was taken aback. He hadn’t paid his income taxes for three years, and the IRS was after him. He was not under attack; he was facing the consequences of his lack of wisdom.

A young lady was dating a non-Christian guy. She knew that it was an unwise choice, but she did it anyway. They ended up getting married. The guy, now her husband, didn’t want to be the spiritual leader of the home. He didn't want to serve God and held her back from reaching her spiritual potential.

A couple of years later, she said, "My marriage is under attack." Now, was her marriage under attack, or was she dealing with the consequences of unwise decisions? Sometimes, it's easy to blame the devil when the problem stems from unwise decisions.

> "Knowledge is the acquiring of facts; understanding is the interpretation of facts; wisdom is the application." – Edwin Louis Cole

I get *knowledge* when I read in the Word of God that Jesus is the Way, the Truth, and the Life and no one goes to the Father except through Him. I get *understanding* when I comprehend and develop my personal relationship with the Lord. I get *wisdom* when I actually make a decision to place my faith in God and live for Him.

Knowledge happens when I read in the Bible that God will work everything out for the best. *Understanding* happens when I am able to see God working in my life. *Wisdom* happens when I stop worrying about my problem and actually put my faith in Him.

> "Knowledge shows up on tests. Wisdom shows up in relationships."
> – Rick Warren

Knowledge happens when I read in God's Word that I am called to love God and love people. *Understanding* happens when I understand how God created people differently than I am created and learn how to love them even through differences. *Wisdom* happens when I love them.

Knowledge. Understanding. Wisdom. Let's apply all three to specific scenarios of life:

Scenario 1: A co-worker talks to your boss about you, and it is not nice. Knowledge tells you that the right thing to do is forgive. Understanding tells you that your co-worker is dealing with some personal issues and is taking it out on you. Wisdom tells you to take the initiative to pray for your co-worker and speak with her – with love – to solve the issue.

Scenario 2: A Facebook friend posts his strong opinion about same-sex marriage, and it is not in alignment with the Word of God. Knowledge tells you that his worldview is based on the liberalism of our world. Understanding tells you that you are not going to change his mind. Wisdom tells you to leave it alone and pray for him.

Scenario 3: You desire to get closer to God. Knowledge tells you that studying the Bible is the key factor. Understanding reveals the different Bible study options. Wisdom gives you the Godfidence to schedule daily time with God and join a small group.

> "The purpose for learning the things of God is the acquisition of wisdom, and we cannot have wisdom without knowledge. Ignorance breeds foolishness, but true knowledge – the knowledge of God – leads to the wisdom that is more precious than rubies and pearls." – R.C. Sproul

PRACTICE MAKES PERFECT

"Therefore everyone who hears these words of mine and puts them into practice is like a wise man who built his house on the rock. The rain came down, the streams rose, and the winds blew and beat against that house; yet it did not fall, because it had its foundation on the rock. But everyone who hears these words of mine and does not put them into practice is like a foolish man who built his house on sand. The rain came down, the streams rose, and the winds blew and beat against that house, and it fell with a great crash."

Matthew 7:24–27

How did Jesus teach wisdom? Here in what we call the Sermon on the Mount, He draws a clear distinction between a wise man and a foolish man. The difference is fairly straightforward. A wise man puts the words of Jesus into practice. A foolish man does not. Pretty simple. A wise man has Godfidence in the words of Jesus, whereas a foolish man does not.

Perhaps someone says, "I need prayer. I need $10,000 to get me out of debt and become financially healthy." You pray for him, and he makes a commitment to learn Biblical financial principles at Financial Peace University. For the next twelve months, he has a gazelle-like approach to applying the truth (wisdom) and gets out of debt. He went from knowledge to understanding to wisdom to victory to blessings. In the middle of all of this is wisdom...anointed common sense. "If any of you lacks wisdom, he should ask God, who gives generously to all without finding fault, and it will be given to him," (James 1:5).

> **GODFIDENCE LESSON**
> Having Godfidence takes you from knowledge to understanding to wisdom to victory to blessings.

GODLY WISDOM VERSUS EARTHLY WISDOM

Blessed are those who find wisdom,
those who gain understanding,
for she is more profitable than silver
and yields better returns than gold.
She is more precious than rubies;
nothing you desire can compare with her.
Long life is in her right hand;
in her left hand are riches and honor.
Her ways are pleasant ways,
and all her paths are peace.
She is a tree of life to those who take hold of her;

those who hold her fast will be blessed.
Proverbs 3:13–18

What are the benefits of godly wisdom? I underlined five of them in the Scripture above. Long life. Riches. Honor. Pleasant ways. Peace. Some people do not use wisdom in how they conduct their lives.

James 3:13–15 gives a contrast between these two types of wisdom. "Who is wise and understanding among you? Let them show it by their good life, by deeds done in the humility that comes from wisdom. But if you harbor bitter envy and selfish ambition in your hearts, do not boast about it or deny the truth. Such 'wisdom' does not come down from heaven but is earthly, unspiritual, demonic."

The three characteristics of man's (worldly) wisdom are (1) earthly, (2) unspiritual, and (3) demonic. Maury was a single guy living at home with his father and working in the family business. When he found out he was going to inherit a fortune when his sickly father died, he decided he needed a wife with whom to share his fortune. One evening at an investment meeting, he spotted the most beautiful woman he had ever seen. Her natural beauty took his breath away. "I may look like just an ordinary man," he said to her, "but in just a few years, my father will die, and I'll inherit $200 million." Impressed, the woman obtained his business card and, two weeks later, she became his stepmother.

Earthly wisdom. Unspiritual. Of the devil.

But godly wisdom is quite different. James 3:17–18 speaks of godly wisdom. "But the wisdom that comes from heaven is first of all pure; then peace-loving, considerate, submissive, full of mercy and good fruit, impartial and sincere. Peacemakers who sow in peace raise a harvest of righteousness."

This list that describes godly wisdom is so much better. (1) Pure, (2) peace-loving, (3) considerate, (4) submissive, (5) full of mercy, (6) full of good fruit, (7) impartial, and (8) sincere.

My expanded definition of "godly" wisdom: seeing and responding to life from God's perspective; an attitude and an action; a skill that you can develop.

Here are a few examples of how the world's wisdom differs from godly wisdom:

Wordly Wisdom	Godly Wisdom
Be first	The first shall be last
Get all you can	Give all you can
Look out for #1	Others are a priority
Fight for your rights	Blessed are the peacemakers
Strive to be great	Strive to be a servant
Speak your mind	Speak your heart
Get revenge	Offer forgiveness
Image is everything	Reflect the image of God
Party like there's no tomorrow	Live like Jesus is coming back tomorrow

"Life is not a straight path from birth to death. There are twists and turns, detours and mazes, mountains and valleys. But, as believers, we have the blessing of divine help in making the right choices in life." – Ray Ortlund

SIX KEYS TO GODLY WISDOM

If any of you lacks wisdom, you should ask God,
who gives generously to all without finding fault,
and it will be given to you.
James 1:5

Brenda and I were watching *America's Funniest Home*

Videos with our grandkids when she made the comment, "Why did he do that?" (speaking of the skateboarder who jumped on the handrail of some stairs).

Yes, we often wonder why so many people make dumb mistakes in life, even when it's not to be on *America's Funniest Home Videos*. I've come to the conclusion that there are two kinds of people in this world: those who do what they want to do ("you do you"), and those who do what God wants them to do. They humble themselves and ask God for wisdom. That's what James 1:5 says to do.

Over the years of my life, I've learned lots of lessons. Many of those lessons were based on my mistakes in life. So, I've learned to do what James 1:5 says, I ask God for wisdom. Someone asked me, "What are the top lessons you have learned in life?" I thought this was an excellent question, so I wrote down my top six lessons using the acrostic WISDOM.

W – Welcome the Holy Spirit in every area of your life.

When Jesus is truly Lord of your life, you will be Spirit-led in everything you do. Your thoughts. Your actions. Your decisions. Your relationships. Your faith. Your finances. Your ministry. Your marriage. Your parenting. Your social life. When the Spirit is there, everything changes!

How does this happen? With the Holy Spirit by your side, you will always have a distinct advantage over the enemy. When you are intentional about your relationship with God, the Holy Spirit steps in to lead and guide everything you do. "For all who are led by the Spirit of God are sons of God" (Romans 8:14).

> **GODFIDENCE LESSON**
> Wisdom tells you to have Godfidence in the Holy Spirit.

I – Intercede in prayer for others.

Prayer is our personal connection with God. Many

individuals have the mentality that prayer is their opportunity to tell God what they want. Wrong perspective. Although it is fine to present your personal needs to God, prayer is designed to draw us closer to God and to pray for others. Intercession (praying for others) must be a priority in our prayer life. Why? Because it keeps us from selfishness, and it activates the power of agreement. "Again, truly I tell you that if two of you on earth agree about anything they ask for, it will be done for them by my Father in heaven" (Matthew 18:19).

S – Speak words of life.

"The tongue has the power of life and death" (Proverbs 18:21). Has someone ever told you something that made your day? Perhaps you were feeling down, and their words were exactly what you needed to hear. Words of life can be like a light switch that turns on the power and presence of God in a person's life, even yours. That is why I have placed a "Words of Life" declaration at the end of every chapter of this book. Plus, your words of life to your children, your spouse, your friends and others can be the encouragement they need to hear to make it through. Speak those words.

D – Discover your spiritual gifts and strengths.

Once you find out how God has wired you in a unique way, not only will you avoid burnout and discouragement, but you will set yourself up for reaching your potential. Self-assessments help you understand your strengths, your spiritual gifts, your personality, and much more. Do you know your love language? Your Enneagram number? Your top five strengths (StrengthsFinder)? Your DISC results? Your EQ? Your primary spiritual gifts?

Knowing how God has uniquely wired you will help you focus on reaching your potential rather than spinning your wheels with your weaknesses. "Each of you should use whatever gift you have received to serve others, as faithful stewards of God's grace in its various forms" (1 Peter 4:10).

O – Own up to a great attitude.

Your attitude in life makes a huge difference. Here are some examples of a great attitude:

Identify problems as opportunities.

See the best in other people.

Have a "can't be offended" attitude.

Love God and love people.

Forgive.

Extend grace to people when they make mistakes.

Don't judge.

Don't retaliate.

Remember this: Life is 10% what happens to you and 90% how you respond. Yep. It's about your attitude. "Now your attitudes and thoughts must all be constantly changing for the better" (Ephesians 4:23 TLB).

M – Make spiritual growth your priority.

Are you satisfied with where your spiritual life is today? I hope your answer is "no." Those who are satisfied with their spiritual life have fallen into a comfort zone of complacency. In my book To Another Level, I ask the question, "On a scale of 1 to 10, where do you rate your spiritual life? One meaning a new believer, and ten meaning perfection." Wherever you rate yourself on this numerical scale, there is room to grow.

What is your current plan for spiritual growth? Godly wisdom tells you to make spiritual growth a priority. Godfidence gives you the ability to carry out your plan, "until we all reach unity in the faith and in the knowledge of the Son of God and become mature, attaining to the whole measure of the fullness of Christ" (Ephesians 4:13).

One man spent more than twelve years of his life putting in lots of time and effort climbing the corporate ladder in his profession. When he finally got the title he was striving for, he said, "For years and years, I've done all I could to climb the ladder of success. Now that I have reached the top, I realize that my ladder was leaning against the wrong building."

GODFIDENCE LESSON

> Wisdom doesn't come from talking.
> It comes from listening...to God.

In a certain small town, there was a man who was known as the wisest man around. A young man came up with a plan to outsmart this wise man. He captured a bird and held it in his hands. He approached the wise man while holding the bird in his hand. He covered up the small bird with his hands and said, "Mr. Wise Man. Can you tell me whether the bird I hold in my hand is dead or alive?"

The young man's plan was this: If the wise man said the bird was dead, he would open his hands and let the bird fly away, proving the wise man wrong. If the wise man said the bird is alive, the young man would crush the bird, killing it. He would open his hands and show the wise man a dead bird; proving the wise man wrong.

So, the young man asked the wise man, "Is the bird dead or alive?" The wise man responded by saying, "Son, you are the one who controls whether the bird is dead or alive. The choice is in your hands." In what direction is your life going? You make the choice. Make it with real wisdom. Godly wisdom.

WORDS OF LIFE

I have anointed common sense. As I choose to make wise choices, I receive the promises of long life, riches, honor, pleasant ways, and peace. I refuse to fall into the trap of earthly wisdom. With Godfidence, I will make great choices with godly wisdom.

GODFIDENCE CHECKUP

1) Think of an instance in your life when you made a poor decision. Why did you make that choice? What have you learned from that choice?

____

____

____

____

____

____

2) What are some ways you can activate godly wisdom in your life? For example, prayer, reading the word, getting advice from a godly mentor, staying away from the wrong crowd, etc.

____

____

____

____

____

____

3) In this chapter, we reviewed the eight characteristics of godly wisdom based on James 3:16–17. Identify three of these characteristics you need to improve on.

____

____

____

____

____

____

PRAYER FOCUS

Lord God Almighty, I come to You in the name of Jesus. Your word says in James 1:5 that if I need wisdom, I should ask of You. I need wisdom in my career, my finances, my health, my relationships, my ministry, and my spiritual life. I ask you for knowledge, understanding, and wisdom. I pray that you would give me the ears to hear, the mind to discern, and the will to become. I pray that with every challenge I face, I will learn from it and grow in wisdom. Amen. So be it.

CH. 11 REAL SPIRIT

While they were praying, the place where they were meeting trembled and shook. They were all filled with the Holy Spirit and continued to speak God's Word with fearless confidence.
Acts 4:31 MSG

The students in the first period chemistry class filed in for the final exam. The teacher had previously told them that they could bring with them and use for the exam a sheet of 8.5 x 11 paper with as much information as would fit. Some students came with sheets that had very small writing on them. Other students had diagrams and formulas, and still others had outlines that had labels for everything.

One student walked in with a blank sheet of paper. That was strange. As they got ready for the exam, this student placed the sheet of paper on the floor beside his desk. He motioned for someone right outside the door to come in. A graduate student, his mentor, walked over to the sheet of paper and placed his two feet on the paper to help give the freshman all the answers he needed. He became the information on the sheet of paper that the student needed to ace the final. The teacher and the other students probably didn't like this idea. After all, they would feel like this student has an unfair advantage over the rest of the class. But now this student had confidence to take the test.

In a spiritual sense, that is what happens when you call on the Holy Spirit to step in and come alongside you to help you pass the tests of life. God has sent someone to reside in *you* as your personal teacher. God wants you to have an advantage – a spiritual advantage. Wouldn't it be great if we had this kind of Godfidence to face our tests in life?

GODFIDENCE LESSON

The Holy Spirit is the voice of God.

NOT JUST A SUPPLEMENT

When speaking about the Holy Spirit, I heard someone say, "Yeah, I think being filled with the Holy Spirit would be a great supplement to my spiritual life." This is the wrong idea. Just like God the Father had a distinct purpose for sending Jesus to us, He had a distinct purpose for sending us the Holy Spirit. God blessed us with the Person of the Holy Spirit. Being led by the Spirit is the way God designed us to live. Every moment of every day. Empowered. Anointed. With Godfidence.

I've always been intrigued by eagles. In his book *The Bald Eagle*, Steve Potts describes how the wind, rain, and other weather-related challenges negatively affect the eagle's flying potential. However, the preening process kicks in a way to overcome. The eagle has a special organ near his tail which produces a type of oil that he spreads over his feathers with his beak while preening, making his feathers waterproof. When the feathers are smooth, the eagle is able to fly properly and reach its potential.

The challenges of life have a way of ruffling our feathers and grounding our hopes. What is the solution? The Holy Spirit is the solution. By the way, oil is one of the symbols of the Holy Spirit. Like the preening an eagle experiences, it is the Holy Spirit that waterproofs your heart, your mind, and your life and prepares you to reach your potential. It's not just a supplement to your spiritual life. The Spirit is life itself!

When speaking of the Holy Spirit, make sure you identify Him properly. The Holy Spirit is not an "it." The Bible always refers to Him in the form of a personal pronoun. He is the third person in the Trinity. God the Father, God the Son, and God the Holy Spirit.

Many believers associate the Holy Spirit with the Acts 2 events of Pentecost. The fullness of Pentecost is understood when studying the Hebrew Feast of Pentecost, which God instructed His people to celebrate. In fact, it was on Shavuot (the Hebrew word for Pentecost) that God gave Moses and His people His Word (the Torah). Then, in the New

Testament, as the people of God gathered on that special holy day, God gave us His Spirit. What a great combination when we unite the old with the new. Spirit and Truth.

GODFIDENCE LESSON

If you allow Him to, the Holy Spirit will give you Godfidence to reach your potential.

A young pilot had just passed the point of no return when the weather changed for the worse. Visibility dropped to a matter of feet as fog descended to the earth. Putting total trust in the cockpit instruments was a new experience to him, for the ink was still wet on the certificate verifying that he was qualified for instrument flying.

The landing worried him the most. His destination was a crowded metropolitan airport he wasn't familiar with. In a few minutes, he would be in radio contact with the tower. Until then, he was alone with his thoughts. His instructor had practically forced him to memorize the rulebook. He didn't care for it at the time, but now he was so thankful.

Finally, he heard the voice of the air traffic controller. "I'm going to put you on a holding pattern," the controller radioed. Great! thought the pilot. However, he knew that his safe landing was in the hands of this person. He had to draw upon his previous instructions and training and trust the voice of an air traffic controller he could not see. Aware that this was no time for pride, he informed the controller, "This is not a seasoned pro up here. I would appreciate any help you could give me."

"You've got it!" he heard back.

For the next forty-five minutes, the controller gently guided the pilot through the blinding fog. As course and altitude corrections came periodically, the young pilot realized the controller was guiding him around obstacles and away from potential collisions. With the words of the rulebook firmly placed in his mind and with the gentle voice of the controller, he landed safely at last.

There are times when we find ourselves going through life and an emergency suddenly strikes. We are facing an issue that we didn't anticipate. What do we do? Where do we go? Who do we turn to?

The first thing we are to do is to refer to our instruction manual, the Bible. The Word of God. It is in the Word that we will find all we need to respond to any situation life throws at us.

Secondly, we are to listen to the voice of someone who can lead us safely home. The voice of the Holy Spirit, who guides us through the maze of life much like that air traffic controller. When you combine the Word of God with the Spirit of God, you are going to be just fine.

> "God often gives us an inner conviction or prompting to confirm which way He wants us to go. This prompting comes from the Holy Spirit."
> – Billy Graham

Until Christ returns, we are blessed with the Holy Spirit. Let's do our best to welcome His presence into our everyday lives. Here are twelve Biblical phrases used to describe the Holy Spirit and what He does:

1) The Gift of the Holy Spirit

On one occasion, while he was eating with them, he gave them this command: "Do not leave Jerusalem, but wait for the ***gift*** *my Father promised, which you have heard me speak about. For John baptized you with water, but in a few days you will be baptized with the Holy Spirit."*

Acts 1:4–5

I admit it. I like gifts. I like new things. And I've noticed that one of the great attributes of God is that He loves to bless you and I with gifts. I personally believe that the greatest gift God gives us is the gift of eternal life (salvation). In Romans 6:23, Scripture says, "For the wages of sin is death, but the gift of God is eternal life in Christ Jesus our

Lord." Have you received and opened up this gift of eternal life?

Here is some good news: That's not the only gift God gives you. 1 Corinthians 12, Romans 12, 1 Peter 4 and Ephesians 4 are chapters from Scripture where various gifts from God are listed. I encourage you to learn about spiritual gifts and which ones God extends to you. One of the many additional gifts God offers you and me is this gift in Acts 1:4 – the gift of the Holy Spirit. This gift is priceless!

"A week before Christmas, you see a gift under the Christmas tree. You don't know what it is, but you are anticipating that gift. You know it's going to be good. Jesus said, 'Wait for the gift that the Father is sending you.' It's going to be good."
– Matt Garcia

2) The Promise of the Holy Spirit

"Do not leave Jerusalem, but wait for the gift ***my Father promised****, which you have heard me speak about."*
Acts 1:4

Do you believe in the promises of God? Some believe in the promise of the Holy Spirit and some do not. It's a matter of faith...do you have enough faith to believe it? When God promises, it's a done deal. All you need to do is believe it.

GODFIDENCE LESSON

Resisting the work of the Holy Spirit will limit your spiritual potential.

3) Baptized with the Holy Spirit

"I baptize you with water for repentance.
But after me comes one who is more powerful than I,
whose sandals I am not worthy to carry.
He will baptize you with the Holy Spirit *and fire."*
Matthew 3:11

"John baptized you with water,
but in a few days you will be ***baptized with the Holy Spirit.****"*
Acts 1:5

The Greek word for baptism is *baptezien*, which means "to immerse." When it comes to your spiritual life, you have a choice. You can choose to live a plain and ordinary life, or you can choose to be baptized in the Holy Spirit.

On a hot summer day, people hang out at the pool. Some choose to sit on the edge and are happy dipping their feet in the water, but others choose to dive into the pool, experiencing refreshment over their entire body. Likewise, many Christ followers are happy sitting on the edge of the water, too hesitant to dive into the deeper things of God. I invite you to dive in. The water's fine.

> **GODFIDENCE LESSON**
> Don't allow your spiritual life to be characterized by shallowness.

4) Filled with the Holy Spirit

All of them were ***filled with the Holy Spirit*** *and began to speak in other tongues as the Spirit enabled them.*
Acts 2:4

In many third-world countries, access to water is a huge challenge. Some villagers must walk a mile or more to simply get some fresh water from a spring or well. Sometimes, water is retrieved from contaminated ditches, drains, or streams, which places lives in danger. There are a few mission organizations who bless these villages by building fresh-water wells. When a well is completed, life is so much easier for the villagers. All they need to do is turn on the faucet, and they have access to fresh water.

Many believers go through life without access to the Holy Spirit. Life gets difficult. Praise God for the well of spiritual water God has created for us. Bring your water bottle. He's ready to fill you up. All you need to do is turn on the faucet.

"Be very careful, then, how you live – not as unwise but as wise, making the most of every opportunity, because the days are evil. Therefore do not be foolish, but understand what the Lord's will is. Do not get drunk on wine, which leads to debauchery. Instead, be filled with the Spirit" (Ephesians 5:15–18). When an individual gets drunk, we often say that they are "under the influence." What Paul is saying is this: like wine puts an individual under a negative influence, the Holy Spirit places an individual under a positive influence.

5) Speak in Other Tongues

All of them were filled with the Holy Spirit and ***began to speak in other tongues*** *as the Spirit enabled them.*

Acts 2:4

I had the privilege of growing up in a Christian home and a Pentecostal church. After coming to faith in Christ at age 11, I began praying for the gift of speaking in tongues. I really wanted that gift. After years of praying for this, nothing was happening. As I went through my teenage years and became a young adult, I had felt God's calling on my life to step into pastoral ministry. I loved the Lord. I was serving the Lord in various capacities, but I had no desire to be a pastor. In a family where pastors, missionaries, and ministers were all around me, I didn't want to be just another pastor. If I was going to pursue pastoral ministry, I wanted to make sure it was God calling me.

When I was twenty-four years old, I was in church one Sunday morning when the guest speaker pointed at me and said, "I don't know who you are, but God has given you the anointing to be a pastor. He is calling you." Well, that was pretty clear. A few hours later, I was crying out to God and asking Him if His calling on me was real.

I remember saying these words, "Lord God, I sense that I have been avoiding my calling in life, so right now, I make a commitment to surrender my everything to You, even if it means quitting my job and pursuing the pastoral ministry." As I expressed my commitment to God in this prayer, something happened for the first time in my life – I began speaking in tongues.

I learned a great lesson that day. Total surrender to God opens the door to His precious gifts. That day, my Godfidence went to a whole new level!

GODFIDENCE LESSON

Surrender to God will give you the Godfidence to reach your potential.

Here in Acts 2:4, the reference to the phenomenon of speaking in other tongues is the term *glossolalia*. When an individual speaks in tongues, it is simply a reflection that God is in control of every portion of their life, e.g. their will, their future, their heart, and even their tongue.

6) The Holy Spirit Comes on You

But you will receive power when the Holy Spirit ***comes on you****; and you will be my witnesses in Jerusalem, and in all Judea and Samaria, and to the ends of the earth.*

Acts 1:8

An old Gatorade commercial asks the question, "Is it in you?" When it comes to the Holy Spirit, I ask the question, "Is He in you?" You see, it's one thing to know about the Holy Spirit, but it's another thing to have Him dwell in you.

In the Scripture above, Jesus describes what happens when you allow the Holy Spirit to come on you. 1) You will receive power, and 2) you will be His witness. Witness where? First of all, these hearers became witnesses in Jerusalem, which is a picture of you right there where you live and dwell. Secondly, in Judea, which is a reference to a larger geographical area. Third of all, Samaria. Wait. Samaria? Prejudice and racism said to avoid the Samaritans, because they were the outcasts. But Jesus makes it a point that we must take the gospel to everyone. Last of all, to the ends of the earth. This is a missions mandate. While you may not be able to personally carry out missions and evangelism in every country in the world, we certainly can pray for and financially support missionaries and missions organizations. We have the privilege of being part of what God is doing around the world through the power of the Holy Spirit.

7) The Holy Spirit Pours Out

And I will ***pour out*** *my Spirit on all people. Your sons and daughters will prophecy, your old men will dream dreams, and your young men will see visions.*

Joel 2:28; qtd. in Acts 2:17

Recently, I walked into a yogurt place, getting ready to indulge a bit. The flavor options were amazing, and it was difficult for me to make a choice. I was deciding between toasted marshmallow, red velvet, and sea salt pistachio, so I asked the guy behind the counter for a taste of sea salt pistachio. He pulled out a little bitty spoon and gave me a taste. It was good. So good that I wanted a ten-ounce cup. When I ate the whole cupful, it was even better.

I've noticed that when it comes to the Holy Spirit, many Christ followers are satisfied with a little bitty taste, not wanting the fullness that we can ask God for. Indeed, God wants to "pour out" His Spirit on us. Are you ready to receive it? Get your cup ready, 'cause He is ready to fill it with Godfidence!

8) The Holy Spirit Brings Deep Conviction

...because our gospel came to you not simply with words but also with power, with the Holy Spirit and ***deep conviction****.*

1 Thessalonians 1:5

Many years ago, I met a young couple who has just given their hearts to the Lord, but they were living together outside the bounds of marriage. I was on the verge of confronting them about their sin, when I sensed a nudge from the Holy Spirit not to do so, that He would take care of it. About a month later, this couple asked me to officiate their upcoming wedding, saying, "Pastor, the Holy Spirit has convicted us that we are living in sin, and we want to make things right with God."

Although I calmly answered their request with, "Yes," I felt like my heart was doing cartwheels. Why? Because they had become mature enough to hear the voice of the Holy Spirit and respond accordingly. That is conviction. And I learned a lesson that day – the Holy Spirit does a much better job in bringing conviction on individuals than I do.

Have you ever been on the verge of giving in to sin, and then there is a feeling in your heart that says, "No, don't go there. Don't do that!" That is the voice of the Holy Spirit carrying out His role to bring conviction over you. Individuals who sin and don't feel any conviction about it are in desperate need of the Holy Spirit.

GODFIDENCE LESSON

The devil will bring guilt on you to separate you from God, but the Holy Spirit will bring conviction on you to draw you closer to God.

Now, there is a difference between conviction and guilt. The Holy Spirit brings conviction over you to get you closer to God. The enemy places guilt on you to take you down. I encourage you to respond to the Spirit, not the lies of the enemy.

When I see a news report of someone who murders another person or of an individual who commits a horrific sin, like child molestation, I can't help but identify those sins as being influenced by Satan. I also identify those sinful individuals as people who do not have the Holy Spirit in them. They have no conscience. No convictions. Which means no Holy Spirit. Oh, how much better our world would be if people would simply live by the convictions of the Holy Spirit. Just sayin'.

9) The Holy Spirit Becomes Our Advocate

And I will ask the Father, and he will give you another ***advocate*** *to help you and be with you forever – the Spirit of truth. The world cannot accept him, because it neither sees him nor knows him. But you know him, for he lives with you and will be in you.*

John 14:16–17

In this quote, Jesus refers to the Holy Spirit as our Advocate, which is defined as "a person who speaks in support or defense of a person; a person who pleads the cause of another in a court of law." The Greek word here is *parakletos*, which means advocate, intercessor, helper, consoler, counselor, or comforter. Would you like someone to fill this role for you?

Picture yourself in court trying to defend yourself against accusations of sin. Your accuser, the devil himself, begins to describe to the judge your list of sins, what you did twenty years ago, ten years ago, two years ago. The list is long, and you know you are guilty of those acts. But then your defense attorney – your Advocate, the Holy Spirit – steps up to speak on your behalf. He tells the Judge, "Father God, my client was guilty of each of those sins described by this accusing prosecuting attorney. But years ago, Jesus Christ stepped in to pay the price for every one of his sins. The penalty has already been paid. So, I say that my client was guilty, but that is now in the past. He is no longer guilty."

The Judge responds by sounding his gavel and saying, "Yes, the price has been paid. I find this man not guilty of these charges, and he is free to go." Wow! I am sure you would be so grateful for your Advocate, the Holy Spirit. He not only stands beside you, but He also has your back.

10) The Holy Spirit Remains with You

And I will ask the Father, and he will give you another advocate to help you and ***be with you*** *forever.*
John 14:16

To celebrate his birthday one year, my son, Randy Sean decided to go sky diving (something that I am not called to do). Afterwards, he showed me a video of him jumping out of the plane and enjoying the fall, but I noticed there was a guy strapped to his back. That guy was there to guide the two of them in the right direction on their journey back to earth and to make sure everything went well. Yes, my son landed safely, along with his traveling buddy. That is what the Holy Spirit does for you. He sticks by your side. He guides you. He directs you. He makes sure you arrive safely. His role is to be with you.

> **GODFIDENCE LESSON**
> When you are filled with the Holy Spirit, you can have Godfidence that He's got your back.

11) The Holy Spirit Clothes Us with Power

I am going to send you what my Father has promised; but stay in the city until you have been ***clothed with power*** *from on high.*
Luke 24:49

If Danny Simpson had known more about guns, he might not have needed to rob the bank. But in 1990 in Ottawa, Canada, this twenty-four-year-old went to jail, and his gun went to a museum. He was arrested for robbing a bank for $6,000 and then was sent to jail for six years. He had used a .45 caliber Colt semi-automatic, which turned out to be an antique made by the Ross Rifle Company, Quebec City, in 1918. The pistol is worth up to $100,000 – much more than Danny Simpson had stolen. If he had just known what he carried in his hand, he wouldn't have robbed the bank. In other words, Danny already had what he needed.[21]

Do you realize all that God has placed in your hands? The Holy Spirit is ready to empower you; all you have to do is call on Him. You don't need to rob a bank, because God is offering you the gift of the Holy Spirit.

> "The Holy Spirit never enters a man and then lets him live like the world. You can be sure of that."
> – A.W. Tozer

Have you ever helped someone jump their car because their car battery went out? It lost its power. If so, you may notice that, on your battery, there is a "positive" and there is a "negative." And when you hook up the cables correctly, power flows out of your battery to the dead one, and the other car is able to start. That reminds me of our lives. There are lots of negative things going on in your life. Stress. Work issues. Health issues. Family issues. What happens when you bring the "positive" impact that the Holy Spirit brings? Positive on the negative results in power and Godfidence!

12) The Holy Spirit Leads Us

*For those who are **led by the Spirit** of God*
are the children of God.
Romans 8:14

The Holy Spirit changes the way we live. Here is what your day might look like if you were led by the Holy Spirit. You wake up in the morning and are led by the Spirit to spend time with your daily devotions. You read the Scripture God wants you to read. You pray for the people God wants you to pray for. You receive the Word that God wants you to receive. You are led by the Spirit.

At work, one of your co-workers shares how she is hurting from all the things being thrown at her, and you spend some time praying for her. You are being led by the Spirit. God's presence is right there with you.

As the day goes on, you stop at the grocery store and run into an old friend from high school who needs to hear the gospel message. You take the time to share your heart with her. You are being led by the Spirit. In the evening, you call a friend of yours who is dealing with a health issue. Your call reached her just at the right moment. You are being led by the Spirit.

At home, you notice that your daughter is not smiling like she usually does, and she is not in the best of moods. You take the time to listen to her story of what happened to her at school. You put your arm around her. Pray with her. Love on her. That's exactly what she needed. You are being led by the Spirit. You know these encounters were not coincidence; you were being led by the Spirit. God's presence is with you in every moment of every day.

> **GODFIDENCE LESSON**
> When you are led by the Spirit, you can have Godfidence that your steps are ordered of God.

WE NEED MORE OF THE HOLY SPIRIT

Every time I see how much sin and evil there is in this world, I think of how there is lack of conviction of the Holy Spirit. Without the Spirit, people often veer away from a Biblical world view. Some people say the answer to our world's problems is love. Others say the answer is peace. Love or peace? Actually, if you have the Holy Spirit, you get both, because love and peace are both fruit of the Spirit (Galatians 5:22, 23). Our world needs more of the Holy Spirit.

Faith and wisdom are two examples of the gifts of the Spirit (1 Corinthians 12:8, 9) What would our world look like if we had more faith in God? Or if we used Godly wisdom to make decisions? I'm sure this world would be a much better place. In response to challenges we face in our world, the answer is the Holy Spirit. When we gain Godfidence from the Holy Spirit, we are blessed with spiritual fruit and spiritual gifts that make a world of difference.

The greatest story ever told is all about God taking the initiative to love you and I and be in a relationship with us. Back about 2,000 years ago, He sent His Son. Why? To be the sacrifice we needed for the forgiveness of our sins. Jesus did die on the cross, but that's not the end of the story. On the third day, Jesus rose from the grave, proving He is God! Wow! But that's not the end of the story. About forty-eight days later, God sent the Holy Spirit so that part of Him could be with us here on earth. Praise God! But the greatest story ever told is still not over. The next part of this story will take place when Jesus returns for His followers, which means that you can take part of the greatest story ever told and spend eternity in heaven. Are you in?

WORDS OF LIFE

I am not alone. The Holy Spirit is with me! I am filled with the Holy Spirit! The Holy Spirit is my Advocate. He is my Counselor. He is my Helper. He empowers me. He is the voice of God to me. I am blessed because I am a Spirit-filled child of God!

GODFIDENCE CHECKUP

1) Why do you believe that many Christians have a fear of being filled with the Holy Spirit or simply lack a desire for more of the Spirit?

____

____

____

____

____

____

2) Which of the descriptions of the Holy Spirit means the most to you and why?

____

____

____

____

____

____

3) In what ways do you believe that you can do better at being led by the Spirit?

____

____

____

____

____

____

PRAYER FOCUS

Lord God Almighty, I thank You for sending me the Holy Spirit. Spirit of God, I realize that I need Your power and I need Your anointing. I am blessed to have You as my Counselor, my Comforter, my Helper, my Advocate and so much more. I want to be filled. I want to reach my spiritual potential. Amen. So be it.

CH. 12 REAL COMMUNITY

They devoted themselves to the apostles' teaching and to fellowship, to the breaking of bread and to prayer. Everyone was filled with awe at the many wonders and signs performed by the apostles. All the believers were together and had everything in common. They sold property and possessions to give to anyone who had need. Every day they continued to meet together in the temple courts. They broke bread in their homes and ate together with glad and sincere hearts, praising God and enjoying the favor of all the people. And the Lord added to their number daily those who were being saved.

Acts 2:42–47

A pigmy was standing over a rhinoceros that he killed. A guy saw this dead rhinoceros and the little pigmy standing next to it. "Excuse me, did you kill this rhinoceros?"

"Yes," responded the pigmy.

"How in the world did you – so small – kill this big rhino?"

"With my club."

"With your club? Well, how big is your club?"

"Well, there are about twenty of us in my club!"

This is a picture of real community.

> **COMMUNITY (N.):**
> a feeling of fellowship with others, as a result of sharing common attitudes, interests, and goals [22]

Life was not meant to be lived alone. In the Bible, we read that the people of God gathered together in synagogues, in temples, in tents, on mountainsides, in boats, in homes, and even in an upper room. The actual place didn't matter as much as the fact that the people of God were gathering together. The church was God's people, not necessarily a place where they met.

Is church really important? Perhaps I can ask this question in another way: Is "real community" important? Yes, it is. For three reasons:

1. For the sake of the individual Christ follower. We are blessed to have a place where we can grow, serve, give, and step into the power of agreement.
2. For the sake of the kingdom of God. When a church is doing what the church is called to do, we can make a powerful spiritual impact on the world around us.
3. For the sake of the unchurched (those who do not attend church). I've heard it time and time again from those who are not Christ followers, "The reason I don't go to church is because so many people who called themselves 'Christian' are fake." Yes, it is true that there are many fake Christians. Wouldn't it be great if we were to rise up and be authentic Christ followers? Real church. Real community.

FIVE CHARACTERISTICS OF THE REAL CHURCH

1) The church is the body of Christ.

Now you are the body of Christ,
and each one of you is a part of it.
1 Corinthians 12:27

In his New Testament writings, Paul makes a correlation between the church and a physical body. Our eyes. Our ears. Our mouth. Our arms. Our legs. Every part of our body is important. How does this correlate to the Body of Christ?

Each one of us has been uniquely gifted in a way that we fit in as part of the Body of Christ, so He creates a supernatural connection. If you have the gift of leadership, you can use your gift to make a career out of it, or you can use it for God's kingdom purposes. Or, you can use that gift of leadership in both ways. Just a thought.

Do you have the gift of administration? The gift of exhortation? The gift of the Holy Spirit? The gift of wisdom?

The gift of craftmanship? You've been given that gift for a kingdom purpose.

GODFIDENCE LESSON

When you activate your spiritual gifts, not only will you reach your spiritual potential but you will help your church reach its potential.

2) The church is the bride of Christ.

I saw the Holy City, the new Jerusalem,
coming down out of heaven from God,
prepared as a bride beautifully dressed for her husband.
Revelation 21:2

This Scripture describes the church as the bride of Christ. This is given to us as a reminder that God wants to have a personal relationship with us. In a wedding ceremony, vows usually include the words, "'til death do us part." In this spiritual picture of the bride of Christ, these words will not apply, because we will be in heaven for eternity. We will never die. This is a real relationship!

3) The church is the group of called out ones.

And I tell you that you are Peter, and on this rock I will build
my church, and the gates of Hades will not overcome it.
Matthew 16:18

This Scripture expresses words from Jesus. And when Jesus uses the words "I will," He is making a promise. So, in this passage, was He saying that He was going to build a physical structure where people can gather together? No. He was giving His promise to build you and me.

The word *church* in the Bible is quite a unique term. While most of the New Testament translates the Greek language to English, the word *church* is not a direct translation. This word, *church*, derives from a German word that means "house of the Lord; temple." Today, when we hear the word *church*, we tend to think of it in the context of a physical building where people go to worship the Lord, but the correct translation for the Greek word used, *ekklesia*, is "the called out ones; assembly." The German word that was substituted is an inaccurate translation.

Jesus did not promise a new building or a new temple. He spoke a promise over you and me. We are the called-out ones. How are we called out? We are…

a. called out by our Savior, Jesus Christ. He is the One who established the church.
b. called out from a sinful lifestyle. We've been transformed to a new life in Christ.
c. called out to a heavenly destiny. We have a hope to look forward to.
d. called out for a God-anointed purpose. There is a reason why we were created.
e. called out under the power of the Holy Spirit. We are led by the Spirit.

4) The church is the family of God.

Therefore, as we have opportunity, let us do good to all people, especially to those who belong to the family of believers.

Galatians 6:10

FAMILY (N.):

1. a basic social unit consisting of parents and their children, considered as a group, whether dwelling together or not…
4. any group of persons closely related by blood, as parents, children, uncles, aunts, and cousins. [23]

As I read this definition of family, I can't help but

associate it with the family of God. A group dwelling together. A group who are brothers and sisters. A group related by blood – the blood of Jesus. A group with a common ancestry, because we have the same Father. We are the family of God.

In 2019, my son Matt and his wife, Jesika, welcomed three little children into their home in a foster-to-adopt program. The first time we were introduced to these three special children, Brenda and I immediately fell in love with them. It's like they were part of the family since birth. Now, they are part of our family, and have the same privileges as those who were naturally born into the family.

When a person makes a decision for Christ, he/she is adopted into the family of God. They become sons and daughters of the Most High God, with full privileges as heirs of God and co-heirs with Christ. Welcome to the family!

5) The church is the community of God's people.

Through followers of Jesus like yourselves gathered in churches, this extraordinary plan of God is becoming known and talked about even among the angels!

Ephesians 3:10 MSG

When a group of people are a real community, the bond is powerful. They learn together. They share together. They grow together. They love together. They hurt together. They celebrate together. If you are not a church member, you may find yourself without a bond with other believers.

Rebecca wrote me a note saying, "Coming to Fortress Church was the best decision I ever made. Every single person I meet is truly a believer, a conqueror, and a person – like me – seeking God's love, comfort, forgiveness and guidance. They are a family full of God's love. I know that I am God's masterpiece. I am an overcomer! I am victorious with God's love!"

CALLED OUT, BUT IMPERFECT

One reason people hold back from being connected to a church is because they've been hurt by the people in the church. Yes, that happens. Why? Because the church is made up of imperfect people, and we do imperfect things. There are those who expect perfection from Christians in the church, and they have to realize it's not going to happen. After all, you are not perfect either, but God can use you greatly to reach out to hurting people.

Perhaps you can look at the church as a spiritual hospital where imperfect individuals go to get spiritually well. Jesus, the One who builds the church, is the Great Physician. He is the perfect One. We know that if we can just get our hurting friends and family to Dr. Jesus, then they will be fine.

> **GODFIDENCE LESSON**
> If you lost your faith in the church because you were hurt there, then your confidence was in man, not God.

Many years ago, an underprivileged boy named Howard Kelly was going door-to-door selling products to earn a little bit of income. He had one dime left, and he was hungry. He decided that he would ask for a meal at the next house. However, he lost his nerve when a lovely young lady opened the door. Instead of asking for a meal, he asked for a glass of water. She thought he looked hungry, so she brought him a peanut butter and jelly sandwich and a glass of milk.

After eating, he asked the lady, "How much do I owe you?"

She said, "You don't owe me anything."

He responded with, "Thank you," and went on his way, very encouraged. You see, he was about to give up, but his faith in humanity and faith in God was given a boost.

Years later, that same woman became critically ill. The local doctors couldn't figure out the core of her health issue, so they sent her to the big city where there were specialists of her rare disease. Dr. Howard Kelly was in for the consultation. When he heard the name of the town she was from, a strange light filled his eyes. He went in to see her and immediately recognized her. He gave this patient special attention and after a while, she was cured of that disease.

Dr. Kelly requested the business office to pass the final bill to him for approval. He looked at it and wrote something on it. When the lady received and opened that bill, she read the following words: "Paid in full with a peanut butter and jelly sandwich and a glass of milk."

BETTER TOGETHER

[Let us not give up] meeting together, as some are in the habit of doing, but [encourage] one another – and all the more as you see the Day approaching.

Hebrews 10:25–26

A Sunday School teacher was talking to the children about the importance of the church. To illustrate her point, she folded her hands together and said, "Here's the church; here's the steeple; open the doors and see all the people."

As she asked the class to do this along with her, she realized that one boy did not have a left hand (that's the way he was born). Before she could do anything about it, a friend of this boy scooted over to him, reached out his left hand and said, "Let's do this together." The two boys proceeded to join their hands together to create a visual of the church, the steeple, and the people. Their teamwork ideally illustrated the concept. Where one of us is weak, another is strong. This is a beautiful picture of real community.

GODFIDENCE LESSON

Jesus designed the church to help you reach your spiritual potential.

I often see discipleship as the *Word of God* working in the lives of the *people of God* empowered by the *Spirit of God*.

What a great combination. We need the Word. We need the Spirit. And we need the people of God, i.e., the church. Who came up with this idea of church? In the Scripture above, Jesus Himself said, "I will build my church." It was His idea, and He is the One who builds it.

Every time I read a "one another" passage in the Bible, I can't help but consider the importance of discipleship in building up an effective church. We are called to love another (Romans 13:8), instruct one another (Romans 15:14), serve one another (Galatians 5:13), carry one another's burdens (Galatians 6:2), be patient with one another (Ephesians 4:2), submit to one another (Ephesians 5:21), esteem one another above ourselves (Philippians 2:3), encourage one another to do good deeds (Hebrews 10:24), be devoted to one another (Romans 12:10), be kind and forgiving to one another (Ephesians 4:32), and extend hospitality to one another (1 Peter 4:9). You have a calling to be a *talmid* (disciple). But your potential rises when you become part of the *talmidim* (disciples).

Question: Do you want to have the power to overcome the gates of hell? Notice that Jesus said that it is "the church" that will overcome the gates of hell. So, if I want to be an overcomer, I must connect with the church. I am better together with the people of God. And when we as the church unite together in the name of Jesus, we win together!

{ "The proper context for every disciple maker is the church." – Francis Chan

These words of John F. Kennedy have become famous, "Ask not what your country can do for you, ask what you can do for your country." One of the things I like about JFK's statement is that it challenges us to focus on serving, not being served. In today's era of American life, many people don't live by this servanthood mentality. They don't hold back from demanding what their country can do for them. And if they don't get what they want, they complain. If they don't like what they see, they get angry. If they don't get their way, they protest.

It's all about me, me, me! This is a selfish attitude. And unfortunately, this mentality has crept into the church world.

I remember having a conversation with a couple who had visited the church I pastor. They were great people. One of their questions was, "What does your church have to offer us?" I quickly realized that I was speaking to a spiritually immature couple.

When an individual or family is in the process of searching for a home church (which we should all do), they have one of two perspectives. They can either have the attitude of, "What does this church have to offer me and my family?" or they can have the attitude of, "What can my family and I do to serve this church?" One attitude is "serve me." The other attitude is "I want to serve you." It's the difference between a consumer attitude and a contributor attitude. Taking versus giving. Think about this: Which attitude reflects spiritual maturity?

> **GODFIDENCE LESSON**
> A spiritually mature believer is a member of a church where God has called them to serve.

What would Christ's attitude be? Matthew 20:28 says, "the Son of Man did not come to be served, but to serve, and to give his life as a ransom for many." I want to be more like Jesus. My priority is to serve others. How about you?

THE POWER OF TEAM

On the night that Michael Jordan scored sixty-nine points in a game, his teammate, Stacy King (who scored one point) said, "Yes, I will always remember that this was the game that Michael Jordan and I combined for seventy points.

Wouldn't it be great to know that you are on a winning team? Actually, if you've placed your faith in Christ Jesus, you are on a winning team. God's team. You are already a champion!

> "Becoming a member is a declaration that you are moving from being a consumer to being an investor; that you are joining not just the community of Christ, but the cause of Christ." – Erwin McManus

SMALL GROUPS

They broke bread in their homes
and ate together with glad and sincere hearts,
praising God and enjoying the favor of all the people.
Acts 2:46–47

The early believers met in the temple *and* in their homes. Small groups give us a picture of a great life-support system. No brain surgeon would operate on an individual without a life-support system. No soldier is ever sent into battle without a life-support system. In the military, it is a unit called a platoon. A platoon is a connect group. It is a band of brothers who support each other, watch out for each other, protect each other, encourage each other, fight for each other, and sometimes give their lives for each other.

As we continue to look at the way Rabbi Jesus discipled the Twelve, we see another distinct characteristic – He used a small group. Looking through the four gospels, we see that there were three or four times that Jesus spoke to the thousands, but the greater portion of his time was spent with His small group. He poured Himself into these twelve men. This is real discipleship.

> "I've never found a better tool for creating and sustaining relationships than healthy small groups." – Larry Osborne

Do you believe that it is easier to personally connect with 5,000 people or with twelve? Obviously, the answer is twelve. If establishing a small group was a priority to Jesus, then it should be a priority to us as well. There is a Hebrew word that describes this Biblical principle of small groups, *haverim*, which literally means, "friends studying the Word together." Here are seven discipleship benefits of *haverim*.

1) Interactive conversation

I love to hear sermons. They have an important place in our spiritual growth. We can benefit from such a monologue, but we can also benefit from a dialogue, where the Bible teaching is interactive. In a *haverim*, we can ask a question or two, give some input, or simply share a story that correlates to the topic.

2) Personal prayer support

Because of the large number of people who attend a typical Sunday morning worship service, most church services don't have time to hear specific prayer needs from every person in the audience. Depending on the number of people, that may take an hour or so, but sharing your personal prayer need in a small group is always welcomed. It is refreshing to know that someone you know is praying for you.

3) Personal encouragement

In Acts 4:36–37, we are told of a man named Joseph who had a very important ministry. He had the gift of encouragement. In fact, he was such a great encourager that people gave him the nickname Barnabas, which means "son of encouragement." His ministry made a difference to the Apostle Paul (Acts 9:26–27; 11:25–27). One of things I have noticed is that every time I finish a small group gathering, I am encouraged. Perhaps it was an individual who encouraged me, or perhaps it was a Scripture or a Bible principle, or perhaps it was the special dynamic of believers sharing together. I walk away encouraged. And hopefully, I encouraged others.

4) Spiritual accountability

One of the primary factors that makes an athlete successful is having a good coach; someone who will teach you, train you, push you, and encourage you. A good coach will get the best out of you. A great place to find a good coach is at a Bible study small group. We need someone to coach us and even ask us the tough questions about our spiritual life. This is spiritual accountability.

5) True friendship

One of the lessons I've learned in life is this: you get close to the people you pray with. True statement. Some people choose the right group of friends, and other people choose the wrong group of friends. Whoever your friends are, they will have an influence over you, and you will have an influence over them. A Bible study small group is a great place to build friendships with individuals on the same faith journey as you. We are better together.

6) Group ministry opportunities

When Jesus ministered to people, He would often use the men of His small group to help or simply prepare them to do the same. When He fed the 5,000, it was the disciples who distributed the fish and bread. They saw how He healed the sick and raised the dead. They were there when He stilled the storm and when He made the deaf man hear. Likewise, those involved in a small group have opportunities to teach, to serve, to host, to pray, to reach out, and to make a difference in the lives of others.

7) Spiritual growth

When you combine interactive conversation, personal prayer support, personal encouragement, spiritual accountability, true friendship, and group ministry opportunities, the result is spiritual growth. You will find yourself in a deeper relationship with the Lord.

"When people who have been stuck find themselves involved in a small group that is actually doing the things the Bible says to do, life change occurs that has never before occurred."
– Dr. Henry Cloud

I love the fact that there are different types of small groups. Here are five examples.

Type of Group	Primary Focus
Discipleship Groups	Bible Study / Spiritual Growth
Fellowship Groups	Connecting with friends
Affinity Groups	Special Interests (e.g., knitting, softball, biking)
Support Groups	Specific Needs (e.g., GriefShare, Divore Care)
Outreach Groups	Action / Ministry (e.g., feeding the homeless)

One morning, I got word that one of my church members had undergone major surgery a few days prior, and I didn't even know. I jumped in my car to drive to the hospital to visit Daniel. After I prayed over him, I said, "Daniel, I am so sorry that it took me a few days to come pray over you, but I just found out this morning that you had surgery."

He said, "Don't worry about it, Pastor. I told my Connect Group about the surgery. They prayed over me and continued to care for me this week. I am blessed!"

Wow! It felt good not to be needed. (Is it ok for me to say that?) The truth of the matter is that Daniel's spiritual life has been positively affected by being in a community (small group).

"Small groups provide the best possible means for the church to actually be the church."
– Gary L. McIntosh

At the 1996 Olympics in Atlanta in the Women's Team Gymnastics competition, the U.S. Team was behind with one more performance to go. In order for USA to win the gold medal, it was up to Kerri Strug. She had two chances to make a high score on the vault. The problem was that she had injured her ankle in the previous event, and she could barely walk.

On her first vault, she fell on her landing, which meant that everything was riding on her last vault. And she had to do it on an injured ankle. As she prepared to do this last vault, she heard the words from her coach, Bela Korolyi, "You can do it! You can do it!" Those words meant the world to Kerri. They gave her the confidence she needed. And, yes, she did it. USA won the gold.[24]

Sometimes, a few words of encouragement can give someone the confidence they need to win an event or complete a task. Then, there are times that a few words of encouragement can help an individual leave their old way of life to become a Christ follower. "You can do it! You can do it!" This is Godfidence, and we have the privilege of giving it to others!

WORDS OF LIFE

I recognize that I am not designed to live my spiritual life alone.
I need my Lord. I need my brothers and sisters in the Lord.
I am blessed with specific spiritual gifts.
I am committed to my church and my small group.
I am a servant of God.
I value my community with my brothers and sisters in the Lord.

GODFIDENCE CHECKUP

1) Suppose someone tells you, "I don't need to go to church, and I don't need to be part of a small group. I can be a Christian on my own." How would you respond?

____

____

____

____

____

____

2) What are your primary spiritual gifts that you are called to use in the church?

____

____

____

____

____

____

3) Taking into account the various tools and resources we use to grow our spiritual life. How important are small groups to you in this spiritual growth process? Why?

____

____

____

____

____

____

PRAYER FOCUS

Lord God Almighty, I come to You in the name of Jesus Christ. I thank You, Lord Jesus, for establishing the church; a place where I can grow, serve, give, pray, fellowship, and worship. I realize that church isn't perfect because it has imperfect people. Help me accept and love others the way You do. I thank You that as you said in Matthew 16 when I connect with the church, not even the gates of hell can stand against me. I want that kind of power. Amen. So be it.

CH. 13 REAL WORSHIP

Therefore, brothers and sisters, since we have confidence to enter the Most Holy Place by the blood of Jesus, by a new and living way opened for us through the curtain, that is, his body, and since we have a great priest over the house of God, let us draw near to God with a sincere heart and with the full assurance that faith brings..."

Hebrews 10:19–22

It happened in 1971 in Eastern Europe. A group of approximately forty people had gathered together to worship God where the worship of God was prohibited. That is when a few communist soldiers burst through the doors of the meeting place, armed with huge machine guns. Fear gripped the hearts of the worshippers.

The communists forcefully yelled, "You are worshipping God, and this is punishable with death. We have come to get rid of every person who worships the Lord. We give you two minutes to decide who is Lord of your life. If Jesus Christ is not Lord of your life, you may walk out of these doors – denouncing your faith in Him – and go home in peace and safety. But if you profess that Jesus Christ is Lord of your life, you must stay and pay the price."

A leader of that church, a man who many looked up to, bowed his head in shame and walked out. A young lady who thought that she was too young to die rose up and walked out. One by one, more than half of the people walked out, denouncing Christ and revealing who they really were. But there were still about twelve who remained. They were strong. They feared nothing or no one but God Himself. The communists said, "Any more? This is your last chance!"

When all who wanted to leave had left, the group of communist soldiers put down their guns and rifles and said, "We acknowledge your faith in Christ Jesus as Lord. We, also, are believers in Jesus Christ, and we were looking for a place to worship, but we didn't want to be with just anyone. We want to be ***real*** worshippers, not the fakes. ***Now, let us worship!"***

GODFIDENCE LESSON

A real relationship with God begins with real and genuine worship.

What does real worship mean to you? Is it singing a song? A hymn? Or is it more than that? Has worship changed since Bible times? What does the Bible say about worship? Throughout every book of the Bible, there is a common theme: God desires a personal relationship with His people. He moves heaven and earth to get closer to us. How we approach God is worship. God's Word is filled with principles of how we can deepen our worship to the Lord.

Question: Why was God so adamant about getting his people out of Egypt?

Many would say, "Because God wanted to take His people to the promised land!" Good answer. Or some might answer, "Because God wanted to deliver His people out of the suffering they were dealing with." Good answer. But the real answer is found in Exodus 7:16, when God was telling Moses to tell Pharoah, "'The Lord, the God of the Hebrews, has sent me to say to you: Let my people go, so that they may worship me in the wilderness.'"

God desires a deep relationship with us. Worship is vitally important to our relationship with the Lord. It reflects how well we are connecting with God. Moses got it. But not all the Israelites did.

In Exodus 20:18, when Moses came back to tell them the commands God had given, we are told that the people stayed at a distance. What? The people stayed at a distance? Yes, they did. Why? We don't know why, but we can speculate. Perhaps there are reasons similar to why people stay at a distance from the presence of God today. Here are the top three reasons in my opinion...

1. Some people don't have a desire for more of God.
2. Some people are content in their spiritual comfort zone.
3. Some people are afraid of commitment with God.

Every day, the Lord invites you into His presence. You get there when you pray, when you get into the Word, and when you worship. Think about it: You are invited to enter into the presence of the Lord. What a privilege. Don't stay at a distance.

{ "God is serious about how we worship him, and we must be serious about it, too." – R.C. Sproul

EXPRESSIONS OF WORSHIP

In John 4, Jesus speaks to a Samaritan woman about being a "true" worshipper. What does it mean to be a "true" worshipper? Does it mean that there are "false" worshipers? Fakes?

"Yet a time is coming and has now come when the true worshippers will worship the Father in the Spirit and in truth, for they are the kind of worshipers the Father seeks. God is spirit, and his worshipers must worship in the Spirit and in truth" (John 4:23–24).

I want to be someone whom the Father seeks. Do you? Then, I must learn the principles of real worship – as Jesus said here, "in Spirit and in truth." I once had a discussion about worship with a friend of mine when he made this comment, "I worship God the way I feel comfortable." Now, although I understand that he was communicating to me that he isn't very expressive, but I still disagree with his comment. Why? Because, in reality, we should worship God the way Scripture tells us to, not the way we want to. It is the difference between truth-based worship and person-based worship.

When we worship "in Spirit," we connect with God from the heart. It is not a response to religion or to a building or to music – worship is a response to God Himself. It is based on your relationship with the Lord. An atheist, for example, cannot have a worship experience with God because he has no relationship with God. He doesn't connect with God, but a Spirit-filled Christ follower longs to spend time with God. When you invite the Holy Spirit into your worship experience, then you become a Spirit-led worshipper. Are you ready to touch the heart of God?

To worship "in truth" is to have a Biblical understanding of what real worship is about. Many worshippers never check their owner's manual. God's Word is our owner's manual, and it tells us how we are to worship. If you would simply understand the Biblical principles of worship, then it will mean so much more to you.

GODFIDENCE LESSON

If you worship with Truth but no Spirit, you dry up. If you worship with Spirit but no Truth, you burn up. If you worship with Spirit and Truth, you grow up!

SEVEN HEBREW WORDS FOR PRAISE

A great place to begin understanding truth-based worship is by studying the seven different Hebrew/Biblical words for praise.

Yadah: "to worship with the extended hand. To throw your praise up to God." The root word *yada* means to acknowledge or confess sin. While praising God, have you ever lifted your hands heavenward as an expression of worship? Yes, it is a Biblical principle to lift up your hands. This is *yadah*.

"Lift up your hands [yadah] in the sanctuary and praise the LORD" (Psalm 134:2). Do you enjoy it when your children express their love to you? So does God!

More Scriptures: Psalm 108:3; 2 Chronicles 30:22; Psalm 86:12.

Towdah: "to praise with a heart of gratitude; to worship with the extended hand in adoration, rejoicing, and thanksgiving." This is usually signified with hands cupped inward.

Like *yadah*, *towdah* is expressed with the lifting up of hands, but it is slightly different. It is expressed with hands cupped inward. What is the significance? It places the worshipper in a receiving mode. The root word *toda* means to thank God for things He has done and for the things to come. It is a combination of thanksgiving and faith. Perhaps you can picture a receiver in football ready to catch the football. What does he do? He cups his hands inward to receive what is coming to him.

> **GODFIDENCE LESSON**
> Gratitude thanks God for what He has done. Godfidence thanks God for what God is going to do.

"Sacrifice thank offerings [*towdah*] to God, fulfill your vows to the Most High" (Psalm 50:14). Are you grateful to God for what He has done for you? Do you have Godfidence in what He will do for you? Then express *towdah* to Him today.

More Scriptures: 2 Chronicles 29:31; Jeremiah 30:19; Psalm 26:7.

Rua: "to praise with a loud tone, to triumph, to glory and shout." Because of your passion to praise God, have you ever raised your voice to the Lord loudly? This is rua. It is a spiritual warfare kind of praise.

> "Worship is not just a reminder of who God is, it is a reminder to Satan of who he was."
> – Mark Batterson

"O clap your hands all you nations, shout [*rua*] to God with cries of joy" (Psalm 47:1).

More Scriptures: Joshua 6:10, Psalm 95:1, Psalm 100:1.

When it comes to being loud in your praise to the Lord, don't use the excuse that you are timid or that you are an introvert. Praise is an expression of your heart, and it is good to speak it out!

Barak: "to worship by kneeling down and blessing God." This physical expression of praise shows reverence and respect to God. *Barak* is a terrific expression of worship because when you kneel down, not only are you bringing reverence to God, but you are humbling yourself before Him.

"Come, let us bow down in worship, | let us kneel [*barak*] before the LORD our Maker" (Psalm 95:6). "I will extol [*barak*] the LORD at all times" (Psalm 34:1). The more you humble yourself before God, the greater He becomes in your life.

Zamar: "to praise God by the touching of strings." This type of praise is associated with music. Take, for example, a guitar player. He can play songs and sound good. But when he uses his guitar to play praise and worship songs, it becomes a form of praise.

"My heart, O God, is steadfast, | my heart is steadfast; | I will sing and make music [*zamar*]. | Awake, my soul! Awake, harp and lyre! | I will awaken the dawn. | I will praise you, LORD, among the nations; | I will sing of you among the peoples" (Psalm 57:7–9).

"Praise the LORD with the harp; | make music [*zamar*] to him on the ten-stringed lyre. | Sing to him a new song; | play skillfully and shout for joy" (Psalm 33:2–3).

Many years ago, I learned an important lesson: Whenever I am feeling down, pull out my guitar and worship God. As I begin to strum my guitar and lift my voice, I am inviting the presence of God into my situation, and my darkness flees. This is what happens when you *zamar*.

Halal: "to boast, to shine, to rave, to celebrate." *Halal* is the root word for "hallelujah." "Praise [*halal*] the LORD, Praise [*halal*] O servants of the LORD, praise [*halal*] the name of the

LORD" (Psalm 113:1).

Many Psalms, like Psalm 106, 111, 148, 149 and 150, begin with *halal*. Here is the underlying principle of *halal*: You can raise your hallelujah in the good, in the bad, in the ups, and in the downs. Our God is worthy of praise!

More Scriptures: Psalm 44:8; Psalm 102:18; Psalm 69:34; Psalm 22:22.

Tehillah: "the spontaneous song of the Lord." This comes from the same root word as *halal*, but it goes a bit further. This type of worship is initiated by the Holy Spirit. Have you ever been worshipping God and the song ends, but then, you keep on singing, perhaps even making up your own personal lyrics with that tune? This is the Hebrew word for praise, *tehillah*. The unending song of the Lord.

On the days that led up to Valentine's Day, I gave Brenda a few Valentine's cards. A few of them had some catchy words written on a Hallmark card. Nice. But I noticed what Brenda enjoyed better than those words on the Hallmark card – my words. She was drawn to my personal notes on the card. Why? Because she knew that those were the words that came directly from my heart to hers.

We can express our love for God in a similar fashion. Song writers have penned some beautiful worship songs to the Lord, and the Lord loves to hear them. But I have a feeling the words from your heart to God's heart makes a bigger impact. This type of worship is described in Hebrew as *tehillah*.

"I will extol [*barak*] the LORD at all times; | his praise [*tehillah*] will always be on my lips" (Psalm 34:1). "He put a new song in my mouth, a hymn of praise [*tehillah*] to our God." (Psalm 40:3).

Have you ever heard this phrase, "God inhabits the praises of his people"? It is actually taken from Psalm 22:3 (KJV), where it says, "But thou art holy, O thou that inhabitest the praises of Israel." The question I ask is this: Which of the types of praise does God inhabit? The answer is: *tehillah*.

More *tehillah* Scriptures: Isaiah 61:3; Psalm 147:1; Isaiah 42:10.

Praising God is what you were created to do. And when you do so, you are bringing completion to your spiritual life. Now that you know the Biblical approach to praising God, I believe it will have much more meaning to you than just singing a song. Praise Him. Raise your hands. Give Him thanks. Shout to Him. Kneel before Him. Pick up your musical instrument and sing. Celebrate His presence. And sing a new song.

SEVEN REASONS WHY WE SHOULD PRAISE THE LORD

1. God commands us to praise. (Psalm 150:6)
2. Praise is the door to God's presence. (Psalm 100:4)
3. God is enthroned in our praise. (Psalm 22:3 ESV)
4. Praise keeps our focus on God, not our problems. (Psalm 3:1-3)
5. Praise is warfare against our enemy. (2 Chronicles 20:22)
6. Praise fills our hearts with joy. (Psalm 16:11)
7. Praise points the way to God's blessings. (Psalm 103:1–5)

FIVE BIBLICAL WORDS FOR WORSHIP

The Word of God speaks so much about praise and worship. Not only do we learn from the original Hebrew language the depth of praise, but we can also learn more about worship from the original Hebrew and Greek. Let's study this.

Paneh (Heb.): "the face of God; His presence." Moses was a worshipper. He knew what it was like to dwell in the presence of God. Exodus 33:11 describes this relationship that he had with God as a "face to face" relationship. Many times during my time of worship with God, I have sensed that He was right there in front of me. This is what Moses experienced, and so can we. "The LORD would speak to Moses **face** to **face**, as one speaks to a friend."

The word "face" in Scripture is a reference to "the presence of God." This is the essence of the Hebrew word, *paneh*. Here is the cool principle of this Hebrew word for worship: You can take the presence of God with you wherever you go. When Moses wondered about leaving the presence of God on Mt. Sinai, God said this... "My Presence will go with you, and I will give you rest" (Exodus 33:14).

GODFIDENCE LESSON

The deeper your worship with God goes, the more Godfidence you will have that His Presence will be with you wherever you go.

Moses understood the importance of real worship. In fact, he had an epiphany. He realized that the presence (*paneh*) of God is what will set the people of God apart from everyone else.

"How will anyone know that you are pleased with me and with your people unless you go with us? What else will distinguish me and your people from all the other people on the face of the earth?" (Exodus 33:16).

What happened to Moses when he had a face-to-face encounter with the Lord? He walked away with such a powerful radiance of God that he had to place a veil over his head. (Exodus 34:33–35) Wow! That is the glory of God!

King David knew the importance of real worship as well. Not only was he known as a man after God's heart (Acts 13:22), but he also wrote many Psalms that reflected His attitude of real worship. "My heart says of you, 'Seek his face!' Your face, LORD, I will seek" (Psalm 27:8).

Seeking the presence of God was David's priority, and it should be ours as well. In this era of advanced technology, many of us often trade face-to-face encounters with people for convenient virtual encounters: FaceTime, text messages, emails, Zoom, etc. Have we become less relational with people? And have we also become less relational with God? Are you a real worshipper? It doesn't matter if you can sing or not, only that you desire to dwell in the presence of God.

Proskuneo (Gk.): "to do reverence to; to kiss or become intimate with."

In Matthew 4, we are given the story of Satan trying to get Jesus to worship him. Jesus said this, "'Worship the Lord your God and serve him only'" (v. 10). The word "worship" here is the Greek word *proskuneo*. In other words, Jesus was saying, "Your reverence and intimacy should be focused on the Lord God Almighty and no one else."

In Matthew 28:9, we are told that the disciples and the ladies who went to the empty tomb worshiped the risen Savior, Jesus! "They came to him, clasped his feet and worshipped him." The term "worshipped" here is this word *proskuneo*. They felt intimacy with the Lord.

In Revelation 4:10, we are given a picture of worship in heaven. "The twenty-four elders fall down before him who sits on the throne and worship him who lives for ever and ever." What is focal point of our worship in heaven? Intimacy with God (*proskuneo*).

{ "Ten minutes in the presence of God is far better than ten days on vacation." – Randall Sean Garcia

Latreuo (Gk.): "to serve and to minister." Using your spiritual gifts to serve the Lord in ministry is worship. When you serve by changing diapers in the church nursery, this is worship unto God. When you help with a downtown outreach project, you are worshipping God. When you lead a small group Bible study, you are worshipping God. Remember, worship comes from worth-ship, which begs the question, "How much is God worth to you?" Is He worth the time and effort it takes to serve Him by serving people? By the way, when the church comes together to worship, we often refer to it as a worship *service*.

"Therefore, I urge you, brothers, in view of God's mercy,

to offer your bodies as living sacrifices, holy and pleasing to God – this is your true and proper worship [*latrueo*]" (Romans 12:1).

"Therefore, since we are receiving a kingdom that cannot be shaken, let us be thankful, and so worship [*latrueo*] God acceptably with reverence and awe" (Hebrews 12:28).

> **GODFIDENCE LESSON**
> Real worshippers are those who are not afraid to step out of their comfort zone to serve God and serve people.

Leitourgos (Gk.): "the priestly ministry of worship." The Old Testament priests were those who were set apart to draw near to the presence of the Lord. What a privilege they had. When Jesus died on the cross, the curtain in the temple was torn – symbolizing that now, you and I have access into the presence of God. What a privilege!

Have you ever heard the phrase, "You lead by example?" Here is the cool thing about *leitourgos*: When you and I draw near into the presence of God, we can take others with us. This is why the apostle Paul used this word in Romans 15:16, "[God gave me the grace] to be a **minister** [*leitourgos*]of Christ Jesus to the Gentiles. He gave me the priestly duty of proclaiming the gospel of God, so that the Gentiles might become an offering acceptable to God, sanctified by the Holy Spirit."

As you read through the following list of responsibilities of an Old Testament priest, perhaps you can correlate them to your role as a New Testament priest.

The Old Testament priest was called...

1. to offer up sacrifices to God (Leviticus 1).
2. to be holy (Leviticus 10:8–10).
3. to pray to God and bless the people (Numbers 6:22–27).
4. to keep the fire on the altar burning (Leviticus 6:12–13).

5. to bear the ark of the Covenant, the presence of God (Joshua 4:10–11).
6. to worship during the battle (2 Chronicles 20:19-20).
7. to seek an anointing from God (Exodus 29:7).

This is *real worship*!

Doxa (Gk.): "glory; honor; the unspoken manifestation of God; splendor."

In Luke 2:14, we read the story of how the angels from heaven appeared to the shepherds in the field when the Baby Jesus was born. How did the angels worship God? They gave him glory: "**Glory** [*doxa*] to God in the highest heaven, and on earth peace to those on whom his favor rests."

In John 1:14, we read how John described the essence of Jesus as He came from heaven to earth, "The Word became flesh and made his dwelling among us. We have seen his **glory**, the **glory** of the one and only Son, who came from the Father, full of grace and truth."

In Matthew 24:30, it is prophetically spoken how Jesus will come for the church and appear in all of His glory: "Then will appear the sign of the Son of Man in heaven. And then all the peoples of the earth will mourn when they see the Son of Man coming on the clouds of heaven, with power and great **glory**."

Jesus is worthy of all honor and glory! Let's give Him what He deserves. Real worship.

IS CHURCH WORSHIP NECESSARY?

Therefore, since we are receiving a kingdom that cannot be shaken, let us be thankful, and so worship God acceptably with reverence and awe, for our "God is a consuming fire."

Hebrews 12:28–29

I've heard it said many times, "I can worship the Lord from the privacy of my home. I don't need to go to church." While it is true that we can worship the Lord in our home, in our car, while we are taking a walk, etc., there is a special dynamic that takes place when the people of God come together.

In 2020, our world was rocked by the pandemic of the coronavirus. We learned the meaning of terms like social distancing, stay at home, and quarantine. To do their part in overcoming the virus, most churches began having worship services online. While it wasn't the best way to have church, we had to make it happen.

During that time, I missed the Sunday gatherings of the people of God in the worship center. I missed the hugs, the handshakes, the smiles, and the face-to-face interaction. Yes, there is a special dynamic that takes place when the people of God come together to worship. Here are my eight reasons why it is important to have church worship services together in a worship center.

1. To bring people into God's presence
2. To encourage and uplift the people of God
3. To release the gifts of the Spirit
4. To bring the anointing of the Holy Spirit
5. To do spiritual warfare against the enemy
6. To bring our sacrificial offerings to the Lord
7. To learn and grow in the teaching of God's Word
8. To serve as New Testament priests

A FEELING OR A CHOICE?

There have been times that I haven't felt like worshipping God. I was physically drained, I was dealing with a crisis, or perhaps someone was pushing my buttons. For some reason, I just did not feel like worshipping God. It was a sacrifice to worship God. What does Scripture say about this?

"Through Jesus, therefore, let us continually offer to God a sacrifice of praise – the fruit of lips that openly profess his name" (Hebrews 13:15).

It reminds me of the guy who told me, "I just don't feel

like I love my wife anymore," to which I responded, "You can't base your love for your wife on a feeling. The day you exchanged vows, you made a choice." Can you imagine how crazy life would be if we acted on our feelings all the time?

> **GODFIDENCE LESSON**
> Whatever circumstance you don't turn into praise turns into pain.

Similarly, a real relationship with the Lord always includes real worship, whether we feel like it or not. I like what Habakkuk says about worshipping God even though we are dealing with challenging situations...

Though the fig tree does not bud
    and there are no grapes on the vines,
though the olive crop fails
    and the fields produce no food,
though there are no sheep in the pen
    and no cattle in the stalls,
yet I will rejoice in the LORD,
    I will be joyful in God my Savior. (Habakkuk 3:17)

The Randy Garcia paraphrased version of this passage would be like this:

Though my car needs new brakes
and my back really aches,
Though my weight keeps on rising
and my company's downsizing,
Though I've got bills to pay
and not enough hours in a day,
Though my car stopped cruising
and the Cowboys keep losing,
Yet I will rejoice in the Lord,
and be joyful in God my Savior!

STIR THE NEST

Stir the nest. I've heard this phrase many times, and then I read where it comes from. It is what as eagle does in the nest to make the little eaglet uncomfortable. The eagle will put broken twigs, sharp objects and the like in the nest to irritate the eaglet. Why? Because the eagle wants to get eaglet out of his comfort zone. When this happens, the eaglet will jump out of the nest and begin to fly.

In a similar fashion, God places certain irritations in your nest to get you out of your comfort zone because He wants you to fly. He wants you to soar. He wants your relationship with Him to soar. And it begins with your worship to Him.

Darren Whitehead tells the story of a conversation he had with his friend, Ken. Ken told him, "Pray for me. I've got a situation going on with my family. My daughter was at a party last night and she never came home, and we don't know where she is."

Darren responded, "You must be worried out of your mind."

Ken assured him, "No, I don't worry. I worship!"

Wow! What a great response. Is that the kind of Godfidence you have? True worshippers don't worry. We worship.

GODFIDENCE LESSON

True worshippers don't worry about the circumstances around them. They are focused on the presence of God within them.

TOUCHING HEAVEN

I really enjoy worshipping God. And if His presence is this good here on earth, I can only imagine how it will be in heaven. Sometimes, I feel that we are just getting a taste of the presence of God here on earth. Revelation 5 attempts to describe how worship will be in heaven.

Then I looked and heard the voice of many angels,

numbering thousands upon thousands, and ten thousand times ten thousand. They encircled the throne and the living creatures and the elders. In a loud voice they were saying:

"Worthy is the Lamb, who was slain,
to receive power and wealth and wisdom and strengthvand honor and glory and praise!"

Then I heard every creature in heaven and on earth and under the earth and on the sea, and all that is in them, saying:

"To him who sits on the throne and to the Lamb
be praise and honor and glory and power, for ever and ever!"

The four living creatures said, "Amen," and the elders fell down and worshiped" (Revelation 5:11–14).

What a grand picture of intense worship. Don't miss it.

WORDS OF LIFE

I was created to worship God. In the good times and in the bad times, I will worship the Lord. When I feel like it and when I don't feel like it, I will worship the Lord. I won't hold back expressing myself to God. I am a worshipper. This is who I am.

GODFIDENCE CHECKUP

1) Which of the Hebrew/Greek words for praise or worship means the most to you and why?

____

____

____

____

____

____

2) In your opinion, what is the relationship between

worship and your personal relationship with the Lord?

____

____

____

____

____

____

3) What was so special about Moses or what did Moses do to warrant being blessed with the glory of God that shone so brightly on his face?

____

____

____

____

____

____

PRAYER FOCUS

Lord God Almighty, I praise You for all that You have done, and I worship You for Who You are. Indeed, You are worthy of all the glory and honor that any of us could ever give You. I pray that I would always be focused on the way You taught us to worship: In Spirit and in truth. Through my ups and downs of life, I will always give You praise. May I never miss an opportunity to worship You. I don't want to wait until Sunday to worship You. I make worship to You my lifestyle. Today and every day, I pray that my worship will be my simple expression of my love and devotion to You. Amen. So be it.

CH. 14 REAL GENEROSITY

But since you excel in everything – in faith, in speech, in knowledge, in complete earnestness and in the love we have kindled in you – see that you also excel in this grace of giving.
2 Corinthians 8:7

A few years ago, my Ford Explorer needed some repairs. My faithful repair guy, Russell, told me that to get it up and running was going to cost me $700.00. I wasn't expecting that, but I needed a vehicle to drive. I went ahead and gave him the ok for the repairs. He said, "It should be ready next Tuesday."

On Sunday, two days before I had to pay for these repairs, I had the thought, "What if I don't pay my tithes to the Lord and use that money toward these expenses? It would really help." Then, I had a brief chat with God, trying to justify what I was thinking of doing. Note to self: No matter how logical your argument is, you will never convince God that doing wrong is ok.

So, I paid my tithes that Sunday. When church was over, I was shaking hands with a number of people. Nancy approached me and said, "God told me to give you this." It was a check, folded in half. I placed it in my pocket, knowing that it would be rude to look at it right then and there. A few hours later, I was home, getting ready to relax, when I emptied my pockets and saw the check. I opened it up, and it was in the amount of $700.00. Wow! Was that a huge coincidence that I received the exact amount of money I needed for my car repairs? No. No coincidence. God doesn't work on the basis of coincidences. It was a supernatural blessing from God, based on my obedience to Him. It was also a reminder that God uses people like Nancy in big ways when they listen to His voice.

This is another example of how our generosity is

connected with the blessings God sends our way. The word "pray" is used about 400 times in the Bible. The word "believe" is used 272 times. The word "love" is used about 700 times. The word "give" is used over 2,000 times. Does this mean that to pray or believe or love is not as important as to give? Not necessarily. I would venture to say that the Bible addresses the action "to give" much more because most of us tend to struggle with it.

> **GODFIDENCE LESSON**
> In the areas of my life where I obey, God blesses. In the areas of my life where I disobey, God disciplines.

We live in a world where we are surrounded by people who deal with the problem of materialism. Consider this: If your annual earnings are $26,500 or more, you are in the top 10% of the world's richest people in the world. If your annual income is $35,000 or more, you are in the top 5% of the world's richest people in the world. If you have food in your fridge, clothes on your back, a roof over your head and a place to sleep, you are richer than 75% of the people in the world.

Money can buy you a bed,
but it can't buy you sleep.
Money can buy you books,
but it can't buy you wisdom.
Money can buy you medicine,
but it can't buy you health.
Money can buy you cosmetics,
but it can't buy you beauty.
Money can buy you a house,
but it can't buy you a home.
Money can buy you entertainment,
but it can't buy you happiness.
Money can buy you companions,

but it can't buy you true friends.
Money can buy you flattery,
but it can't buy you respect.

"How you handle or mishandle your money tells us who you are and more important, it tells you who you are. Your priorities, passions, goals and fears are shown clearly in the flow of your money."
– Dave Ramsey

When I was in school, there were certain things I enjoyed, like P.E. and lunch time, and there were other things I didn't enjoy, like taking tests. In fact, when my teacher informed us of an upcoming test, I would automatically raise my hand to ask, "What will be covered on the test?"

Why would I ask that question? Because I was not about to study anything that was not going to be on the test. Needless to say, when I completed my college education, I was so glad that I didn't have to take any more tests. Well, I was wrong. I failed to understand that living life is a series of tests. Whether we like it or not, we have to deal with relationship tests, career tests, family tests, physical tests, and much more. When it comes to generosity, here are three ways in which we are tested.

1) Generosity Is a Test of Priorities

Honor the LORD with your wealth,
with the firstfruits of all your crops.
Proverbs 3:9

Let's say that I am out shopping for shoes. I see this nice pair of shoes – really nice – and the price tag says $89. Then, I see another pair of shoes – lesser quality, may not look quite as nice – on sale for $29. I am debating which to purchase. It is a test. Have I already been generous to God? Have I paid my bills? Is the higher-priced pair of shoes a need or a want? If I make the right choice, then I have passed the test.

As noted in the Scripture from Proverbs above, the Bible addresses our generosity priorities by using the term "firstfruits," which is a simple reminder to put God first. Much like what a farmer would do as he collects his crop, he gives his firstfruits to the Lord, not his leftovers.

2) Generosity Is a Test of Obedience

"Give, and it will be given to you. A good measure, pressed down, shaken together and running over, will be poured into your lap. For with the measure you use, it will be measured to you."

Luke 6:38

The words of this Scripture come from Jesus Himself. He says, "Give." It is not an option; it is a mandate that simply needs to be obeyed. The good news is that being generous comes with a promise of a blessing. How much blessing? A good measure. How big of a measure? Jesus said, "For with the measure you use..." In other words, the bigger your generosity, the bigger your blessing.

I once heard a man tell me, "I'm going to pray about whether to give to God." He didn't realize that there are some things we don't need to pray about. For example, I don't need to pray about whether or not I should love my wife. Ephesians 5:25 tells me to do that. It's not a matter of prayer, it's a matter of obedience. Let's pass this test.

GODFIDENCE LESSON

When you pass your test,
you end up with a testimony!

The Message version of the Bible translates Luke 6:38 this way, "Give away your life; you'll find life given back, but not merely given back – given back with bonus and blessing. Giving, not getting, is the way. **Generosity** begets **generosity**."

The Bible is filled with promises of blessing to those with a heart of generosity. The Old Testament book of Malachi speaks about the blessings that flow when we tithe. What is the tithe? It is a Scriptural mandate to pay 10% on one's income to the church for the support of the kingdom of God. That sounds like a lot of money, but the good news is that paying tithes opens the door to many promises from God. Malachi 3:8–11 says...

> "Will a mere mortal rob God? Yet you rob me.
> "But you ask, 'How are we robbing you?'
> "In tithes and offerings. You are under a curse – your whole nation – because you are robbing me. Bring the whole tithe into the storehouse, that there may be food in my house. Test me in this," says the LORD Almighty, "and see if I will not throw open the floodgates of heaven and pour out so much blessing that there will not be room enough to store it. I will prevent pests from devouring your crops, and the vines in your fields will not drop their fruit before it is ripe.... Then all the nations will call you blessed, for yours will be a delightful land," says the LORD Almighty.

Here is a list of four promises from God listed in this passage. To those who tithe, God says...

> I will open the floodgates of heaven.
> I will pour out blessings to you.
> I will protect your resources.
> Nations will call you blessed.

Based on these promises of God, I would expect to believe that most every believer tithes, but that is not true. Statistics show that between 7% to 9% of Christians tithe. Looking at this from a different angle, I see that more than 90% of Christians cheat themselves out of the best of God's promises.

GODFIDENCE LESSON

Faith in God leads to salvation.
Obedience to God leads to blessings!

3) Generosity Is a Test of Lordship

As Jesus started on his way, a man ran up to him and fell on his knees before him. "Good teacher," he asked, "what must I do to inherit eternal life?"

"Why do you call me good?" Jesus answered. "No one is good – except God alone. You know the commandments: 'You shall not murder, you shall not commit adultery, you shall not steal, you shall not give false testimony, you shall not defraud, honor your father and mother.'"

"Teacher," he declared,
"all these I have kept since I was a boy."

Jesus looked at him and loved him. "One thing you lack," he said. "Go, sell everything you have and give to the poor, and you will have treasure in heaven. Then come, follow me." At this the man's face fell. He went away sad, because he had great wealth.

Mark 10:17–22

What is the point of this story that Jesus told? Do you need to sell everything you have for the sake of the kingdom of God? Is this story about money? Not really. It is primarily about lordship. It is evident that the young man in this story worshipped the god of money. In order to make Jesus his Lord, he needed to get rid of his god of money. It was a test. And this young man failed it.

One young lady began tithing 20% of her income to God. Why in the world would she do that? She said, "Because I have faith, and I am believing God to give me a promotion. And if I get that promotion, my income will double. So, I am simply tithing that in faith."

GODFIDENCE LESSON

God blesses you, not just to increase your standard of living, but more importantly, to increase your standard of giving!

GO

One of the characteristics of individuals with Godfidence is that we take advantage of great opportunities. When it comes to giving, I often refer to this as GO: Generosity Opportunities. When I receive my paycheck, I think "GO," a generosity opportunity to tithe. Sometimes, God wants me to give to His kingdom above the tithe. When God moves my heart to give to a missionary doing great kingdom ministry, I think "GO." This is a Generosity Opportunity. When God moves my heart to contribute to a ministry, like Adult & Teen Challenge or HIS Bridge Builders, or Convoy of Hope, I think "GO." This is a Generosity Opportunity. When God moves my heart to bless a needy family who is struggling, I think "GO." This is a Generosity Opportunity.

GODFIDENT TRUST

When Jesus looked out and saw that a large crowd had arrived, he said to Philip, "Where can we buy bread to feed these people?" He said this to stretch Philip's faith. He already knew what he was going to do.
Philip answered, "Two hundred silver pieces wouldn't be enough to buy bread for each person to get a piece."
One of the disciples – it was Andrew, brother to Simon Peter – said, "There's a little boy here who has five barley loaves and two fish. But that's a drop in the bucket for a crowd like this."
Jesus said, "Make the people sit down." There was a nice carpet of green grass in this place. They sat down, about five thousand of them. Then Jesus took the bread and, having given thanks, gave it to those who were seated. He did the same with the fish. All ate as much as they wanted.

John 6:5–11 MSG

This is one of my favorite miracles. Jesus feeds 5,000 with just a little bit of fish and bread. Wow! While there are many lessons we can learn from this great story, I would like to see it from the perspective of this boy who took his lunch to this huge gathering. It seems as though he was the only one in the crowd who came prepared for lunch. And now, Andrew asks him to give it up. That's not fair. Of course, Andrew was asking on behalf of Jesus. Would this boy trust Jesus enough to give Him his lunch? Here are three lessons we learn here about Godfidence trust.

Lesson 1: Godfident trust opens doors. Fear shuts doors.

Could Jesus have performed this great miracle without this boy's lunch? Yes. He could have, but He chose to use something that the boy had and to multiply it. For the boy, it was a test. A test of his trust in Jesus.

The good news is that the boy made the right choice and gave it to Jesus, which opened the door to see a great miracle unfold. I am sure the boy had to think about it – even if for just a moment. Perhaps there was a slight bit of fear the boy had, i.e., "I'm hungry, and I won't get the food back." But he trusted Jesus, and the door was opened for everyone to see a miracle right before their eyes.

> **GODFIDENCE LESSON**
> You make a living by what you get.
> You make a life by what you give.

Lesson 2: Godfident trust is the foundation of a solid relationship.

Have you ever used these words in your prayer to the Lord, "Lord God, I don't understand why I'm having to deal with this, but I trust You." I've prayed that many times because I tend to want to understand why I am dealing with my issues in life. Finances have a way of challenging our trust in God and the strength of our relationship with Him.

Have you read the book *The Five Love Languages* by Gary Chapman? It's a great book that deals with relationships. The premise of the book is that each of us receives love best in one of five ways...quality time, words of affirmation, acts of service, physical touch, and gifts.

Real generosity reflects using these "love languages" toward God. When you give God the priority of your quality time, you are showing love to Him. When you vocalize your praise to God (words of affirmation), i.e., "Lord, You are great and mighty! I praise You for what You've done, and I worship You for Who You are," you are expressing love. When you volunteer at church or at a homeless shelter (acts of service), you are expressing your love for God. When you tithe and give generously to the Kingdom of God (gifts), you are expressing your love for Him. These are examples of real generosity. Real relationship.

Lesson 3: Godfident trust stretches your faith.

Reading this story from John 6, there is a phrase from the Message version of the Bible that caught my attention. It says in verses 5 and 6, "When Jesus looked out and saw that a large crowd had arrived, he said to Philip, 'Where can we buy bread to feed these people?' He said this **to stretch Philip's faith**. He already knew what he was going to do."

God has a way of stretching our faith. He did it for Philip, and He does it for you. To forgive someone who has hurt you, it's a stretch. To embrace someone who is different than you, it's a stretch. To take time out of your busy schedule to have daily devotions, it's a stretch. To give to the kingdom of God when you would rather put that money away in savings, it's a stretch. But every time you stretch, your Godfidence grows.

> “Generosity is what keeps the things I own from owning me. In other words, the point of my generosity isn’t just to bless others, it is also to liberate me.” – Eugene Cho

THE BLESSING

Many years ago, a sixteen-year-old teenager left home to seek his fortune. All his worldly possessions were tied in a bundle, which he carried in his hand. As he was walking away from his home, he ran into a neighbor who asked, “William, where are you going?”

“New York City,” the boy said. “My father is too poor to keep me at home. I need to make a living on my own. The only thing I know how to do is make soap and make candles.”

The neighbor said, “William, can I pray for you and then give you a little advice?” They both knelt down, as the old man prayed and then spoke these words of life over William. “Someone soon will be the leading soap maker in New York; it may as well be you. Be a good man. Give your heart to Christ. Pay the Lord all that belongs to Him of every dollar you earn, and I am certain that God will bless you.”

When the teen arrived in New York City, he focused on Matthew 6:33 that says, “Seek first the kingdom of God.” He found a good church and made a commitment to tithe.

William soon became a partner in the business he was working for. After a few years, his partner died, and William became a sole owner of the business. He prospered. His soap sold well, and his family was blessed. So, he began to give God 20% of his income, and then 30% of his income. And then even 50%, as the Lord kept on blessing him and his family. His name was William Colgate, and his legacy went far beyond soap and toothpaste. Because he had the Godfidence to be generous to the kingdom of God, Mr. Colgate left a powerful legacy that continues to be passed on from generation to generation.

GODFIDENCE LESSON

Before you can expect God to bless you, you must first bless Him!

In January of 2018, I issued a 90-Day Challenge. I invited the people of my church to tithe for ninety days. I told them, "When the ninety days are completed, if you believe that God has not blessed you, then you can ask for your money back." It turned out that sixty-four individuals signed up for the challenge. During the ninety days, I received countless testimonies of how God was blessing the people. Would you like to guess how many of these sixty-four people asked for their money back? The answer is zero. God is faithful. And many more individuals now had Godfidence to be generous to God.

GODFIDENCE LESSON

Money is the key indicator of your spiritual life and spiritual priorities.

In his book *The Treasure Principle*, Randy Alcorn says, "In fact, 15 percent of everything Christ said relates to this topic (money and possessions) – more than His teachings on heaven and hell combined. Why did Jesus put such an emphasis on money and possessions? Because there's a fundamental connection between our spiritual lives and how we think about and handle money. We may try to divorce our faith and our finances, but God sees them as inseparable."

A man and his seven-year-old boy were spending time in the waiting room of a car dealership as the oil was being changed in his car. The boy was getting hungry and saw a candy bar in a nearby vending machine. He asked his daddy for a dollar. Dad pulled out his wallet and all he had was a twenty-dollar bill. He handed it to his son and said, "You can have this."

The boy argued, "No, daddy, I want a dollar bill."

Dad said, "But I'm giving you much more than a dollar."

The boy said again, "But I want a dollar bill."

This kind of conversation happens many times between God and us. "God, this is what I need. This job. This boyfriend. This house. This career. This is what I want!"

Then God says, "Here, I have something much better and more valuable for you. Here it is."

But we often respond by saying, "No. God, I don't want what you are giving me. I want this other thing." And we miss out on the big blessings God has waiting for us.

> "There are two ways to get enough. One is to continue to accumulate more and more. The other is to desire less." – G. K. Chesterton

"For where your treasure is, there your heart will be also" (Matthew 6:21). Whatever I invest in, that is where my heart is. If I were to spend money on my wife, it means my heart is with her. If I were to spend money on some nice amenities for my house, then it could be said that my heart is there. If I spend money on Apple stock, then my heart is there. But if I am generous to God and His kingdom, then it would be obvious that my heart is with God.

PRIME THE PUMP

A man found himself in a hot desert, very thirsty, and he knew his life was at stake if he didn't get water soon. Off in a distance, he saw this water pump. When he got up to it, there was a twenty-ounce glass of water next to it. Next to the water was a note that read, "This pump will give you all the water you need, but in order to prime the pump, you must pour all the water from the glass into the pump."

This man had a decision to make. Should he pour the glass of water into the pump and, if it doesn't work, run the risk of losing his life. Or, on the other hand, if there is indeed a well underneath this pump and he uses this water to prime it, then he can get all the water he would need.

After debating this with himself, the man made the right choice. He poured the twenty ounces of water into the pump and began to work the handle. At first, nothing was happening. No water was flowing. He began to sweat. But then, a few drops of water appeared, and then came a huge gush. He grabbed his empty gallon container and filled it up. He found another container nearby and filled it up. He drank all he wanted and freshened up.

The last portion of the note said, "When you finish, fill the twenty-ounce glass with water, and leave it next to this note for the next person that comes along, so that they will have what they need to prime the pump." He did so. And he was so grateful that he obeyed what the note next to the pump said.

When it comes to generosity, you and I have the same choice. Do we use all of the resources we have for our benefit, or do we trust what the Bible says and prime the pump? Those who have primed the pump will always tell you they made the right decision. Because that is when the blessings of God flow in ways that supersede what you previously had. When it comes to giving to God, do you have the Godfidence to prime the pump?

WORDS OF LIFE

I speak life into my finances. As I am generous, I believe that I will receive the blessings of God. When I give, I believe that missionaries will be supported, lost people will come to faith in Christ, and the church will be blessed!

GODFIDENCE CHECKUP

1) Take some time to review your financial budget. Is it evident that you are generous to the kingdom of God? What steps can you take to be more generous?

____

____

____

____

2) In your opinion, why do most believers today fail to trust God with the tithe?

PRAYER FOCUS

Lord God Almighty, I come to You in the name of Jesus. I ask for your wisdom over the way I handle my finances. Teach me how to be more generous and place my priorities in the right order. I understand that You entrust me to help support your kingdom purposes financially. I believe that You are Jehovah Jireh, my Provider. Amen. So be it.

CH. 15 REAL WITNESS

He who wins souls is wise.
Proverbs 11:30 NKJV

Freddy was dealing with so much pain in his life that he made a decision to take his life. He turned his oven to 400 degrees and stuck his head in it. As his head began to get hotter and hotter, he began thinking about how hot hell must be.

So instead, he pulled his head out of the oven, went to his living room, knelt down and gave his heart to the Lord, telling Him, "Lord, I don't want to experience hell. Forgive me of my sins. Thank You for the cross. Today, I surrender my life to You and will serve You from this day forward. Amen."

Freddy was so excited about his new-found faith that he wanted to tell his best friend, who was at a party that night. So, he got in his car and went over to where the party was at, pulled his buddy aside and talked to him about the Lord. His friend said, "Wow! That sounds terrific. What do I need to do to receive Christ?"

Freddy said, "First, you turn on your oven to 400 degrees, and I will show the rest."

Well, hopefully you know that you don't have to turn on an oven to lead someone to Christ, but there are some great lessons from Scripture we can learn from this story to effectively share our faith with Godfidence.

As Christ followers, one of the great privileges we have is to tell others about Christ. Think about it. Not even the angels in heaven have these blessed opportunities that we have. God has entrusted this life-changing gospel message to you and I for the purpose of sharing it with others.

GODFIDENCE LESSON

In a world of people searching for answers, we have the answer: Jesus. All we need is some Godfidence to share it.

The word evangelism comes from the Greek word *euaggelízo*, which means to verbally declare good news. My Bible dictionary says, “evangelism has to do with the proclamation of the message of good news.”[25]

Evangelism is such an important aspect of our Christian life. When Jesus was getting ready to depart earth and return to the Father, He spoke His famous last words. He said, “Therefore go and make disciples of all nations, baptizing them in the name of the Father and of the Son and of the Holy Spirit, and teaching them to obey everything I have commanded you. And surely I am with you always, to the very end of the age” (Matthew 28:19–20).

We often refer to this statement as the Great Commission. Some people interpret these words as a call to evangelism. Others believe this is a call to discipleship. I believe it is both. Jesus strategically addressed the importance of what our task on earth is to be. It is not an option. This is not called The Great Suggestion. It is called the Great Commission; it is a mandate.

In order to equip the believers to do this great work, God the Father sent the Holy Spirit to empower us to be His witnesses. “But you will receive power when the Holy Spirit comes on you; and you will be my witnesses in Jerusalem, and in all Judea and Samaria, and to the ends of the earth” (Acts 1:8). Yes, evangelism is very important.

In a court room, there’s a judge, a prosecutor, a defense attorney, a defendant, and witnesses. Witnesses give testimony. They don’t prosecute the defendant. They don’t convict the defendant. Witnesses do their best to give an honest and true testimony of what they saw or experienced. Their only job is to testify. As a Christ follower, your role is to be a witness of what Christ has done for you. Judging people is not your job, let’s leave that up to God. Convicting people of their sins is not your job, let’s leave that to the Holy Spirit. God has given you power to be His witness.

A witness is a person who testifies for a cause or has personal knowledge of a particular event that has taken place. Webster defines the word "testify" in three ways:

1. to make a statement based on personal knowledge or belief,
2. to serve as evidence or proof, or
3. to express a personal conviction.[26]

"So do not be ashamed of the **testimony** about our Lord" (2 Timothy 1:8).

> That which was from the beginning, which we have heard, which we have seen with our eyes, which we have looked at and our hands have touched – this we proclaim concerning the Word of life. The life appeared; we have seen it and **testify** to it, and we proclaim to you the eternal life, which was with the Father and has appeared to us (I John 1:1–2).

> **GODFIDENCE LESSON**
> Your light shines brighter when the world is darker.

HOLY HUDDLE

If indeed the message of the gospel is so important, then why are so few believers sharing their faith? Studies have shown that less than 5% of the Christ followers in America are consistently sharing their faith with others. Less than 5%. Pretty sad. What is the problem?

I enjoy watching football. In fact, I believe that being a football fan helps my spiritual life. This is because my team, the Dallas Cowboys, needs lots of prayer. When I watch a football game, I enjoy seeing the action on the field, e.g., the running, the passing, and the tackling. I don't really care to see them in their huddle. Yes, there is a purpose in the huddle. That is where they call the play and plan their execution.

There is something that I call the Holy Huddle that happens every Sunday morning. Christians enjoy getting together and huddling up and hearing God's game plan for their life. The problem is this: Many believers don't go and carry out God's plan. They enjoy the Holy Huddle but are hesitant to put it into action.

Question: In the last six months, how many people have you led to faith in the Lord? I don't ask that question to condemn you; I ask it to inspire you.

No matter what that number is, I believe you would say that you can do better. You can take it up a notch or two. This chapter is designed to give you specific strategies to share your faith and gain Godfidence as a witness for Christ.

> "I think our culture is changing, which is making evangelism difficult...people are shrinking back because it's not politically correct. They're not even sure how to engage in spiritual conversation."
> – Garry Poole

TEN WAYS TO OVERCOME YOUR FEAR OF SOULWINNING

We have experienced the greatest miracle of all (salvation). And we have the assurance of eternal life in heaven, yet most believers choose not to share the gospel. Why? I believe the primary reason is this: fear. Simply put, many believers have a fear of sharing their faith. Here are a few suggestions to overcome those fears.

1) Memorize a few Scriptures.

The Bible is our evangelism textbook. It is filled with stories of God's love for us and how we can experience it for ourselves. To be an effective soul-winner, you don't have to have a Bible college degree, just a few Scriptures and a heart for people. Look up these examples and consider memorizing them: John 3:36, Proverbs 11:30, Luke 19:10, John 3:3, John 14:6.

GODFIDENCE LESSON

The more soul-winning Scriptures you memorize, the more Godfidence you will have to share your faith.

2) Pray about your fears.

"I sought the LORD, and he answered me; he delivered me from all my fears" (Psalm 34:4).

Fear is the opposite of faith. The more fear you have, the less faith you have. So, if you want your faith to increase, pray for God to remove your fears and replace it with faith. Every time you share your faith with someone, your faith will grow.

GODFIDENCE LESSON

The more you share your faith with others, the more your Godfidence will grow.

3) Recognize that the Lord is with you.

"One night the Lord spoke to Paul in a vision: 'Do not be afraid; keep on speaking, do not be silent. For I am with you...'" (Acts 18:9–10).

Keep on speaking about the Lord. Do not be silent. You are Christ's ambassador. There are many individuals you know who need to hear this life-changing message of the gospel. And remember that last portion of the Great Commission, "And surely I am with you always, to the very end of the age." Matthew 28:20.

GODFIDENCE LESSON

When you realize that you have God's authority and God's anointing, you can't help but share your faith with Godfidence.

4) Don't be afraid of making mistakes.

"So is my word that goes out from my mouth: | It will not

return to me empty, | but will accomplish what I desire | and achieve the purpose for which I sent it" (Isaiah 55:11).

A while back, I delivered a message to the church on a Sunday morning that was, in my opinion, terrible. I don't know why, but my thoughts seemed jumbled, and my delivery was shaky. I just didn't have Godfidence that day. Later on, I found out that two people came to faith in Christ as a response to the message I preached. Wow! I was reminded how God can take an imperfect person and use his imperfect message to reach imperfect people. How? Because we serve a perfect God.

5) Don't be afraid of being asked questions you don't have answers for.

Years ago, I used to be hesitant to share my faith with people because I thought I would look dumb if I didn't have an answer to a question they might throw in my direction. Finally, I learned how to overcome this. As I was sharing my faith with a friend, he asked me, "Why do bad things happen to good people?"

I responded by saying, "That is a great question! I tell you what: I will research the answer to that question and get back with you. Are you free for lunch next Thursday so that we can talk about that?"

He answered, "Sure!"

What happened? Three things: (1) I admitted that I didn't know the answer to his question. People today are drawn more to people who are real rather than people who come across as "know-it-alls." (2) I created a second opportunity to meet up with my buddy and further our spiritual discussion. (3) I listened to him and valued what he had to say. There is power in listening.

It doesn't matter how long you've been a believer or how much Bible training you have, you are never going to have an answer to every question people ask you. Be honest. Be real. And take note of divine opportunities.

GODFIDENCE LESSON

Godfidence doesn't mean that you will always have an answer. It means that God is always directing your conversations.

6) Be determined to win souls.

I've noticed that many believers get discouraged when they share their faith but don't see results. Indeed, we would love it if everyone who we share Christ with placed their faith in Him, but that's not the case. Studies show that when a person does make a decision for Christ, they have heard the gospel message an average of 6.7 times.[27] So, perhaps the person you shared Christ with did not make a decision, but you've helped them get one step closer to making the best decision they could ever make. Be determined!

GODFIDENCE LESSON

Although you can't force anyone to accept the Truth, you can have Godfidence to plant spiritual seeds.

7) Be prepared to share your testimony (short form).

One of the best ways to connect with people is to share what God has done for you. God has given you a testimony. He has rescued you. He has healed you. He has turned your life around. He has given you new hope. It's time to share it. Make it short and sweet.

"There is nothing more powerful than sharing your own story." – Herbert Cooper

8) Allow the Holy Spirit to assist you.

"But you will receive power when the Holy Spirit comes on you; and you will be my witnesses…to the ends of the earth." Acts 1:8. What is the primary purpose of the Holy Spirit in you? To empower you to be His witness. There have been several occasions when I've walked away from a conversation thinking to myself, "Wow, how in the world did I come up with that approach and those words?" Then I realize that it was the Holy Spirit working in me and through me.

9) Visualize these lost souls in heaven.

"Where there is no vision, the people perish" (Proverbs 29:18 KJV). Vision and hope go hand in hand. We live in a world where so many people are dying without the knowledge of Jesus Christ as Lord. But those who are Christ followers have hope. Hope for today and for eternity.

How eager are you to take the message of hope to a lost world? Can you picture these individuals in heaven? This is vision. Without it, people perish.

> "If we as followers of Christ are overwhelmed by what Jesus has done, and the benefits of His grace transform our lives, then sharing our faith should be natural." - Derwin Gray

10) Learn an evangelism approach.

There are a few really good soul-winning approaches. My favorite approach is the Romans Road to Salvation. Four Scriptures. Four principles. Here is a synopsis.

Principle 1: Each person must realize that they have sinned. Romans 3:23: "All have sinned and fallen short of the glory of God."

Principle 2: Each person must understand that there are consequences for their sin. Romans 6:23: "For the wages of sin is death, but the gift of God is eternal life through Christ Jesus our Lord."

Principle 3: Each person must understand that Christ Jesus paid the price for our sins. Romans 5:8: "While we were yet sinners, Christ died for us."

Principle 4: Each person must believe in their heart and speak with their mouth that Jesus is Lord to obtain salvation. Romans 10:9–10: "If you declare with your mouth, 'Jesus is Lord,' and believe in your heart that God raised him from the dead, you will be saved. For it is with your heart that you believe and are justified, and it is with your mouth that you profess your faith and are saved."

When I first learned this approach, I used a simple strategy. I would open my Bible and first go to Romans 3:23. Then, in the side column of my Bible, I wrote 6:23, which was a reminder to go there next. Then, next to Romans 6:23, I wrote 5:8, which was a reminder to go to Romans 5:8 next. You get the picture. After using this method a few times, I was able to quote each of these Scriptures by memory and didn't even need a physical Bible in my hands.

Take the time to learn a soul-winning approach. It will give you Godfidence to share your faith, and it could make the difference in someone's eternity.

A MATTHEW LIST

Based on Matthew 9:9–13, the Billy Graham Evangelistic Association makes a great suggestion called "The Matthew List." One of the first things Matthew did after making a choice to follow Christ was to invite his friends over to his house for dinner. And he invited Jesus as well. Matthew wanted his friends to meet Jesus.

It is likely that you have friends in your life who need Jesus. The first thing to do is develop a "Matthew List," a list of people you want to see come to faith in Christ. This list also serves as a reminder to pray for them.

> "Prayer is crucial in evangelism. Only God can change the heart of someone who is in rebellion against Him. No matter how logical our arguments or how fervent our appeals, our words will accomplish nothing unless God's Spirit paves the way." – Billy Graham

Is there an old friend who you have lost touch with lately? Write their name on your Matthew List and begin praying for them. And also, pray for an opportunity to share your faith with them.

Is there a family member of yours who needs Jesus? Write their name on your Matthew List. Is there someone in your life who has done you wrong? Well, they need Jesus. Write their name on your Matthew List. Begin praying for them.

Is there someone in your life who you used to be friends with, but something happened to break your friendship? Write their name on your Matthew List and perhaps reconciliation will take place. There is power in prayer. It's time to gain the Godfidence that your prayers can help make a difference in the lives of each of these individuals.

FRIENDOLOGY

Five-year-old Tracy asked her mom if she could play at a friend's house, and her mom said, "Yes, as long as you are back at 6 p.m. for dinner." When 6 p.m. came, little Tracy was not yet home. Mom waited and waited. Finally, at 6:25 p.m., Tracy came in. Mom was mad.

Tracy said, "I'm sorry I am late, Mom, but my friend's doll broke right before I was going to leave. "

Mom said, "Oh, I see. So, I suppose that you were helping her fix it?"

Tracy said, "No, mom. I was helping her cry. She needed a friend."[28]

A friend is "(1) a person attached to another by feelings of affection or personal regard, (2) a person who gives assistance; patron; supporter, and (3) a person who is on good terms with another; a person who is not hostile."[29]

One statistic states that 61% of Americans are lonely.[30] This makes me think that there are many people in our world who lack genuine friendships. George Barna said, "Americans are friendly, but lonely." Have you heard of "Rent a Friend?" It is a company that first became popular in Japan but is now spreading across our world. "Rent a Friend"? I suppose people are willing to pay for a temporary friend, because they do not have a real, genuine friend to count on.

> "If we remove friendships from the world, half our joy goes right out with it. This is because friendship is the ultimate end of our existence and our highest source of happiness. Friendship – with one another and with God – is the supreme pleasure of life, both now and forever, and no one can fully enjoy life without it." – Drew Hunter

One of the most popular sitcoms of all time is *Friends*. The humor and the storylines are great. But what really grabs the viewer's attention are the real relationships of genuine friends. People long for that.

It is my belief that being a true friend to others is a key to bringing them to faith in God. Here are six characteristics of a true friend…

F – Fights for you
R – Respects you
I – Intercedes for you
E – Encourages you
N – Never gives up on you
D – Demonstrates unconditional love

In the 1990 movie *Castaway*, a man is deserted on an island. All alone. He was lonely. He needed a friend. So, he befriends a volleyball "Wilson," a piece of leather filled with air.

Church consultant Thom Rainer believes the traditional door-to-door evangelism that was effective many years ago is no longer as effective today. He says, "I began to see the trends shift in the 80s. People were becoming less receptive, even hostile, to drop-by visits."

Jesus' way of evangelism can be summarized in one word: relationships. He built a relationship with Nicodemus (John 3), with the woman at the well (John 4), with a blind man (John 9), with Matthew's friends (Matthew 9:10), with Peter and Andrew, James and John (Matthew 4), with Zacchaeus (Luke 19:5), and the list goes on.

The University of Virginia studied thirty-four students.

They set these students at the bottom of a very steep hill and gave them each a weighted backpack, instructing the students to walk up the hill. Some of the students walked up the hill alone, and some of the students were allowed to walk up the hill with a friend.

> ## GODFIDENCE LESSON
> God places certain individuals in your life for a reason. He has Godfidence in you to give them the gospel.

At the end, they were asked to rate the steepness of the hill. Every one of the students that walked up the hill by themselves rated the steepness of the hill higher than the students who walked up the hill with a friend. Further responses proved that the closer the friendship the companions had, the less steep the hill seemed.[31] Never forget that close friends make a world of difference. Who is God calling you to befriend?

I'd like to tell you about a friend Who will never let you down. I've had this friend in my life for forty-seven years. He has never let me down. He encourages me. He loves me. He never leaves me. Because of this friend of mine, I am reaching my potential in life. This friend, He never forsakes me. He has an agape kind of love – so much so that He died for me. And in fact, He died for you as well. His name is Jesus. And you will never find a friend like Him. I wonder...do you know Him?

DIVINE OPPORTUNITIES

God does not do things by coincidence. Often times, He sends divine opportunities your way. These are God-ordained encounters with individuals for the purpose of sharing your faith.

It's not by coincidence that God has you in your particular workplace...in your particular family...in your particular classroom...in your particular circle of friends...or in your particular neighborhood. God blesses you with divine opportunities. Don't miss those appointments.

> "Our tendency is to pray for miracles. But in most situations, it is more appropriate to pray for opportunities." – Andy Stanley

Take Jimmy, for example. His health was failing, and he had to go through dialysis treatments. At first, he was pretty down about having to deal with this major health issue. But as the treatments began, he realized that God had a purpose in it all. He explained,

> You see, there is a group of people sitting in a room with me hooked up to dialysis machines. This is terrific! This is a great opportunity to share my faith with them because they can't walk away from the conversation. And these are people who are hurting. They have questions about life and questions about God. Many of them have given up on life. What a terrific opportunity that God has given me.

Yes, Jimmy made the most of his divine opportunity. He is living out Romans 1:16: "For I am not ashamed of the gospel, because it is the power of God that brings salvation to everyone who believes."

LET'S GET PRACTICAL

Perhaps we don't always see it, but we are blessed with divine opportunities to share our faith every day. Maybe we are waiting for others to come to us, when God is waiting for us to take the initiative. Here is my list of ways we can take initiative to tell others about the Lord.

- Ask your restaurant server, "How can I pray for you?" Then, do it (and make sure you tip well).
- As you are paying for your meal at the drive-thru window, tell the worker, "What is the amount of the bill for the car behind me?" Pay their bill and include a gospel tract or church invite card.
- Accept the BBQ invite from your non-Christian friends.

Bring some good food and connect with them.

- Talk to your hair stylist about what God has done for you. You have their undivided attention for a good amount of time (and tip them well).
- Invite your neighbors over your house for dinner – even if they are not believers. Build friendships with them.
- On Halloween, give out good candy and include a gospel tract and a church invite card.
- Always be prepared. Have gospel tracts and church invite cards at your fingertips.
- Be intentional about reaching out to people who are hurting. Take note if they are dealing with the four Ds: divorce, depression, death, or debt.
- Join your homeowners' association to connect with people.
- Join a community interest group to connect with people.

> "Jesus defines servant leaders as those who humbly serve others because they love them."
> – Aubrey Malphurs

REAL WITNESS – REAL REVIVAL

In Christian circles, we often talk about revival. We pray for revival. We long for revival. The word "revival" is quite simple to define: "restoration to life."[32] In a spiritual sense, some will say that revival is having longer worship services, or more weeknight worship services, or having an evangelist preach, or allowing the gifts of the Holy Spirit to flow, or supporting missionaries around the world. Amen! I love all of the above. And each of these things open the door for God to do His purpose in our lives

But we cannot forget what the fruit of true revival is all about: evangelism. People coming to faith in Christ. When it comes to revival and all that God wants to do, Joel 2:28–29 is a key Scripture:

"And afterward,
I will pour out my Spirit on all people.
Your sons and daughters will prophesy,
your old men will dream dreams,
your young men will see visions.
Even on my servants, both men and women,
I will pour out my Spirit in those days."

I love this passage. It is a promise of God. But sometimes, we stop at verse 29, and fail to get the entire context of this Biblical thought. If we continue to read, we see that verse 32 says..."And everyone who calls on the name of the Lord will be saved."

Did you catch that? Scripture teaches us that the fruit of true revival is people coming to faith in Christ. People whose lives were headed for spiritual death and not having purpose for life are now revived and brought to life, receiving eternal life in Christ Jesus. If you want to see revival in your life, then share your faith. Bring people to Christ. Revival is at your fingertips.

WORDS OF LIFE

I believe that I am called to bring others to faith in Christ.
I will overcome any fear I have of sharing my faith.
I will take advantage of every divine opportunity.
I will be salt and light to a hurting world.
I am a soul-winner!

GODFIDENCE CHECKUP

1) Create your Matthew List: your list of ten people who need Christ and whom you will pray for on a consistent basis.

_______________ _______________

_______________ _______________

_______________ _______________

2) How will sharing your faith differ when you are speaking to a twenty-two-year-old versus speaking to a sixty-year-old?

3) In addition to the practical suggestions listed in this chapter, what are some other ways you can create opportunities to share your faith...in your workplace, in your community, in your extended family, etc.?

PRAYER FOCUS

Lord God Almighty, I thank You that I am a child of God. It is my desire that more individuals come to faith in You as well. I am asking You to equip me and prepare me to have the Godfidence to share my faith. I pray for divine opportunities. I pray for creative ways to share my faith. I pray for a sensitive spirit to notice individuals who are hurting or just simply need to hear the gospel message. Use me to reach others. No more excuses. I am Your ambassador. Amen. So be it.

CLOSING

Do you remember where you were on September 11, 2001 when you heard the news that terrorists had destroyed the Twin Towers in New York City? I was driving my kids to school that Tuesday morning. I also remember what happened the following two Sundays. Churches across America were filled with people. Many people were crying out to God. Most of us had questions about why this happened. Was the world coming to an end? Is my life at risk? Is this going to change the way we live?

Everyone was turning to God...at least for two weeks or so. Then, the spiritual life of America slipped back to where it was before 9/11. Complacent. Non-committed. Lukewarm.

Fast forward to 2020. Our nation is still in a mess. Racism. Social injustice. Coronavirus. Unemployment. Political upheaval. Social media opinions. Secular worldviews. And more. It is obvious that we – for the most part – have pulled away from strong faith in God. In today's society, many people place their faith in their money, their career, their opinions, their news media source, and most anything else but God. No Godfidence.

Researcher George Barna says, "Our research collected information about attitudes and behaviors related to practical matters like lying, cheating, stealing, pornography, the nature of God, and the consequences of unresolved sin. That's what makes the discrepancy between the percentage of people who consider themselves to be Christian – more than seven out of every 10 – and those who have a biblical worldview – just one out of every 10 – so alarming."[33] In other words, the great majority of them don't possess Godfidence or faith. Their confidence is elsewhere. I believe that this is the primary reason why our nation is dealing with so much immorality and discord.

How is your Godfidence? Do you have it? How much Godfidence do you really have? One of the most popular

Scriptures in the Bible is Jeremiah 29:11, which says, "'For I know the plans I have for you,' declares the LORD, 'plans to prosper you and not to harm you, plans to give you hope and a future.'" Great Scripture. Great promise. But don't stop there. If you keep reading, the Scriptures teach us how we can live and dwell with hope and a future. The next two verses say this, "'Then you will call on me and come and pray to me, and I will listen to you. You will seek me and find me when you seek me with all your heart'" (12–13).

There it is. This is the answer. Call on God. Go to Him. Pray to Him. Seek Him. But not just in any way – seek Him with all your heart. That's what it says. This is Godfidence. Scripture says that when we have this kind of Godfidence, we can find Him.

Some people complain about the world they live in. Others do something about it. Some people are part of the problem. Others are part of the solution. Some people give up. Others step up. Some people give God a half-hearted commitment. Others go all in.

How about you? If not you, then who? If not now, then when? There are chapters in your life yet to be written. There is a legacy to establish. There is a God to serve. You can do it! You can make it happen when you dedicate yourself to live with Godfidence.

My final prayer for you is that you would have...

The Godfidence of Abraham to have great faith in God,
The Godfidence of Moses to experience the glory of God,
The Godfidence of Joseph to pursue the will of God,
The Godfidence of Ruth to step into the favor of God,
The Godfidence of David to be have a heart after God,
The Godfidence of John to embrace the love of God, and
The Godfidence of Peter to be led by the Spirit of God.

For a moment, think of the best strategy to win a game of checkers. When one of your pieces makes it across the board, which is not an easy task, it gets crowned. Getting crowned makes a huge difference. A crowned checker piece can move in ways the other pieces can't. It can jump over and defeat its opponents like it wasn't able to do before, all because it was crowned. Getting crowned sets the player up for victory. Life is not an easy task. It takes effort on your part and the power of the Holy Spirit to get your spiritual life to where it needs to be and find your purpose in life. Once you get there, you are crowned. You become a daughter of the King or the son of the Most High God. Once you put on that crown, you will have the Godfidence to defeat your enemy and live in victory. You've been crowned! Now, it's time to live like it.

Amen. So be it.

END NOTES

[1] Dictionary.com Unabridged, "Confidence (n.)," dictionary.com.

[2] George Barna, "The State of the Church 2016," (Ventura, CA: Barna Group 2016), https://www.barna.com/research/year-review-barnas-10-read-articles-2016/.

[3] Dictionary.com Unabridged, "Worry (v.)," dictionary.com.

[4] Donna Washburn, PhD, Heather Kelly, PhD, Christine Arnzen, PhD, Emma Hale, Adult and Teen Challenge Outcome Study Report, (Evangel University, October 2019), https://teenchallengeusa.org/wp-content/uploads/2019/10/Adult-and-Teen-Challenge-Outcome-Study-Report-Final-REV-101519.pdf.

[5] Andy Stanley, Irresistible, (Grand Rapids, MI: Zondervan, 2018), ##.

[6] Mark Berman, "'I forgive you.' Relatives of Charleston church shooting victims address Dylann Roof," Washington Post, June 19, 2015, https://www.washingtonpost.com/news/post-nation/wp/2015/06/19/i-forgive-you-relatives-of-charleston-church-victims-address-dylann-roof/.

[7] Elyssa Smith, "Surrounded (Fight My Battles)," https://genius.com/Upperroom-surrounded-fight-my-battles-live-lyrics.

[8] Jerry D. Porter, "Desperate Prayer" Holiness Today, (2017), https://www.holinesstoday.org/desperate-prayer.

[9] Dictionary.com Unabridged, "Heresy (n.)," dictionary.com.

[10] Ibid., "Deity (n).

[11] Josh McDowell and Bob Hostetler, Beyond Belief to Convictions (Wheaton, IL: Tyndale House, 2002), 24.

[12] Thomas Ryan, "25% of U.S. Christians Believe in Reincarnation." America, the Jesuit Review, October, 2015. https://www.americamagazine.org/faith/2015/10/21/25-percent-us-christians-believe-reincarnation-whats-wrong-picture.

[13] Claire Gecewicz, "New Age Beliefs Common Among Both Religious and Non-Religious Americas," Facttank, Pew Research Center (October 1, 2018), https://www.pewresearch.org/fact-tank/2018/10/01/new-age-beliefs-common-among-both-religious-and-nonreligious-americans/.

[14] McDowell and Hostetler, 7.

[15] Misty Bernall, She Said Yes: The Unlikely Martyrdom of Cassie Bernall (New York: Pocket Books, 1999).

[16] "Passion for Memorizing God's Word," Senior Living, CrossCards (December 10), https://www.crosscards.com/devotionals/senior-living/senior-living-december-6-1454751.html.

[17] Gideons International, "Miner Died Signing His Daughter's Bible," Family Times (2020), https://www.family-times.net/illustration/Commitment/201312/?translation=50.

[18] Ray Vander Laan, In The Dust of the Rabbi (Grand Rapids, MI: Zondervan, 1995-2016), www.thattheworldmayknow.com/in-the-dust-of-the-rabbi.

[19] Frances Chan, "BASIC Follow Jesus – Clean Your Room," https://www.godtube.com/watch/?v=WGL6PGNX.

[20] Dictionary.com Unabridged, "Wisdom (n.)," dictionary.com.

[21] Mark Leigh, Epic Fail (New York: Random House Books, 2013), 47.

[22] Oxford English Dictionary, "Community (n.)," lexico.com.

[23] Dictionary.com Unabridged, "Family (n.)," dictionary.com.

[24] Gaby Del Valle,"Karolyi's 'You Can Do It' Made All the Difference," Bustle (August 11, 2016), https://www.bustle.com/articles/178073-who-did-bela-karolyi-say-you-can-do-it-to-the-moment-of-encouragement-went-down.

[25] "Evangelism," Holman Bible Dictionary, Trent C. Butler, General Editor, (Nashville, TN: Holman Bible Publishers, 1991) 446

[26] "Testify," Webster's Ninth New Collegiate Dictionary (1989), 1219.

[27] Deborah Smith, "Sharing Your Faith," Calvary Chapel Magazine (53:12–17), https://www.calvarychapelmagazine.org/images/PDFs/share_your_faith.pdf.

[28] Martha Whitmore Hickman, qtd. in Molly Brumfield, "I Helped Her Cry," Molly Brumfield (November 6, 2017), https://www.mollybrumfield.com/i-helped-her-cry/.

[29] Dictionary.com Unabridged, "Friend (n.)," dictionary.com.

[30] "CIGNA Takes Action to Combat the Rise of Loneliness and Improve Mental Wellness in America," Cigna Insurance (January 23, 2020), https://www.cigna.com/newsroom/news-releases/2020/cigna-takes-action-to-combat-the-rise-of-loneliness-and-improve-mental-wellness-in-america.

[31] Simone Schnall, Kent D Harber, Jeanine Stefanucci, and Dennis R. Proffitt, "Social Support and the Perception of Geographical Slant," Journal of Experimental Social Psychology, 44:5 (2008), https://www.semanticscholar.org/paper/Social-Support-and-the-Perception-of-Geographical-Schnall-Harber/1ad7f199a9a18755d10c45aa7e8d79652fdfbbd8.

[32] Dictionary.com Unabridged, "Revival (n.)," dictionary.com.

[33] Brandon Showalter, "Only 1 in 10 Americans Have Biblical Worldview; Just 4% of Millennials: Barna," The Christian Post (February 28, 2017), https://www.christianpost.com/news/1-in-10-americans-have-biblical-worldview-just-4-percent-of-millennials-barna.html.

BIBLIOGRAPHY

Barna, George. America at the Crossroads. Grand Rapids, MI: Baker Books, 2016.

Barna, George. Growing True Disciples. Colorado Springs, CO: Waterbrook Press, 2001.

Barna, George, and the Navigators. The State of Discipleship. Colorado Springs, CO: Barna Group, 2015.

Batterson, Mark. If. Grand Rapids, MI: Baker Books, 2015.

Bevere, John. The Bait of Satan. Lake Mary, FL: Charisma House, 2004

Bonhoeffer, Dietrich. Discipleship. Minneapolis, MN: Fortress Press, 2003.

Bridges, Jerry. Growing Your Faith. Colorado Springs, CO: Navpress, 2004.

Carden, Paul. Christianity, Cults & Religions. Torrance, CA: Rose, 2008.

Chan, Francis. Multiply. Colorado Springs, CO: David C. Cook, 2012.

Chan, Francis. Forgotten God. Colorado Springs, CO: David C. Cook, 2009.

Cloud, Henry. 9 Things You Simply Must Do. Nashville, TN: Thomas Nelson, 2004.

Cloud, Henry and John Townsend. Making Small Groups Work. Grand Rapids, MI: Zondervan, 2003.

Coleman, Robert E. The Master Plan for Evangelism. Grand Rapids, MI: Fleming H. Revell, 1993.

Earley, Dave and David Wheeler, Evangelism Is, B & H Publishing, Nashville, TN, 2010.

Eims, Leroy. The Lost Art of Disciple Making. Grand Rapids, MI: Zondervan, 1978.

Gibbs, Paul Clayton. Talmidim, How to Disciple Anyone in Anything. Colleyville, TX: Harris House, 2016.

Gibbs, Paul Clayton. Haverim, How to Study Anything with Anyone. Colleyville, TX: Harris House, 2017.

Hayward, Chris. The End of Rejection, Venture, CA: Gospel Light, 2007.

Horton, Stanley, ed. Systematic Theology. Springfield, MO: Legion Press, 2020.

Ingram, Chip. The Real God. Grand Rapids, MI: Baker Books, 2016.

McDowell, Josh and Bob Hostetler. Beyond Belief to Convictions. Wheaton, IL: Tyndale House, 2002.

McDowell, Josh and Sean McDowell. The Unshakable Truth. Eugene, OR: Harvest House, 2010.

McIntosch, Gary I. and Charles Arn. What Every Pastor Should Know. Grand Rapids, MI: Baker Book, 2013.

McPherson, Miles. The Third Option. New York, NY: Howard Books,

2018.
McRaney, Will Jr. The Art of Personal Evangelism. Nashville, TN: B & H Publishing, 2003.
Parrott, Dr. Les and Leslie. Saving Your Marriage Before It Starts. Grand Rapids, MI: Zondervan, 2015.
Potts, Steve. The Bald Eagle. Mankato, MN: Capstone Books, 1998.
Putman, Jim and Bobby Harrington. Discipleshift. Grand Rapids, MI: Zondervan, 2013.
Rainer, Thom. I Am a Church Member. Nashville, TN: B & H Publishing, 2013.
Sprinkle, Preston. Charis. Colorado Springs, CO: David C. Cook, 2014.
Tough, Alan. The Adult's Learning Projects. Toronto, Canada: Ontario Institute for Studies in Education, 1971.

APPENDIX 1

Scriptures of Life

For greater Godfidence, meditate on these Scriptures

When you feel like giving up . . .

And God is faithful; he will not let you be tempted beyond what you can bear. But when you are tempted, he will also provide a way out so that you can endure it.
1 Corinthians 10:13 (NIV)

When you are heart-broken . . .

The LORD is close to the brokenhearted and saves those who are crushed in spirit.
Psalm 34:18 (NIV)

When you are dealing with grief . . .

I cry to you for help when my heart is overwhelmed. Lead me to the towering rock of safety, for you are my safe refuge, a fortress . . ."
Psalm 61:2, 3 (NLT)

He will wipe every tear from their eyes. There will be no more death or mourning or crying or pain, for the old order of things has passed away.
Revelation 21:4 (NIV)

When you are dealing with fear . . .

For God has not given us a spirit of fear, but of power and of love and of a sound mind.
2 Timothy 1:7 (NASB)

So do not fear, for I am with you; do not be dismayed, for I am your God. I will strengthen you and help you; I will uphold you with my righteous right hand.
Isaiah 41:10 (NIV)

When you are dealing with worry . . .

Therefore I tell you, do not worry about your life, what you will eat or drink; or about your body, what you will wear. Is not life more than food, and the body more than clothes?
Matthew 6:25 (NIV)

Do not be anxious about anything, but in every situation, by prayer and petition, with thanksgiving, present your requests to God.
Philippians 4:6 (NIV)

When you are dealing with rejection . . .

For the LORD will not reject his people; he will never forsake his inheritance.
Psalm 94:14 (NIV)

(speaking of Jesus) He was despised and rejected by mankind, a man of suffering, and familiar with pain.
Isaiah 53:3 (NIV)

When you are dealing with your calling in life . . .

Brothers and sisters, think of what you were when you were called. Not many of you were wise by human standards; not many were influential; not many were of noble birth.
1 Corinthians 1:26 (NIV)

I press on toward the goal to win the prize for which God has called me heavenward in Christ Jesus.
Philippians 3:14 (NIV)

Nevertheless, each person should live as a believer in whatever situation the Lord has assigned to them, just as God has called them.
1 Corinthians 7:17 (NIV)

When you are dealing with a health issue . . .

But He was wounded for our transgressions, He was bruised for our iniquities; The chastisement for our peace was upon Him, and by His stripes we are healed.
Isaiah 53:5 (NKJV)

He said, "If you listen carefully to the LORD your God and do what is right in his eyes, if you pay attention to his commands and keep all his decrees, I will not bring on you any of the diseases I brought on the Egyptians, for I am the LORD, who heals you."
Exodus 15:26 (NIV)

When you are in a battle . . .

For the LORD your God is the one who goes with you to fight for you against your enemies to give you victory.
Deuteronomy 20:4 (NIV)

Have I not commanded you? Be strong and courageous. Do not be afraid; do not be discouraged, for the LORD your God will be with you wherever you go.
Joshua 1:9 (NIV)

When you have sinned . . .

But he said to me, "My grace is sufficient for you, for my power is made perfect in weakness." Therefore I will boast all the more gladly about my weaknesses, so that Christ's power may rest on me.
2 Corinthians 12:9 (NIV)

If we confess our sins, he is faithful and just and will forgive us our sins and purify us from all unrighteousness.
1 John 1:9 (NIV)

When you need encouragement to overcome . . .

I can do all things through Christ who strengthens me.
Philippians 4:13 (NIV)

What then shall we say to these things? If God is for us, who can be against us? Romans 8:31 (ESV)

When you are lonely . . .

GOD said, "My presence will go with you. I'll see the journey to the end."
Exodus 33:14 (MSG)

I will not leave you as orphans; I will come to you.
John 14:18 (ESV)

When you have a decision to make . . .

Commit your actions to the LORD,
and your plans will succeed.
Proverbs 16:3 (NLT)

Trust in the LORD with all your heart, and do not lean on your own understanding. In all your ways acknowledge him, and he will make straight your paths.
Proverbs 3:5, 6 (ESV)

APPENDIX 2

Ten Ways to Pray Over Your Children

1. Pray for your children to accept Christ as their Savior. 2 Peter 3:9
2. Pray for your children to enter into Godly relationships, especially in marriage. 2 Corinthians 6:14
3. Pray for your children to have the mind of Christ and make wise choices in life. Philippians 4:8
4. Pray for your children to experience the favor of God. Psalm 5:12
5. Pray the needs of your children will be met. Philippians 4:19
6. Pray your children would find their purpose in life. Exodus 9:16
7. Pray a hedge of protection over your children. Job 1:10
8. Pray your children would be covered by the blood of Jesus. 1 John 1:7
9. Pray your children would know and do the will of God. Romans 12:2
10. Pray your children would experience success and reach their potential in life. Joshua 1:8

APPENDIX 3

Ten Ways to Pray Over Your Wife

1. Pray your wife would have a deep relationship with the Lord. 1 John 4:10-12
2. Pray your wife would be sensitive to the voice of God. 1 John 5:15
3. Pray your wife would experience good health. Psalm 139:14
4. Pray your wife would be filled with the joy of the Lord. Nehemiah 8:10
5. Pray your wife would have a desire for inner beauty. 1 Peter 3:3, 4
6. Pray your wife would respect and encourage you. Ephesians 5:33
7. Pray your wife would be a Godly mother to your children (and grandchildren). 2 Timothy 1:5
8. Pray your wife would be a virtuous woman. Proverbs 31:30, 31
9. Pray that the Lord would bless your wife's hands as she works in the home and outside the home. Proverbs 31:13-19
10. Pray your wife would be an overcomer. Romans 8:37

APPENDIX 4

Ten Ways to Pray Over Your Husband

1. Pray your husband would be a man after God's heart. Acts 13:22
2. Pray your husband would be a wise and courageous spiritual leader. Joshua 1:9
3. Pray your husband would love you as Christ loves the church. Ephesians 5:25
4. Pray your husband would prosper in his career. Psalm 90:17
5. Pray your husband would exhibit love to all people. John 13:35
6. Pray your husband would be a Godly father to your children (and grandfather to your grandchildren). Psalm 71:18
7. Pray your husband would handle finances with wisdom and be willing to be generous to the kingdom of God. 2 Corinthians 8:7
8. Pray your husband would speak words of life. Deuteronomy 30:19
9. Pray your husband would choose Godly friends. Proverbs 27:17
10. Pray your husband would always pursue the will of God. 1 John 2:17

APPENDIX 5

Names of God

Elohim – The Strong, Creator God (Genesis 1:1, 2)
Abba Father – God our Father (term of endearment, Galatians 4:6)
Adonai – Master Over All (Deuteronomy 3:24)
Jehovah – Lord, Master and Relational God (Genesis 2:4)
Jehovah Shalom – The Lord is my Peace (Judges 6:23, 24)
Jehovah Rapha – The Lord is my Healer (Exodus 15:26)
Jehovah Roi – The Lord is my Shepherd (Psalm 23:1)
Jehovah Jireh – The Lord is my Provider (Genesis 22:14)
Jehovah Nissi – The Lord is my Banner of Victory (Exodus 17:15)
Jehovah Gibbor Milchamah – The Lord, Mighty in Battle (Psalm 24:8)
Jehovah Tsidkenu – The Lord is my Righteousness (Jeremiah 23:6)
Jehovah Shamma – The Lord is Always There (Psalm 139:7)
Jehovah Mauz – The Lord is my Fortress (Jeremiah 16:19)
Jehovah M'Kaddesh – The Lord Who Sanctifies (Leviticus 20:7, 8)
I Am – The God Who Is (Exodus 3:14)
Yahweh – Lord/Adonai (Psalm 2:11)
El Elohe Israel – The Mighty God of Israel (Genesis 33:20)
El Elyon – The God Most High (Colossians 1:16, 17, Daniel 3:26)
El Emunah – The God Who is Faithful (Deuteronomy 7:9)
El Hakabodh – The God of Glory (Psalm 29:3)
El Moshaah – The God of Deliverance/Salvation (Psalm 68:20)
El Olam – The Everlasting God (Psalm 90:1, 2)
El Shaddai – God Almighty, the All-Sufficient One (Genesis 17:1, 2)
Elohei Marom – The Lord of Heights (Micah 6:6)
Christ – The Anointed One; The Messiah (Matthew 16:16)
Emmanuel – God With Us (Matthew 1:23)

APPENDIX 6

Names of Jesus

Almighty One (Revelation 1:8)
Alpha and Omega (Revelation 22:13)
Advocate (1 John 2:1)
Author and Perfecter of Our Faith (Hebrews 12:2)
Bread of Life (John 6:35)
Bridegroom (Matthew 9:15)
Chief Cornerstone (Psalm 118:22)
Deliverer (1 Thessalonians 1:10)
Faithful and True (Revelation 19:11)
Good Shepherd (John 10:11)
Great High Priest (Hebrews 4:14)
I Am (John 8:58)
Immanuel (Matthew 1:23)
King of Kings (Revelation 17:14)
Lamb of God (John 1:29)
Light of the World (John 8:12)
Lion of the Tribe of Judah (Revelation 5:5)
Living Stone (1 Peter 2:4)
Lord of All (Philippians 2:9-11)
Mediator (1 Timothy 2:5)
Messiah (John 1:41)
Mighty One (Isaiah 60:16)
Morning Star (2 Peter 1:19)
Our Hope (1 Timothy 1:1)
Passover Lamb (1 Corinthians 5:7)
Peace (Ephesians 2:14)
Rabboni (John 20:16)
Redeemer (Job 19:25)
Risen Lord (1 Corinthians 15:3-4)
Rock (1 Corinthians 10:4)
Savior (Luke 2:11)
Son of Man (Luke 19:10)
Son of the Most High (Luke 1:32)
Resurrection and the Life (John 11:25)
The Door (John 10:9)

The Way, the Truth, the Life (John 14:6)
The Word (John 1:1)
True Vine (John 15:1)
Wonderful Counselor, Mighty God, Everlasting Father, Prince of Peace (Isaiah 9:6)

APPENDIX 7

Three Types of Bible Translations

One of the blessings we have at our fingertips is the variety of Bible translations. A common question many people have is this: What is a good Bible translation to read and study? This is a good question. The Old Testament was primarily written in Hebrew and the New Testament was written in Greek. With that in mind, any type of interpretations from one language to another, there are challenges. Here are three categories of Bible translations.

1) Exact Equivalency Translations (Literal). These are described as "word for word translations." Do you speak more than one language? If so, then you know what it's like to translate from one language to another. Sometimes, you choose to use a "word to word" way of interpretation. Some Bible translations take each word from the original Hebrew and Greek and translate it to English accordingly. Examples of these are the King James Version, the New King James, the New American Translation, and the English Standard Version.

2) Dynamic Equivalency Translation. These are described as "thought by thought translations." Perhaps you have used this format when translating from one language to another, as a way of being more accurate in relaying the thoughts in a more authentic way. Dynamic Equivalency Translations of the Bible take thoughts and sentences from the original Hebrew and Greek and interpret those thoughts into English. Examples of these are the New International Version, The New Living Translation, and Today's English Version.

3) Paraphrase Versions. While the first two types of Bible translations use the original Hebrew and Greek manuscripts, there are paraphrase versions which, instead, primarily use the Exact Equivalency or Dynamic Equivalence versions and translate them into modern language. Perhaps not quite as accurate, but much easier to understand. Examples of these are The Living Bible and The Message.

So, which version is right for you? Check them out. I like to use different versions for different purposes. If I want an accurate study Bible, I may use the New International Version. If I want to use phrases I am more familiar with, I may use the King James Version. If I want some positive encouragement, I may open up The Message. They each serve a purpose.

APPENDIX 8

Here are some examples of Blessings and Words of Life:

Randy Sean, You are a man of God! Today, I speak blessing and favor over you in the Name of Jesus Christ! As Ephesians 3 states, may you be able to grasp the width, length, height and depth of the love of God. I speak blessing over your role as a husband and spiritual leader to Selina and to your children, Cole, Riley and Raeanne. As you lead at home, may you win at life. I speak blessing over your career and your calling as a pastor. May your gift of leadership and influence bring many people to follow you as you follow Christ. In the Name of Jesus Christ, I bless you with the ability to Love, Live and Lead. I love you! Pops

Matthew David, Today, I speak blessing to you in the Name of Jesus Christ! As an apprentice of Jesus, you are already pursuing your purpose and fulfilling your calling. I speak words of life upon your calling to be a husband and spiritual leader to Jesika and a dad to Major, Annacelli and Maliah. I speak life into your calling in ministry and calling to be an advocate for orphans. I speak prophetically that – like David – you would be a man of the *Word*, a man of *Wisdom*, a man of *Worship*, and a mighty *Warrior*! May God's anointing on you be greater than you can ever imagine. I believe in you! I love you! Pops

Shalyse, My beautiful daughter. I speak blessing to you in the Name of Jesus Christ! You are blessed with beauty, from the inside out. I cherish your God-given uniqueness. You are so very valuable to me. I speak blessing over your role as a Godly mom to Cam. I bless you with great *faith* - that no matter what happens around you, your faith in God will grow within you. I bless you with God's favor. May you receive *favor* from people and *favor* from God. I bless you with an anointed future. May you keep on looking ahead to the destiny God has set apart for you. I speak words of life into your future marriage. I love you and believe in you! Pops.

Brenda, I speak words of life over you. May you realize how much of a blessing you are to me and to many people. I affirm your strengths of Discipline, Harmony, Connectedness, Analytical, and Achiever. I speak blessings over your gift of administration as you use it in the workplace, in ministry and our home. As your name means "sword," may God's Word, the sword of the Spirit, be your source of strength and direction. I bless you with the anointing of the Holy Spirit to fulfill your calling as a mom, a grandma, a pastor's wife, a marketplace missionary and a leader to ladies. Know that I believe in you, and so does God. You are the love of my life! I love you! Randy

Example of Family Mission Statement with Young Children:

I am an apprentice of Jesus.
I am not afraid
because God has adopted me and called me by name.
I am not alone
because I am a part of a family team.
My purpose is to love God
with all my heart, mind, soul, and strength,
and love everyone because God loved me first.
I rejoice in suffering,
speak life in pain,
and know that God is with me.